Gendered Speech
in Social Context

Gendered Speech in Social Context

Perspectives from Gown and Town

Edited by Janet Holmes

Victoria University Press

VICTORIA UNIVERSITY PRESS
Victoria University of Wellington
PO Box 600 Wellington

Copyright © Editor and Contributors 2000

ISBN 0 86473 402 6

First published 2000

Printed by Publishing Press, Auckland

Contents

Section 3:
The Town Perspective:
Language and Gender in the Workplace

Introduction

This volume represents the full range of issues discussed at the first ever Language and Gender Symposium to be held in New Zealand. The Symposium was organised as a Victoria University Centennial event, under the auspices of the School of Linguistics and Applied Language Studies at Victoria University of Wellington in October 1999. I hope that it will be the first of many such occasions.

The material has been organised into three distinct sections, representing the major themes addressed by contributors to the Language and Gender Symposium. The papers in the first section represent current leading edge international academic research in the language and gender area. The second section comprises contributions to a panel discussion on the issue of the potential value of such language and gender research in the workplace, illustrating the dialogue that the Symposium was designed to engender. The papers in the third section explore different aspects of the implications and applications of language and gender research in the 'real world'.

The three Plenary speakers, all international researchers in language and gender studies, have each contributed their papers to this volume. Jennifer Coates, whose visit was funded by the British Council, is one of the leading British researchers in the area, Sally McConnell-Ginet, funded by the Fulbright Foundation, is widely regarded as the foremost American researcher in this area, and Anne Pauwels, invited by Victoria University's Faculty of Humanities and Social Sciences, is undoubtedly the outstanding Australian researcher in language and gender. These papers provide a strong contribution to the sections in which they appear.

Section 1, the 'gown' section, covers a very wide range of current academic issues in language and gender research. It opens with Jennifer Coates' paper on masculinity and narrative, a topic which recurs later in section 3, where Su Olsson's analysis of women's stories extends the theme into workplace contexts. Jennifer Coates analyses narratives in which men's stories accomplish hegemonic masculinity through topic choice, language use, and through an emphasis on achievement and competition. But she also notes that some of the men's stories reveal

7

them struggling to reconcile competing discourses of masculinity. The advantages of moving on from essentialist approaches in gender analysis are also demonstrated by Ann Weatherall's discourse analysis of children's conversations while at play. She explores ways in which the concept of gender is mobilised by the children to co-ordinate and order their ongoing play activity, and in doing so challenges some earlier generalisation in language and gender research.

Miriam Meyerhoff and Andrew Barke focus on different pragmatic aspects of language and gender research in non-English-speaking communities, one exploring the gendered meanings of apologies and expressions of empathy in a Vanuatu community, and the other examining the many meanings of the pronoun 'you' in Japanese over time. The themes introduced in Jenifer Coates' paper are also picked up in Damian O'Neill's analysis of the accounts provided by violent men involved in rehabilitative therapy. He explores ways in which the men's discourse may provide insights into the way they construct their 'masculine' identity, and may also give indications of identity shift as a result of the therapy.

Finally in this section, some gender-differentiated aspects of the New Zealand sound system are examined. Paul Warren and Nicola Daly describe evidence that differences in the positioning and prominence of pitch on final rises in intonation-only questions clearly distinguish the speech of the Pakeha speakers of New Zealand English they analysed. In a paper which focusses on New Zealand vowels, Margaret Maclagan's analysis indicates the important role that women have played in contributing to the development of New Zealand English over the last century.

The Symposium was unique in bringing together a large number of people concerned with issues in language and gender both from academia (representing the 'gown' component) and from the workface (the 'town' group), and in promoting extensive discussion and constructive debate between these very different groups. This enthusiastic engagement is represented most obviously by the Panel discussion in section 2, where two practitioners, Vicky Noble, a Senior Executive Nurse, and Judy Lawrence, the Chief Executive of a government department, explore with three academics, Jennifer Coates, Sally McConnell-Ginet and Anne Pauwels, the relevance of language and gender research to practitioners in the workplace.

Section 3 is where the applications and implications of language and gender research are explored most thoroughly. The first two papers focus on different aspects of sexist language. Anne Pauwels provides extensive evidence that inclusive language is not just politically correct, it also captures audiences and engenders commitment. The extent to which feminism has impacted on advertising is illustrated by Uta Lenk's analysis of the language of German job adverts. Su Olsson's paper revives the narrative theme, focussing on 'mythical' and heroic dimensions of women's work stories, and highlighting their potential for challenging the dominant (male) organisational order.

Deborah Jones and Jennifer Peck take linguistic analysis into the corporate world, the former examining explicitly the problems that practitioners often have with academic analysis, and the latter picking up Anne Pauwels' theme and focussing on the economic benefits of gender-sensitive practices in the 'real world'. The research of Victoria University's Language in the Workplace project also reflects a number of earlier themes, providing evidence that women can foot it very effectively in the workplace, but also echoing a point made by others that simple gender dichotomies are at best misleading and at worst positively counter-productive in the workplace. The point is tellingly elaborated in the final paper from Sally McConnell-Ginet, which indicates clearly that some of the major obstacles to women's success in the workplace are the pre-conceptions and stereotypes which face them from cradle to boardroom. Her suggestions for raising workplace consciousnesses provide a fittingly constructive conclusion to the collection.

I would like to take this opportunity to express my gratitude to all those anonymous referees who willingly and constructively assessed papers for this volume. The high standard of the final selection owes a great deal to their trenchant comments and valuable suggestions. I am also grateful to Louise Burns for her reliable and careful assistance with copy-editing, and to Vivian Trott who meticulously checked the references. I hope that readers find the collection as stimulating and enjoyable as did those who participated in the Symposium.

Janet Holmes
10 April 2000

'So I thought bollocks to that': men, stories and masculinities

Jennifer Coates

University of Surrey

My aim in this paper is to look at the way masculinity is constructed in conversational narrative, that is, in stories told in spontaneous conversation involving male friends. Narrative is an important resource for speakers in the construction of self (Bruner 1990; Kerby 1991; Linde 1993). Telling stories not only allows us to give shape to our lives and to maintain our sense of self, it also allows us the possibility of exploring alternative selves. And given that the self is gendered (Benjamin 1990; Jukes 1993: xxiii), then narrative is a key resource for speakers in the construction of gender.

The following extract is taken from a contemporary NZ song, a song written and sung by men, but which takes a critical look at contemporary masculinity.

(1) HOW YOU DOING?

1	Mike:	Oh how you doing? I haven't seen you for–
2	Kevin:	Yeah, it's quite a while isn't it?
3	Mike:	What are you up to these days?
4	Kevin:	Oh, keeping busy, how about you?
5	Mike:	Oh yeah, yeah. It's Kevin isn't it?
6	Kevin:	What did you call me?
7	Mike:	Kevin? It's Kevin isn't it?
8	Kevin:	Yeah. John.
9	Mike:	Mike.
10	Kevin:	Mike!
11	BOTH:	Yeah, Mike, that's it.
12		Oh how you doing? I haven't seen you for–

```
13           Oh how you doing? I haven't seen you for–
14  Kevin:   Oh how you doing? I haven't seen you for–
15  Mike:    It's quite a while isn't it?
16  Kevin:   What are you up to these days?
17  Mike:    Oh, keeping busy, how about you?
18  Kevin:   Oh, you know. So where are you living anyway?
19  Mike:    Well you'd hardly call it living. I lost my job. I'm
             having quite a few emotional problems . . .
20  Kevin:   Hamilton? Wellington? Palmerston North?
21  Mike:    Grey Lynn
22  Kevin:   Oh. Yeah, it's nice out there eh!
23  Mike:    Yeah it's nice.
24  Kevin:   Yeah.
25  Mike:    Grey Lynn, yeah.
26  BOTH:    Oh how you doing? I haven't seen you for–
27           Oh how you doing? I haven't seen you for–
```
[from *Songs from the Front Lawn*]

This song sketches a meeting between two men, men we are led to assume have been friends in the past. The men are portrayed as socially inept (they have trouble remembering each other's names), and they stick to platitudes and well-worn conversational routines. When one of them attempts to answer the question *where are you living anyway?* with an answer that involves self-disclosure rather than just bare facts, the other speaker quickly steers the talk back to the impersonal.

The song makes fun of masculine inarticulateness and inexpressivity – and I know from personal observation that it makes people laugh. The laughter seems to be the kind that arises from the shock of recognition, which suggests that this song contains some truth, however stereotyped its portrayal of male interaction.

In an attempt to find out whether the masculinity portrayed in the song corresponds in any way to the reality of men's lives today, and more specifically, to try to get a better understanding of the way men talk to each other, I have collected a corpus of all-male talk.[1] The corpus consists of 30 spontaneously-occurring conversations involving male friends. Participants were simply asked to record themselves when they were with their friends. This resulted in recordings being made in a wide range of social contexts: the most popular setting was the pub, but male participants also recorded themselves in their homes, in the workplace – both in a university office after hours and during the tea break in a car repair workshop – in a youth club, even in a garden shed for one group of dope-smoking adolescent boys. And also, because they were very sophisticated in their use of lapel microphones, in unexpected places like men's toilets and walking along the street to the chip shop!

Rather than look at the totality of men's conversational behaviour, I focus specifically on conversational narrative, that is, on the stories told by speakers to each other in the course of everyday conversation. Narrative provides the researcher with invaluable materials for exploring the presuppositions of cultural life. As Polanyi puts it, 'story materials [can be used] as an entry into the cluster of basic interwoven ideas which lies behind and supports our daily lives' (1989: 112). The stories discussed in this paper are used as an entry into the basic cultural ideas which lie behind men's lives in late 20th century Britain – and I assume these cultural ideas are not dissimilar to those around in New Zealand today.

Storytelling plays a significant role in friendly conversation. The writer Ursula LeGuin argues that 'Narrative is a central function of language' (1992: 39). Storytelling among friends allows us not just to catch up with each other's lives, with what's been happening to us, but more importantly it plays a key role in the construction of the self. If we accept that the self is gendered, in other words, if we accept there can be no sense of 'I' without the 'I' being either 'I a woman' or 'I a man', then in friendly all-male conversation, one of the main functions of narrative is the construction of masculinity. In this paper the stories the men tell each other are analysed in order to explore some of the tensions arising from competing versions of what it is to be a man today.

Up to this point I have spoken of 'masculinity' in the singular. But this is a convenience: there is no singular masculinity – masculinity is fluid and variable and at any point in time there will be a range of masculinities extant in a culture, masculinities which differ in terms of class, sexual orientation, ethnicity, age, etc. And these masculinities intersect in complex ways. Moreover, masculinity cannot be understood on its own: the concept is essentially relational. In other words, masculinity is only meaningful when it is understood in relation to femininity and to the totality of gender relations (Connell 1995: 68, Kimmel 1987: 12, Roper and Tosh 1991: 2). But bearing in mind these caveats, I hope the reader will tolerate my use of the singular form 'masculinity' as well as the plural 'masculinities' in this paper.

So what does the data reveal about the accomplishment of masculinity? In some ways, the masculinities portrayed and performed in the stories conform to the stereotypes. But some of what we find in these stories challenges the stereotypes in unexpected ways.

Four extracts

I first examine four brief extracts from the stories in the corpus, extracts chosen because, despite their differences, they all draw on dominant discourses of masculinity.

(2) CAR WOULDN'T START [MN04B-2]
[Four young men aged 18/19 in garden shed in Surrey][2]
   [% = very quiet]
1   can't believe my car
2   it's ((2 sylls)) [really]
3   mhm, speedo's fucked [oh no]
4   I was just about to– wind[screen]wipers are fucked [oh right]
5   and now the fucker won't start [oh no]
6   [. . .]
7   I mean last time I just banged the bonnet [yeah]
8   and I mean it started up straight away [yeah]
9   and this time I was banging it and kicking it and shouting at it
     ((xxx)) [oh my god]
10 so then I– .hh I had a look at the fuses
11 and the fuses were alright
12 so I pulled the wires off
13 and cleaned them all up
14 and put them back again [%fuck it%]
15 did that three or four times
16 it still wouldn't start so–
17 what a bastard
18 ((xxx)) ((hope it)) starts first time tomorrow
19 <R laughs quietly>

(3) Extract from THE PSION SWAP [MJ06-3]
[3 men in their 20s talk in a pub in Somerset]
1   Yeah, like the most basic Psion he got was this one that he bought ages ago,
2   and he went and bought one from Argos
3   and totally swapped the cases over so he got like the new innards in his old case
4   and then took it back to Argos
5   and said he didn't want it any more. <LAUGHTER>
6   And then later on he changed it for the upgraded version again at Curry's,
7   took all the serial numbers off,
8   switched them over and the badges,
9   And this customer brought this back,
10   and he said 'This is only a five twelve k'.
11   'Oh that's strange it's meant to be two megabytes.'
12   Cos he– it was a five twelve k
13   but he put the two megabyte stickers on there and kept a five twelve k on his.
14   He was a dodgy bastard wasn't he?
15   he knew all the tricks though.
16   Yeah but look what's happened to him now
17   yeah now he's in prison.

(4) Extract from TABLETS AND DRINK [MW01-7]
[Two middle-aged men in a pub in Birmingham]
1   and you know where Amble Road is?
2   I was takin that fucking corner
3   and everything went (2) woozy
4   y'know what I mean <FASTER>
5   so straight away ((then–)) pull into the fucking side
6   eh?
7   started seeing double vision
8   so I pulls in to the side
9   and I thought 'well I'll be alright in a couple of minutes' <FASTER>
10   I'd only had two pints.

11 the next thing I knew were fucking four o'clock in the morning
12 and the fucking copper was knocking on the doo–. on the windscreen.

(5) Extract from THE GOOD SAMARITAN [MK02-3]
[Two middle-aged men in a University office after work]
1 and I was doing erm in 1969 a dialect survey
2 of the languages round about erm a town called Yola
3 and er . for our lunch with our interpreter one day we had sandwiches
4 and we decided after visiting this or that village in the area . to walk up to the top of one of these clusters of– of rocks and have our lunch.
5 This was about er four hundred miles or so from Ibadan,
6 erm about a hundred and fifty miles from any erm sizeable town,
7 pretty remote one might think.
8 It took us about half an hour to wend our way up this er jumble of very very large boulders,
9 and er we got close to the very top,
10 and the top was obscured from us by a boulder.
11 We walked round this boulder
12 and there sitting on the top . was er a European couple
13 with their backs to us.
14 As they heard us approach they turned round,
15 and lo it was my Vice Chancellor and his wife.

These stories obviously accomplish a lot more than gender: age is a significant factor, and the first two stories perform being young as well as being masculine. Class is also a significant variable: the differences between examples 4 and 5 have a great deal to do with the social class of the two speakers. The narrator of 'Tablets and drink' is a working class Birmingham man for whom the pub is an extension of home; the narrator of 'The good Samaritan' is a highly educated middle-class man who has got into the habit of meeting his friend and colleague after work to chat. They agreed to tape these conversations because, like all linguists, they could not resist collecting data!

But despite these disparities of age and class, there are some important commonalities. I shall discuss five of these in some detail: the topic of the stories, the gender of characters in the stories, the attention to detail, the use of taboo language, and the use of technical vocabulary and formal syntax.

First, the topics of these extracts are stereotypically masculine: they are about cars, about modern technology, about drinking, about travel. Other stories in my corpus have topics such as going out drinking, fighting, pornographic videos, sporting achievement. One of the functions of such topics is that they keep talk away from the personal: very few stories in my corpus involve self-disclosure of a kind parallel with that found in women's friendly talk (see Coates 1996).

Second, these extracts all portray a world peopled by male human beings. The only woman mentioned in these four extracts is the Vice-Chancellor's wife. In the sub-corpus of 67 stories analysed, 94% of the stories have male protagonists, and 71% of stories depict an all-male world.[3] This corresponds to Johnstone's findings for male narratives in Indiana USA: 'when men are not the protagonists of their own stories, they tell stories about other men' (Johnstone 1990: 67).[4]

Third, these extracts display a great deal of attention to detail. In example 2, the narrator talks about his car in detail: he mentions the speedometer, the windscreen wipers, the bonnet, and the fuses, and tells us how many times he cleaned the wires. In example 3, the narrator talks about two megabytes and five twelve K, details which position him as technically competent. In example 4 the narrator gives the name of the road at the beginning of the extract, tells us he had only had two pints, and specifies the time the policeman knocked on his windscreen. Example 5 also provides lots of detail about place and time. This is precisely what Johnstone (1990; 1993) found in her analysis of stories told by white MC males in Indiana USA. This attention to detail constitutes an important strategy in men's conversation: it enables men to avoid talk of a more personal nature. That this is often a deliberate strategy is revealed by the following admission by David Jackson in his 'critical autobiography':

> I often turn to the sports page in the daily newspaper, concerning myself with the raw material for endless non-emotional, non-conversations with other men . . . (Jackson 1990: 221).

The detailed naming of objects, then, is one way the language of these stories accomplishes masculinity. The use of taboo words is another, one that is difficult to overlook, and which compares markedly with the language of the women's conversations and the language of the mixed conversations collected. To give an example, the word *fuck* and words deriving from it (*fucking, fucked, fucker*, etc.) appear 72 times in the stories in the all-male sub-corpus, 12 times in the mixed sub-corpus, and not at all in the all-female sub-corpus. Examples 6-12 give some more examples of taboo language from the all-male data:

(6) it's fucking crap here today [The Area Manager's call]
(7) Oscar was very fucked off [Oscar was very fucked off]
(8) he just fucking uses whatever's around [The paint dispute]
(9) Just one of those moments you know life's turned to shit like that [You can't not know your name]
(10) cos I'd been driving like a dangerous cunt [Lucky thirteen]
(11) he used to come out with so much bollocks like that [Skin disease and stress]
(12) I was fairly pissed by the time we got to the fucking park if you remember [Quadruple Jack Daniels]

Taboo language in these stories functions in many ways: it gives verisimilitude to direct speech; it adds emphasis to points the narrator wants to foreground; but most importantly it performs hegemonic masculinity. Swearing and taboo language have historically been used by men in the company of other men as a sign of their toughness and of their manhood. Jock Phillips, in his classic account of early settlers in New Zealand, writes that swearing 'signalled the colonial man's readiness to live a hard and physical life and his unconcern for the genteel formalities of civilised life. It also showed contempt for the female world of manners' (96: 32). Swearing has played this role for men all over the world, not just in the colonial setting. In the late twentieth century there is ample evidence that taboo language is used in all-male sub-cultures such as the army and in the rugby changing room as well as in male peer groups on the street as a way of constructing solidarity (Kuiper 1997; Labov 1972; Moore 1993). Jackson (1990: 156) talks of the enormous pressure put on boys in Britain by the male peer group to swear and talk tough, while Gough and Edwards' (1998) analysis of the spontaneous talk of four male friends under the influence of alcohol demonstrates the ubiquity of taboo language in informal all-male talk.

Another highly significant function of the language in men's narratives is its role in maintaining emotional restraint. Male inexpressivity is recognised as a major feature of contemporary masculinity by commentators, and is increasingly seen as problematic (Pleck 1995; Seidler 1989). Jackson (1990: 156) claims that 'the non-adult public arena was dominated by language routines that taught me to bury the language of personal feeling'. These language routines include swearing, boasting and talking tough, and men's narratives often function as boasts, and construct a world peopled by swearing, tough-talking males. But emotional restraint is also accomplished through the use of technical vocabulary and formal syntax. 'The Psion swap', example 3 above, is a good illustration of a story that uses technical language: the technical vocabulary is skilfully used to make the story convincing, but it also keeps the focus away from the personal and the emotional.

The use of more formal syntax as a way of accomplishing emotional restraint is more apparent in the narratives told by older well-educated men, who swear a great deal less than their working class peers and also less than younger speakers of all classes. Example 5 is a good representative of the narratives told by these older middle-class men. First, some of the lines (determined largely by prosodic features, but also corresponding often to sentence boundaries) are long by normal narrative standards, for example, lines 3 and 4. Second, the verb is in the passive in line 10 (*the top was obscured from us by a boulder*); passives occur only rarely in narrative. Third, note the use of highly literate set phrases as this chunk builds to a climax in line 12: *and there sitting on the top was a European couple with their backs to us*, where the opening words *and there* followed by a non-finite clause starting with V + ing is readily recognised by English speakers as a rhetorical flourish often found at the climax of a story. The narrator then caps this in line 15 with his use of the archaic phrase *and lo* to introduce his climactic line *it was my Vice Chancellor and his wife*; this line uses a syntactic pattern which self-consciously mimics the language of the King James Bible. The overall effect of the language in this extract is to make the narrative stylistically very formal, and this has the effect of distancing the speaker from the addressee.

What emerges from this analysis of a few examples is that a variety of resources are exploited to accomplish dominant masculinity: topic choice, the virtual exclusion of women from the storyworld, and linguistic patterns, both lexical and syntactic. All these features contribute to emotional restraint, one of the key values inherent in dominant masculinity (Connell 1995; Jukes 1993; Seidler 1989; Tolson 1977).

Stories of achievement: men as heroes

Apart from emotional restraint, the other aspect of these stories which is most striking is their stress on achievement. Achievement is another key value of dominant masculinity. Storytelling has a key role to play in enabling male narrators to perform hegemonic masculinity through presenting themselves, or their male protagonists, as successful, as winners, as heroes.

Examples 13 and 14 are both tales of achievement and triumph.

(13) THE PAINT DISPUTE [MA01-1]
[Three young men in their mid-20s are talking at T's flat about a difficult art student]
1   did I tell you recently?
2   he rea– he u– u– used up all– he used up a–
3   like I had a palette with like loads of black paint on it
4   and he used it all up
5   and I said 'Get me some more paint'
6   and he refused [what?]
7   I– I told him to get me some more paint and he was going– he was going to refuse
8   and he could tell that I was getting more and more serious about it
9   cos he was getting more and more refusey about it
10   he y– y– YOUR paint?
11   it was MY paint [yeah]
12   he was a complete cunt about using other people's paint
13   and in– in the end I had to– er in the end I got REALly annoyed with him
14   and I kicked a chair into bits

15 and then he r– he sort of . ran– ran out of the studio
16 and stayed away for half an hour before coming back
    <LAUGHING>
17 back and sort of shaking my hand and being apologetic
    <AMUSED>
18 and then–
19 [HE STILL DID– DIDN'T GET YOU MORE PAINT
    THOUGH?]
20 well in fact he did
21 I mean he took a while about it cos he kept saying 'I've got no
    money'
22 and I at one point lost my temper with him
23 I couldn't do it a second time
24 it was really pathetic
25 but in the end he gave– he gave me a tube of white.

(14) AMAZING LEFT [ME04-1]
[Three 16-year-olds are talking in Julian's room at boarding school]
1   in the June in the– in the final of the Ties
2   I did the most amazing left with this half-volley you will ever
    see.
3   ((it)) came down
4   it was like quite– it was quite like– quite a– quite high but quite
    hard
5   it came down ((here))
6   I had someone running up
7   it was on my left so I didn't have time to ((1 word)) change
    ((feet))
8   so I took it on the half-volley
9   and it just went flying <EMPHATIC>
10 and Neil ran on from an on-side position
11 and he was away
12 and he ((was))–
13 and it was just the most beautiful ball I've ever ever ever seen.
    <EMPHATIC>

In both these examples the narrator presents himself as the protagonist in a story where he performs heroically, whether in contest with another person, or on the sportsfield. In 'The paint dispute', the narrator is relatively modest about his achievement: the evaluative clause *it was really pathetic* focuses on the inadequacy of Robin, the other student, rather than on Tim's victory. However, we are left in no doubt as to who came out on top in this dispute. Julian, in 'Amazing left', frames his story explicitly as a celebration of triumph with the phrase *the most amazing left* in line 2, and the final line *it was just the most beautiful ball I've ever ever ever seen.*

I also want to include an example from stories told by older speakers: a good example is a first-person narrative told by a middle-aged man about collapsing with acute appendicitis and having to survive with incredible stoicism a series of events which prevent him getting to hospital. The story is very long – 126 lines – so the following is only an extract from the epic tale:

(15) Extract from APPENDICITIS [MR02A-12]
[Three middle-aged men in a pub after work]
49   the next morning thing's were no better
50   so . I walked round the street a couple of hundred yards to the doctor's surgery
51   unfortunately . the doctor . lived out in Essex
52   and he'd been snowed in
53   so . I spent a couple of hours sitting around in his surgery
54   and then finally the receptionist says, 'Look you know,
55   the doctor isn't going to be able to make it till this evening,
56   he's stuck in the snow,
57   would you mind coming back'.
58   so I shuffled off around the street <LAUGHING>
59   and spent the day thinking . ((you know)) This is really getting bad,
60   because .hh oddly enough the sort of classic appendicitis pain didn't appear until very late
61   you know 'god only knows what is wrong with me,
62   but this is– this is definitely rough'.
63   So I spent the whole day um–

64   finally five or so . o'clock came round
65   and I staggered around the street again to the doctor's surgery
66   and this time I got to see him
67   and I was standing in front of him
68   and I was going like this
69   sort of swaying in the breeze
70   and he said um 'I need to get you a bed,
71   suspected appendicitis' he said.

Tony is then whisked into hospital, where it becomes clear that he has a ruptured appendix and needs to be operated on immediately if he is not to die. Like examples 11 and 12, it is a tale of heroism, but heroism of a different kind. The protagonist has to endure a terrible ordeal; he becomes increasingly ill, and circumstances such as bad weather conspire against him. He comes through the ordeal with stoic fortitude. As we see from these examples, heroic behaviour can mean winning a dispute, or making a perfect move on the sportsfield, or bearing pain and coming through an ordeal.

There are other stories in the men's conversations which deal with pain or illness. Typically, the narrator will only foreground the pain or the illness if it serves to illustrate how brave the protagonist was, or how successful in outwitting a significant other. In her analysis of the stories told by male and female speakers in a town in Indiana USA, Johnstone (1990; 1993) found that the men's stories emphasised contest. Achievement in these stories, that is the winning of the contest, was associated with the male protagonist acting alone. (By contrast, the women's stories emphasised community and the importance of acting in collaboration with others: women were portrayed as failing when they acted alone.) The stories in my corpus seem to support her findings: in example 13, Tim acts alone – and violently – to make Robin replace the paint he'd used; in example 14, Julian is clearly part of a team, but the story celebrates his solo contribution; in the Appendicitis story, the narrator portrays himself as battling alone against the odds.

Competition in storytelling

This focus on achievement in men's stories has a consequence that Johnstone (1990; 1993) does not discuss. It is that narrative activity in all-male groups can be face-threatening in a way that it is not in all-female groups. In other words, when men tell stories which present them as heroes, as the victors in conflict with various kinds of other, they are performing a particularly competitive version of masculinity which can be called one-up-man-ship. The result is that telling stories becomes in itself a competitive activity, with speakers competing to boast about their triumphs or their cock-ups. The *Can You Match That* aspect of all-male talk is well illustrated by stories in my corpus: adolescent speakers compete to tell ever more extreme stories about getting drunk; young men (in their 20s) tell stories which exaggerate feats of aggression and getting the better of authority figures (eg. by kicking down a door at work, about skiving off work, about a fight with a workmate); older men with a more working class background tell stories about run-ins with the police, while older men with a more middle-class background vie with each other to appear widely-read or well-travelled or up-to-date in terms of technology and science – or even good wine. In one story sequence, the narrator of the second story begins his story with the words *tell you what, I'll beat all of that* [MN06A-7], which explicitly labels his narrative as a competitive speech act.

With younger speakers, this competitive element can be overt, with so-called friends ganging up on each other. The following extract comes from a series of boasting stories about drinking and getting drunk, told by three 16-year-old boys. It is the kind of narrative that Polanyi (1989) calls a 'diffuse story' because the story is not told as a neat chunk, but instead 'blocks of story materials [are] interleaved with blocks of conversation in which points of the story are discussed or amplified' (Polanyi 1989: 66).

(17) Extract from QUADRUPLE JACK DANIELS [ME01-11]
[Three 16-year-old boys at public school]
1   Henry: that evening you were in such a bad mood/ cos me and
               Robert were pissed and you weren't/
2   Robert: I'm serious you know/ I've never seen you pissed/

3   Julian: oh crap/
4   Robert: I've never seen you pissed/
5   Julian: how will that– hang on/
6   Robert: how have you ever been pissed? <R AND H LAUGH>
7   Julian: oh fuck off/
8   Robert: tell me now/ <MOCKING>
9   Julian: fuck you/

This is a particularly vicious bit of competitive talk. Note how none of the speakers mitigates the force of their remarks with any face-saving devices. In particular, Robert's attack on Julian's drinking ability is a face-threatening act, pure and simple. Julian responds by swearing, as a feeble attempt at counter-attack, but he is in an impossible situation since he can only lose face whatever he chooses to do: if he attempts to provide evidence that he has been drunk (which he does at another point), that still allows Robert the victory of having forced him onto the defensive.

A more subtle way of competing is to undermine another's story by adding a deflating comment at the end. In this way, the current narrator's heroism can be punctured so that the next narrator is free to take the floor. The talk following the story 'Amazing left' (example 12) is a good illustration of this: after the narrator's triumphant *it was just the most beautiful ball I've ever ever ever seen*, one of his co-participants at the talk asks, 'Who?'. The narrator answers, with considerable bathos, 'Me'. The faux naif question 'Who?', undermines the whole point of the story – if the addressees can claim not to know who the story is about, it fails as a piece of one-up-man-ship.

This strategy is also used by older speakers: a middle-aged middle-class male tells a long story about a Volkswagen Beetle which was swept off a bridge into a river somewhere in Africa, but which proves to be watertight and starts first time once it is back on dry land. The story is well-constructed, but the narrator's friend adds comments both during and at the end of the story which undermine the narrator; the final section of the story is given in example 18.

(18) Extract from WATERTIGHT VOLKSWAGEN [MK02-5]
84   The punchline of this tale was that he sent this er reel of film
     which he'd taken back for developing in Germany
85   and had addressed it to his wife
86   and it arrived when his wife's–
87   it arrived at his home
88   and his wife saw the pictures before a letter from him arrived
     explaining (.h) what was ((up))
89   she was no end surprised to see her husband's Volkswagen in the
     middle of a river
90   and no husband
91   and no husband
92   all was well <IN HUSHED RITUAL TONES>
93   yes that seems to be the sort of thing one might attribute to the
     publicity department of Volkswagen

It is actually a very aggressive move to make a comment of this kind
after a fellow speaker has invested so much time (this is one of the
longer stories in the corpus) and creative energy in building a storyworld, in animating characters, in constructing a coherent plot. What
the story-recipient is in effect saying is that he is not fool enough to
think this is a genuine story, since in his view it is probably a fiction
spread around by 'the publicity department of Volkswagen'. The fact
that he is relatively indirect in making this accusation – he uses the
hedges *seems, sort of thing*, and *might* and employs the impersonal
pronoun *one* – does not alter the fact that this is still a 'so what?' move,
and a 'so what?' of a particularly sophisticated and middle-class kind.

The struggle to express vulnerability

But in fact the picture is not as simple as this. While the stories discussed
so far reproduce the dominant values of masculinity – emotional restraint,
ambition, achievement, and competitiveness – these values inevitably
jostle for position with other, competing, values. We are all involved,
whether we like it or not, in the ceaseless struggle to define gender
(Weedon 1987: 98), and it is not the case that the men whose conversations I have listened to adopt the dominant discourses of masculinity
at all times and without protest. Some of the stories reveal men struggling

to reconcile competing discourses of masculinity.

The next story is a good example of this: in many respects this story performs conventional masculinity, but alternative discourses are voiced, and the discussion which follows the story shows the men struggling to reconcile these competing discourses. The story comes from a conversation involving four men, all carpenters, aged between 25 and 40, having a drink in a pub after work; the narrator is Alan.

(19) THE DIGGER [ML02-2]
1   should of seen Jason on that digger though
2   yeah he . he come down the ((park)) part
3   where it's– the slope
4   then he's knocking down the front wall
5   and there was this big rock
6   and he couldn't get it out
7   so he put a bit more . power on the thing
8   and . and the thing– the digger went <<SCOOPING NOISE>>
9   it nearly had him out <LAUGHS>
10 he come out all white.

This story constructs a dominant version of masculinity, where masculinity is bound up with physical strength. It tells of a man using a huge and powerful machine to knock down a wall. The point of the story, though, is that when Jason tries to employ more power to dig out the recalcitrant rock, he almost loses control of the machine.

The last line of the story, however, positions the audience slightly differently: Alan ends the story with the line *he come out all white*. 'To go white' is recognised as being a physical manifestation of fear, so Alan here portrays Jason not as a hero but as someone who nearly lost control of a powerful machine and who is frightened by the experience. Note that in lines 2-7 Jason is the subject of active verbs, but in lines 8 and 9, the climax of the story, the machine becomes the subject, with Jason becoming the object. This twist in the power relations between the man and the machine results in Jason *com[ing] out all white* in line 10.

As the following extract shows, two of Alan's co-participants orient to the narrator's evaluation of the story, but the third resists. The talk following Alan's story is transcribed here in stave format to allow the interplay of voices to be clearly seen.

(20) THE DIGGER

8   Alan: it nearly had him out/ <LAUGHS> he come out all white/
Chris: <LAUGHS>
Kevin: <LAUGHS>
John:

9   Alan:
Chris: <LAUGHS>
Kevin: I bet that could be dangerous |couldn't it/
John: ((|hurt himself/))

10   Alan:
Chris:
Kevin: if it fell |on your head)) it's quite–
John: |he– you know/ –

11   Alan:
Chris: <LAUGHS> |can I have some
Kevin: |it's quite big/
John: |he crapped himself/ he |crapped himself/

12   Alan:
Chris: pot noodles please Kevin <SILLY VOICE>
Kevin: <LAUGHS> |no/
John: |did he have to sit down

13   Alan: he– he– well . he was quite frightened |actually/
Chris:
Kevin:
John: and stuff? . |I know/

14   Alan: cos– cos– |well yeah/
Chris: was it for you as well |mate?
Kevin:
John: I must admit–

15   Alan:
     Chris: did you go a bit white as well then did you?
     Kevin:
     John: god/

16   Alan:
     Chris: don't get
     Kevin:
     John: he was thinking 'god please don't wreck it'/

17   Alan:
     Chris: any blood on it/ <SARCASTIC>
     Kevin: is that the one with all the loa–
     John:

18   Kevin: lots of different things on it?

[Discussion continues about different types and sizes of diggers]

Kevin and John both orient to Alan's move to bring Jason's fear into focus: Kevin comments on the danger of such machines, while John surmises that Jason could have got hurt, and that he crapped himself, another physical manifestation of fear. Kevin's comments are met by taunting from Chris – at least, that is how I interpret Chris's remark *can I have some pot noodles please Kevin*. Chris uses a silly voice to say this and since at face value the remark is totally irrelevant, we have to use conversational inferencing to interpret it. Superficially this utterance is a polite request for food, the sort of thing you might expect somebody relatively powerless – a child, for example – to say to someone more powerful – a mother or a dinner lady. By saying this, is Chris implying that Kevin's utterances *I bet that could be dangerous couldn't it if it fell on your head, it's quite– it's quite big* would be more appropriate in the mouth of a caregiver or food-provider, i.e. in the mouth of a woman? Certainly, Chris seems to be trying to humiliate Kevin, to position him as being cowardly, a wimp, of being un-masculine. Perhaps by producing an utterance as irrelevant as this, he is implying that Kevin's utterances are equally out of place. Chris clearly finds Kevin's view of Jason's near-accident threatening. However, Kevin does not seem to be intimidated: he laughs and says 'No' to Chris, meaning 'No you can't have any pot noodles', which defuses the challenge by treating it humorously.

John continues to explore the theme of Jason and fear with his question to Alan: *did he have to sit down and stuff?* This leads to Alan, who was an eye witness, admitting: *he– he– well . he was quite frightened actually.* Note the hesitations and false starts in this response, as well as the presence of several hedges; Alan is clearly uncomfortable with his answer. Predictably, given his taunting of Kevin, Chris now has a go at Alan with the direct challenge *was it for you as well mate?*, that is, 'was it frightening?'. Alan replies, *well yeah*, with *well* again signalling that this is a dispreferred response. Chris's subsequent question *did you go a bit white as well then did you?* ends with an aggressive tag. It is aggressive in that it demands an answer from Alan, and at the same time the repetition of *did you?* has overtones of motherese (*does he want his dindins, does he?*) which rudely suggests that Alan is behaving like a baby. Chris's question is highly face-threatening. His use of the phrase *go a bit white*, which picks up Alan's earlier utterance, mocks the euphemistic aspect of it and implies that to go white is un-manly. This question challenges Alan to align himself with Jason and, by extension, with un-manliness. Alan begins a reluctant response: *well I still–* before he is rescued by John's intervention: *god/ he was thinking 'god please don't wreck it'.* John in effect answers for Alan with the claim that if Alan had gone white it was because he was worried about the machine. This utterance shifts the ground of the discussion by suggesting that the men's anxiety is to do with damaging the machine rather than with their own vulnerability. This interpretation of events is obviously more palatable to Chris, who here stands for hegemonic masculinity, but he still adds the sarcastic comment *don't get any blood on it* as if determined to wrong-foot Alan. But Kevin and John then steer the conversation into a discussion of exactly what kind of digger it was and how it compares to a fork-lift truck, an impersonal discussion involving lots of detail which re-establishes the solidarity of the group and their alignment with dominant norms of masculinity.

The tension and conflict in this short extract demonstrate how difficult it is for male speakers to discuss vulnerability, and how peer group pressure works to silence those who try to voice alternative masculinities. Alan, Kevin and John attempt to explore their feelings, and thus to push at conventional gender boundaries, but violations of gender boundaries will always be resisted, and will be met with sanctions ranging from ridicule, as here, to violence (Davidoff and Hall 1987: 29).

Self-disclosure

Finally, I turn to self-disclosure in all-male talk. As mentioned above, the majority of the stories in my corpus are first-person narratives, that is, the narrator and the chief protagonist are one and the same. First-person narratives in all female talk very often involve self-disclosure, because the narrative will tell of an event that occurred in the speaker's life, usually very recently, which had some kind of emotional impact. Men's first-person narratives, by contrast, focus more on achievement and triumph, or on the more banal happenings of everyday life, and are not designed to reveal feelings or to lead into talk where feelings can be compared and discussed. The only stories I could really label as self-disclosing came in conversations involving older rather than younger men, middle-aged men who seem more solid in their masculine identity.

Example 21b is an example of a story involving self-disclosure. The participants in this conversation were four middle-aged middle-class men in the pub after work. They are having a general discussion about peaks and troughs in social history. Example 21a gives a brief chunk of the preceding conversation to contextualise the story:

(21a) SUICIDAL [MR03B]
Brian: we keep having this idea that things are going to get
        better/ which was an earlier part of the conversation/
Tony: yes/
Brian: it's paralleled by this– I think what tends to happen/
        you– you ((just)) have peaks and troughs/ you know the
        thing goes– there's a wave/ it does– it doesn't suddenly
        turn into an exponential growth pattern/
Pete: right/
Brian: you know it goes up and it comes down again/
        |you know and I think–

Pete: but Ido you think– do you think– but do you think that
            there's a– within the p– peaks and troughs/ do you think
            there's a– there's a upward or a downward trend?

At this point Brian gives an example from his own life (note how it is
Pete's question that allows Brian this opportunity):

(21b) SUICIDAL [MR03B]

1   well at the moment ((I mean)) this is partly personal
2   cos I mean I– my own life sort of has been (ah) up and down
3   and I've . you know sort of– . if you'd t– if you'd had this
     conversation with me about a term ago
4   I mean I was just about as down as you could get
5   because I'm er– really was quite seriously suicidal
6   and . it HAS come up again
7   you know my life HAS improved/ (mhm/ mhm/)
8   ((xx)) it hasn't actually got any better
9   but my attitude to it and psychologically I'm a lot straighter and
     clearer about what's going on
10   so it has picked up
11   and it was just literally a case of hanging on in there
12   I mean about . towards . about the middle of last term
13   I quite seriously– . I went out and I bought a big bottle of pills
14   they were codeine and aspirin mix
15   and a bottle of whisky
16   and I went and sat on Twickenham Green
17   and I was going to kill myself [mhm]
18   I was going to eat the pills and drink the whisky
19   er well it was only a little bottle of whisky <GREATER SPEED>
20   err sitting there y'know TOTALLY just about as depressed as you
     could possibly get
21   and then I just thought 'you stupid sod'
22   so I threw away the pills
23   drank the whisky
24   and went home
25   [everyone laughs]
26   but y'know that was the turning point

27   I started coming up again <LAUGHING QUALITY TO VOICE>
[Pete: good/ Tony: good/]

This rare example of a man talking about a difficult moment in his life is introduced with some tentativeness. First, he warns his fellow conversationalists that he is about to talk about something partly personal (the hedge partly here is semantically nonsense, but functions to soften the force of his utterance and protect his addressees' face). Secondly, he ties his story in very carefully to the theme of peaks and troughs which has been established in the preceding conversation. This careful tying in of his story to the more general conversational theme reveals his anxiety about telling the story, anxiety which is expressed in the many hedges which appear in lines 1-5 (three tokens of *I mean*, two tokens of *sort of*, and one each of *you know* and *really*). This density of hedging is unusual in men's talk (but is typical of all-female conversation where sensitive topics are under discussion). After this he seems to settle down to tell his story, perhaps reassured that his fellow conversationalists have not raised any objections.

However, the reactions of the other men – laughing with Brian at line 25, then saying *good* after Brian's coda – express both relief and embarrassment. They do not seem very comfortable with Brian's self-disclosure, and this interpretation is borne out by a conversation which takes place the following week involving just Pete and Tony. Pete and Tony arrive at the pub ahead of their friends, and mull over Brian's self-disclosing behaviour the previous week. Example (22) gives an extract from this conversation:

(22) **Extract from ENGLISHNESS [MR01B]**
[% = very quiet]
Tony: I don't know Brian THAT well/ but every time I've met
            him/ he's been pretty free with whatever happened to be
            on his mind at the time/
Pete: I don't know many people like that/ . you know who are
            able to sort of [no] just tap into . their– I don't know
            their situations their problems/ I know I take a long time
            to sort of er . warm to people I think=

Tony: =you . might wonder really how he . overcame the– the
           education that the rest of us obviously Isuccumbed to/
           <LAUGHS>
Pete: II<LAUGHS> yeah/ %yeah%/ (1.0) I think I must be
           quite . a typical Englishman in that sense/ being quite
           sort of er–
Tony: I k– I'm less English than I was/ <LAUGHS>
Pete: is that because you've been ab– abroad?
Tony: no/   I((xx))I
Pete: er   Ihow did you– how did you manage to– to become
           less English?
Tony: I think it's because I decided that– . that (1.0) I ((really))
           didn't like this way of relating to people very much/ and
           that . life actually would be improved by . people being
           more open with each other/ . not that I'm brilliant at it/
           <QUIET LAUGH>
Pete: makes you vulnerable though don't you think? . um
           don't– don't you feel vulnerable? . sometimes?
Tony: yeah but . I suppose that . that's a useful reminder really
           isn't it/ ((I mean)) . vulnerability is er– (1.0) all the– all
           the– the– the masks and so on are supposed to keep
           vulnerability at bay/ but . .hh they only do this at a very
           high cost/
Pete: yeah/ I suppose that's another kind of pain isn't it/
Tony: yeah/
Pete: you know putting up barriers/ distancing yourself/ and
           maybe– . maybe more damage is done that way than
           actually=
Tony: =it's not impossible/

This is an extraordinary stretch of talk. I have found nothing comparable
anywhere else in the conversations in the corpus. Pete and Tony not
only address a topic that demands reflexivity, something men normally
avoid; they also stick to the topic and explore the issues that arise from
it in a way that is relatively common in women friends' talk but is
extremely rare in all-male talk. It is probably significant that there are
only two speakers present: this conversation arises when two friends

meet in the expectation that other friends will join them. When three or more males meet, it seems that peer group pressures make talk of this kind difficult, but where there are just two males, then a kind of intimacy is possible that is precluded otherwise.

Peter and Tony make some fascinating observations on men's talk (though note that they gloss male inexpressivity as 'Englishness' and seem to overlook the gendered nature of the masks they are forced to wear). Tony argues for greater openness, which Pete responds to with a series of three questions: *makes you vulnerable though don't you think?, um don't- don't you feel vulnerable?, sometimes?* Pete obviously feels vulnerable just talking like this, but wants to question Tony's assertion that it is better to be more open. Tony accepts that being open can make you vulnerable, but pursues his line of thinking by asserting that vulnerability is not necessarily bad but may be a useful reminder of our humanity. While feeling vulnerable can be uncomfortable, wearing masks all the time is a much worse option.

Tony here voices an alternative discourse which challenges hegemonic masculinity and asserts the value of emotional honesty and openness. The metaphor of the mask is a powerful one, and seems to express the experience of many men. Tolson (1977: 10), for example, describes conventional male interaction as follows:

> we would fall into the conventional 'matiness' of the pub, a mutual back-slapping, designed to repress as much as it expresses. It was impossible to talk to other men about personal feelings of weakness or jealousy. A masculine 'mask of silence' concealed the emptiness of our emotional lives.

It is this 'mask of silence' which Tony challenges in his bid for fuller, more honest interpersonal interaction.

Conclusions

I've discussed in this paper only a fraction of the stories told in the conversations in the corpus. But I have tried to show how narrative is used in all-male talk to construct and maintain masculine identity. Conversational narrative is our chief means of constructing the fictions that are our lives and of getting others to collude in them. But storytelling also allows us to order or to re-order our everyday, normally taken-for-granted experiences. So while storytelling reinforces hegemonic masculinity, it can also provide a space where what is normally taken for granted can be questioned or challenged.

Men's stories accomplish hegemonic masculinity through topic choice, language use, and through an emphasis on achievement and competition. But male speakers struggle with issues of vulnerability, and struggle to come to terms with more 'feminine' aspects of themselves. Some of them explicitly struggle to form more meaningful relationships with each other, in place of the back-slapping camaraderie typical of male friendship.

As Roper and Tosh (1991: 18) put it:

Despite the myths of omnipotent manhood which surround us, masculinity is never fully possessed, but must perpetually be achieved, asserted and renegotiated.

What I have tried to do in this paper is to show some of the ways that conversational narrative is used by male speakers as a way of achieving, asserting, and renegotiating the conflicting masculinities available to them at the turn of the century.

Notes

1   I am enormously grateful to all the men and boys who agreed to allow their conversations to be used in this project. Some of the recordings were made initially by other researchers, including students taking my Conversational Narrative course at the University of Surrey Roehampton. I am also grateful to those who helped in the collection and transcription of data. Needless to say, all names have been changed, to preserve the anonymity of speakers.

2   I have followed the normal convention of those who work on conversational narrative, presenting the story in numbered lines, each line corresponding to one of the narrator's breath-groups or intonation units, typically a grammatical phrase or clause (see Chafe 1980).

3   In order to give some statistical backing to my observation, I undertook a detailed analysis of a sub-set of the narratives in the conversational data: this sub-set consists of 67 stories selected to give full coverage of all 30 conversations, with more or fewer stories selected depending on the total number in that conversation. So, for example, a conversation containing only one or two stories will have just

one in the sub-set, while a conversation containing eleven or twelve stories will have three or four in the sub-set. Stories chosen cover the whole range from minimal narratives of two lines to very long stories of 165 lines.

4   The following table summarises the gender of characters in the all-male sub-corpus of 67 stories (only 66 appear in the total here because in one story – 'Overheard between two cleaners', the gender of the two cleaners is not clarified).

	MALE	FEMALE	BOTH	TOTAL
Gender of protagonist	62 [94%]	3 [5%]	1 [2%]	66
Gender of other characters	47 [71%]	1 [2%]	18 [27%]	66

Table 1: Distribution of characters by gender in the sub-corpus
[Percentages rounded up to the nearest whole number, so totals are sometimes more than 100.]

References

Benjamin, Jessica 1990. *The Bonds of Love*. London: Virago.

Bruner, Jerome 1990. Autobiography as self. In J. Bruner (ed), *Acts of Meaning*. Cambridge MA: Harvard University Press, 33-66.

Chafe, Wallace (ed) 1980. *The Pear Stories: Cognitive, Cultural and Linguistic Aspects of Narrative Production*. Norwood NJ: Ablex.

Coates, Jennifer 1996. *Women Talk: Conversation Between Women Friends*. Oxford: Blackwell.

Connell, R.W. 1995. *Masculinities*. Cambridge: Polity Press.

Davidoff, Leonora & Hall, Catherine 1982. *Family Fortunes: Men and Women of the English Middle Classes 1780-1850*. London: Hutchinson.

Gough, Brendan & Edwards, Gareth 1998. The beer talking: four lads, a carry out and the reproduction of masculinities. *The Sociological Review*, August 1998, 409-435.

Jackson, David 1990. *Unmasking Masculinity*. London: Unwin Hyman.

Johnstone, Barbara 1990. *Stories, Community and Place*. Bloomington: Indiana University Press.

Johnstone, Barbara 1993. Community and contest: Midwestern men and women creating their worlds in conversational storytelling. In Deborah Tannen (ed), *Gender and Conversational Interaction*. Oxford: Oxford University Press, 62-80.

Jukes, Adam 1993. *Why Men Hate Women*. London: Free Association Books.

Kerby, Anthony 1991. *Narrative and the Self*. Bloomington: Indiana University Press.

Kimmell, Michael S. (ed) 1987. *Changing Men: New Directions in Research on Men and Masculinity*. London: Sage.

Kuiper, Koenraad 1997. Sporting formulae in New Zealand English: two models of male solidarity. In Jennifer Coates (ed), *Language and Gender: A Reader.* Oxford: Blackwell, 285-294.

Labov, William 1972. The transformation of experience in narrative syntax. In *Language in the Inner City.* Philadelphia: University of Pennsylvania Press, 354-396.

LeGuin, Ursula 1992. *Dancing at the Edge of the World: Thoughts on Words, Women, Places.* London: Paladin.

Linde, Charlotte 1993. *Life Stories. The Creation of Coherence.* New York: Oxford University Press.

Moore, Bruce 1993. *A Lexicon of Cadet Language.* Canberra: Australian National Dictionary Centre.

Phillips, Jock 1996. *A Man's Country? The Image of the Pakeha male – a History.* Auckland: Penguin Books.

Pleck, Joseph H. 1995. Men's power with women, other men, and society: a men's movement analysis. In Kimmel, M.S. & Messner, M.A. (eds), *Men's Lives* (3ed). Boston: Allyn & Bacon, 5-12.

Polanyi, Livia 1989. *Telling the American Story: A Structural and Cultural Analysis of Conversational Storytelling.* Norwood: Ablex.

Roper, Michael & Tosh, John (eds) 1991. *Manful Assertions: Masculinities in Britain Since 1800.* London: Routledge.

Seidler, Victor 1989. *Rediscovering Masculinity: Reason, Language and Sexuality.* London: Routledge.

Tolson, Andrew 1977. *The Limits of Masculinity.* London: Tavistock.

Weedon, Chris 1987. *Feminist Practice and Poststructuralist Theory.* Oxford: Blackwell.

Re-visions of gender and language research for the 21st century[1]

Ann Weatherall

Victoria University of Wellington

Introduction

This paper revisits the formative questions of the field of gender and language in the light of a more recent theoretical shift favouring social constructionist over essentialist explanations about the nature of gender, of language and of the relationships between gender and language. It would probably surprise those new to the field that satisfactory answers to questions first posed in the early 1970s, about sexist language and gender difference in language use, have not yet been found. Indeed some disappointment has been expressed about the lack of closure on gender and language research, because it has failed to develop the anticipated social critique to end sexism and other forms of discrimination.

Perhaps more worrying than the lack of definitive answers to those early questions has been that successive paradigms in language and gender research have been turned so easily to anti-feminist purposes. For example, research documenting women's indirect speech style has been used to blame women for not making their meaning clear. In an analysis of cases of date rape, Crawford (1995) noted that men were blaming women for saying 'no' in a way they felt did not mean 'no'.

One explanation for the lack of definitive answers to questions about gender and language is that there are problems with the assumptions on which those formative questions were based. This paper highlights those assumptions, and considers the impact they have had on gender and language research. It also indicates how a more social constructionist approach may begin to overcome some of the difficulties associated with earlier gender and language research. Using transcripts of children's conversations, the theoretical arguments are illustrated with research practice.

Rethinking the terrain of gender and language research

Throughout the history of gender and language work, two concerns have typically organized research in the field – sex bias in language and sex differences in language use. In an early review essay, Kramer, Thorne and Henley asked, 'Do women and men use language in different ways? In what ways does language – in structure, content and daily usage – reflect and help constitute sexual inequality? How can sexist language be changed?' (1978: 638) Robin Lakoff provided the inspiration for many researchers when she argued that, 'the marginality and powerlessness of women is reflected in both the ways men and women are expected to speak and the ways in which women are spoken of' (1973: 45).

So in the past there has been a sharp division between studying the way women and men use language, and studying their representation in language and texts. In more recent work the distinction between those areas has become less marked. Now these two areas are just as likely to be regarded as aspects of one process – the social construction of gender. As Deborah Cameron noted in a recent review article,

> When a researcher studies women and men speaking she is looking, as it were, at the linguistic construction of gender in the first- and second-person forms (the construction of *I* and *you*); when she turns to the representation of gender in, say, advertisements or literary texts she is looking at the same thing in the third-person (*she* and *he*). In many cases it is neither possible nor useful to keep these aspects apart, since the *I–you–she/he* is relevant to the analysis of every linguistic act or text (1998: 957).

More recently, then, some of the old boundaries that have divided up the area have been removed. Cameron (1998) suggests one reason for the breakdown of these old boundaries is that 'discourse', as in the frameworks and meaning systems that guide social interaction and social action, rather than language per se, has become the main locus for the construction (and contestation) of gendered and sexist meanings.

Sexist language

Despite the breakdown of old boundaries, however, there is still value in the traditional concerns of sexist language. A good illustration of this is Anne Pauwels' (1998) language planning approach to feminist oriented linguistic reform. However, even in her work she acknowledges the crucial role of what might be called a 'patriarchal world of discourse'. For example, in English, preference for gender-unmarked generic terms means that terms like 'partner abuse' rather than the gender-marked 'wife basher' hide the fact that men tend to be the perpetrators and women the victims of that crime. In her book Pauwels documents other attempts to neutralise language that have been frustrated

Language planning aside, careful consideration needs to be given to making language prescriptions. Prescribing language forms, whether sexist or not, can be understood as a form of censorship. On this matter Judith Butler's comment is pertinent: 'One is not simply fixed by the name one is called – the injurious address may appear to fix or paralyse the one it hails, but it may also produce an unexpected and enabling response.' (1997: 2). If we accept Butler's proposal, any attempt to 'cleanse' the language of certain terms may in fact be censoring out the very stuff that may motivate social change. The term *girl* is a potential example. In early feminist work there were attempts to outlaw calling adult women *girls*. However, if we erase this term from our speech it becomes difficult, for example, to express our pride and solidarity with adult female athletes. The All Blacks are 'our boys', thus the Silver Ferns deserve to be a similar symbol of national pride – 'our girls'.

One possible way of avoiding the problems associated with prescriptive language policies is to consider sexist language not as the problem itself but as indicating a 'higher level' bias within frameworks of meaning. In this way the use of certain gender-marked terms in language could be understood as creating and reinforcing a 'patriarchal world of discourse' or an 'ideological-symbolic' level of language and communication that disadvantages women. This shift is largely interpretative but has consequences for social practice.

If the use of sexist language is not treated as the problem itself, but as a manifestation of the problem, then the use of 'sexist' forms need not be the focus of intervention strategies.[2] Instead, if the use of sexist language is emphasised as indicating that the broader systems of meaning that we operate in have an androcentric bias, then the emphasis should be on more fundamental changes. One thread of the empirical work presented below is to document the use of gender-marked terms, and to consider the significance of them for the way that children understand their social world.

Gender identity

Aside from 'sexist language', the second question that has dominated the field has been that of whether women and men use language in different ways. As Crawford (1995) pointed out, a phenomenal amount of published research has investigated virtually every possible source of linguistic variation for sex difference. The result has been a general acknowledgement that men's and women's language use does sometimes differ. However, there is neither agreement on the exact nature of the differences, nor any consensus about the theoretical explanation of them.

Cameron (1997) pointed out that despite the lack of theoretical agreement, an assumption shared by different explanations of gender and language use is that speech is understood to index something that pre-exists language. Gender identity – whether it emerges from shared experiences of oppression or from the development of subcultural values – comes first, and then language is used to mark it. Talking like a man or like a woman is understood to be one of a set of social behaviours that results from an internalised gender role. Thus the presupposition shared by different theoretical explanations of gender and language is that 'women' and 'men' pre-exist the language. A consequence of this presupposition is that gender is seen as something essential to the individual – that is, whether through biology or social learning, women and men are essentially different.

This tendency towards gender essentialism has had at least two unfortunate consequences for gender and language research. It has meant that language research has tended to polarise sex/gender into two and only two categories. It has also encouraged the view that gender differences are essential differences so they will be fairly stable across time and social context. However, the realisation that women's and men's speech styles are not stable but particular to the local communicative context has been an important influence on gender and language research in the 1990s. For example, in an important review paper, Eckert & McConnell-Ginet (1992) made a compelling case for the need to 'look locally and think practically' when examining gender and language use. They made the point that expressions of gender will vary depending on the interpersonal and social context, as well as the function of the communicative event.

Conceptualising the way women and men speak, not as a reflection of their identity but as something that is a particularised event, is a shift from an essentialist to a constructionist framework for understanding gender. When gender is understood as a socially constructed category then questions of difference are fundamentally flawed, since they locate sex/gender inside the individual rather than something that is realised between people in the nuances of any particular social interaction. Cameron (1998) has suggested that the recent renewed vigour of research in the field of gender and language can be attributed to the shift towards understanding the socially constructed nature of gendered identities. Analysts are no longer interested in gender difference, but rather how people 'do' gender in social interaction.

In summary, the present research was motivated by a wish to avoid the limitations of past research that seem to have arisen from the assumptions underlying the formative questions of the gender and language field. Instead of investigating sexism in language and gender differences in language use, I was interested in finding evidence of how gender was mobilised in children's conversations in a way that structures and orders their understanding of the world and their behaviour. Furthermore I wished to highlight some aspects of language use that may have been missed by research that focused on differences.

Children's conversations – a social constructionist approach to gender

Data set

The data used for this study were conversations involving six four-year-old children attending the student crèche at Victoria University of Wellington, New Zealand. The children were grouped in an all-girl triad (Ann, Deb and Jen), an all-boy triad (Ben, Ian and Ross), and two mixed sex triads (Ian, Jan and Ross; Ann, Ben and Deb). Each group was recorded during two different types of play activity: making party food with playdoh and playing with a train set. The resulting conversations were transcribed and my analysis of them was informed by a social constructionist approach to gender.

The use of gender marked terms

One aspect of my analysis was to investigate the children's use of gender reference terms (*dad, lady* etc). Out of a total of the 7829 recorded and transcribed utterances made by the children while playing, 3% (n=218) were coded as using gender reference terms. The majority of gender reference terms (88%) were male terms. Many of the male gender reference terms were used when the children anthropomorphised objects. For example, the train was 'Mister Train' the different shaped train tracks were 'Mister Turny' and 'Mister Downhill'. A toy dog was assigned a masculine gender and called 'Joey'. Male cartoon characters were referred to (e.g. 'Cookie Jar man', 'Batman') and masculine specific terms were used for job titles (e.g. 'fireman'). In addition children referred to each other together as 'guys'. The much higher frequency of male terms compared to female terms was an indication of how androcentric-meaning systems were created and reinforced in the children's discursive world.

Mobilising gender in interaction

Evidence that gender as a concept was being mobilised by the children to co-ordinate and order their ongoing play activity emerged when the children played with a train-set. The train-set came with three dolls. One of the dolls wore blue clothes, had a blue cap and was depicted on the train-set box as the train driver. A second doll, in a red dress, was clearly identifiable as a girl. The third doll was dressed in white and blue. Its sex was ambiguous.

The following extracts are examples of how the gender of the dolls was mobilised by the children to co-ordinate their play. Gis(elle) is the adult supervising the children's play:

Extract 1
[Transcription conventions at end of paper]
JAN: which one is this one go in?
GIS: any one that. <2>
ROS: front.
JAN: I can put it in the in the back if I want
ROS: no it goes in the front cos he's the driver.
JAN: no [I can put it.]
IAN: [or the red one] could be the driver.
JAN: I can put which [ever one].<>
ROS: [yeah but you have but <>you ha put the red
         one in cos <> um you can put anyone
JAN: it's a girl one the red one so it doesn't go there.

In extract 1 Jan asks Gis(elle) where in the train the blue boy doll goes.
Gis(elle), trying to avoid directing the children's play, responds
'anywhere'. Ross answers Jan's question, stating that the blue doll should
go in the front of the train because 'he' is the driver. Using Gis(elle)'s
comment as her guide, Jan insists that she can place the blue doll
anywhere she likes. Ian suggests that the red doll could be the driver.
Then Jan realises the importance of gender in determining where the
dolls should be placed and acknowledges that it would be inappropriate
for the girl doll to go where the boy doll belongs. What is evident from
the above exchange is that gender was an important concept that the
children were using to construct a shared understanding.

Extract 2 is another example of how gender was explicitly used to
make sense of the ongoing play activity. This exchange between Ben
and Ross occurred when the three boys were playing with the train-set.

Extract 2
BEN: [see he's] dead eh? have to take him to your hospital [eh?]
ROS: [that's] a her.
BEN: him.
ROS: it's a her <2>
BEN: did your cousin say?
ROS: yeah. <>so it's a her.

In extract 2 the ambiguously sexed doll has fallen out of the train. Ben refers to the doll as 'him' and suggests that a trip to the hospital might be necessary. Ross claims the doll is 'a her'. Ben initially disagrees but finally concurs when he finds that Ross's cousin also said the (ambiguously sexed) doll was female.

The next extract is interesting because Jan has to resolve an incongruence between the train driver doll's sex and Ann who wants to play being the driver:

Extract 3
JAN: an this is the train driver. the train driver's a boy [it's a boy.]
ANN: [I know] I'm a boy I'm a boy.
JAN: well we could make it a girl.

Gender was clearly an important concept that the children used to construct shared meaning and to organise their play activity. Rather than focusing on gender as an attribute of individuals which affects speech, as essentialist approaches are prone to do, research informed by social constructionism places more emphasis on how gender as a category is mobilised in conversation to construct shared meanings and co-ordinate activities.

Girls competing; boys co-operating

Research informed by essentialist theories of gender has tended to highlight gender differences. In the present research the similarities in the boys' and girls' speech is striking. For example both boys and girls tended to use similar linguistic devices to get attention or justify their behaviour.

Extract 4
ROS: I know <> cause I I've seen one at my friend's house <> you
        know. <> now let nis person get on.<>
IAN: and you [gotu just]
BEN: [but they don't] go in there (angry and shouted)
ROS: so I can put them in there as well if I want to.

In extract 4 Ross and Ben disagree over where the dolls can be placed.

Ross uses an 'I can do it if I want to' linguistic formulation to justify his actions. Interestingly Jan used exactly the same formulation to justify her behaviour in extract 1.

Extract 5
DEB: hey look. I made it all. Jan I made it all

Extract 6
IAN: look Ben. look Ben. look at that side.

Extracts 5 & 6 are from an all-girl play group and an all-boy play group respectively. Both Deb and Ian use the directive 'look' in combination with a personal name to attract attention. Numerous other examples exist in the transcripts where the children use similar repertoires of linguistic devices to organize and coordinate their interactions. Claims of general differences in the way males and females speak create a false polarization of how the sexes communicate.

A focus on difference obscures the similarities in the way males and females speak, and it disguises the fact that differences are partial and not absolute. There were numerous examples in conversations where both boys and girls demonstrated linguistic behaviour that is usually attributed to the other gender group. For instance both boys and girls demonstrated cooperative linguistic behaviour. In extract 7 Jan, Ian and Ross are playing together cooperatively in a tea party game:

Extract 7
ROSS: who wants a cup of tea?
IAN: not me.
JAN: not me. can I have a cup of tea please?<3> (Ross gives her one) thank you.
ROSS: do you want a cup of tea Ian?
IAN: no
JAN: oopsy. how are you? . . . .
IAN: I want some tea.
JAN: where's that E? here's a E?
ROSS: your cup of tea that's there.
IAN: I drunk it I have and I want some more tea.<> . . . . . .

ROSS: I've finished my cup of tea.
JAN: and I've finished my cup of tea but I but I've still got a teeny
        bit left.
ROSS: do you want some more tea?
IAN: no

In extract 8 Ross cleverly negotiates a cooperative solution to a situation
of conflict between Jan and Ian who are both trying to get a piece of
track out of the train-set box:

Extract 8
ROSS: how do you get nese fings out? <> I got one.
IAN: [I'll get the other.]
JAN: [I'll get] I can I get that?
ROSS: yeah [you can both.]
JAN: [I'll get it.]
ROSS: [you can both] get it out

In extract 9 Jan, Ian and Ross are playing with Playdoh. All three children
contribute to the competitive tone of the conversation where each child
claims the playdoh colour which is theirs. Jan begins by asserting her
competence at being able to open the playdoh container. She stakes her
claim over the 'pink one' quite categorically.

Extract 9
ROSS: these are hard to get open you know.
JAN: I opened mine. I got pink one.
IAN: I got green.
JAN: I [got] pink.
ROSS: [I got]
ROSS: blue.
IAN: I got green.

In extract 10 Jan and Ann are competing both for turns at speaking
(note the overlapping speech) and for the right to claim the position of
train driver.

Extract 10

JAN: don't put the they go together [eh?]
ANN: [I'm] the train driver
        I am [I'm the train drive.]
JAN: [no I'm the] train driver.

Extracts 7, 8, 9 and 10 illustrated that differences in the boys' and girls' speech are not absolute, but are only differences of degree. In extract 7 the boys demonstrate a co-operative interactive style with Jan which ensures the success of the make-believe tea party. In extract 8, Ross takes on a type of consolatory role more usually considered typical of a co-operative interactive style. In extracts 9 and 10 the girls demonstrate speech features more usually associated with a competitive interactive style. Jan, in extract 9, asserts that she opened the top of her playdoh container soon after Ross has claimed that the containers are hard to open. In extract 10, Jan and Ann compete for the right to be the train driver. So, extracts 7 and 8 are examples where boys are demonstrating a cooperative style of interaction usually attributed to girls, and extracts 9 and 10 are examples where girls are using a competitive style of interaction normally attributed to boys.

Concluding comments

Boundaries marking the traditional territory of gender and language research are breaking down. Instead of treating questions about gender in language as separate from the language used by women and men, the two questions are seen to be about the same process – the social construction of gender. When the traditional boundaries of the discipline blur there is more potential for innovative investigation into the social construction of gender categories and the consequences those constructions have for understanding and social action.

Sex difference has been a dominant theme in gender and language research. Despite a substantial research effort by scholars in English speaking countries over the last 25 years, no straightforward sex differences have been found. Theoretical explanations of sex specific speech styles have polarised and stereotyped gender. More menacingly, this work has also been used to support rather than challenge the gendered status quo.

Gender categories are clearly important social categories and at present there is ample evidence that the masculine category is viewed as more normative and valued more highly than the feminine category. The present move in gender and language research, to view gender as a social rather than an individual concept, has the potential to avoid the gender polarising and sex-stereotyping that has typically been supported by work on gender differences.

However, treating gender as an ideological-symbolic construct and examining how people 'do' gender is not without its problems. For example, how is it that the analyst knows when one is 'doing being a woman' or when one is 'doing being a man'? In analysing 'doing gender', the researcher is deciding what counts as 'doing femininity' or 'doing masculinity'. Thus the analyst may, as in the sex difference research, be reinforcing ideas about gender, since any commentary that treats women and men as different categorical groups reinforces this dichotomy.

How then may we study gender and language/discourse without re-treading old paths? One suggestion, emerging from an ethnomethodological or conversation analytic approach is to invoke gender as an analytic category only when it is explicitly made relevant and constructed by the participants in the interaction (e.g. Stokoe 1998). The extent to which it is desirable, or even justifiable, to invoke gender as an analytic category when it is not absolutely transparent that it is relevant to the participants in the interaction itself, is an issue attracting lively debate (see Wetherell 1998). It is an issue which I hope will continue to engender debate in the gender and language field for some time to come (Weatherall 2000).

Notes

1   'Re-vision – the act of looking back, of seeing with fresh eyes' (Rich 1972: 35).
2   Institutional policies against the use of sexist language are a worthwhile exercise. However, the danger with such policies is that they are used as an excuse for not making more fundamental changes in organisational cultures.

References

Butler, Judith 1997. *Excitable Speech: A Politics of the Performative.* London: Routledge.

Cameron, Deborah 1997. Theoretical debates in feminist linguistics: questions of sex and gender. In Wodak, Ruth (ed), *Gender and Discourse.* London: Sage, 21-36.

Cameron, Deborah 1998. Gender and language gender, language, and discourse: A review. *Signs: Journal of Women in Culture and Society* 23, 4, 945-967.

Crawford, Mary 1995. *Talking Difference.* London: Sage.

Eckert, Penelope & Sally McConnell-Ginet 1992. Think practically and look locally: Language and gender as community-based practice. *Annual Review of Anthropology* 21, 461-490.

Kramer, Cheris, Barrie Thorne & Nancy Henley 1978. Perspectives on language and communication. *Signs: Journal of Women in Culture and Society* 3, 3, 638-651.

Lakoff, Robin. 1973. Language and woman's place. *Language in Society* 2, 45-80.

Pauwels, Anne 1998. *Women changing language.* London: Longman.

Rich, Adrienne 1972. When we dead awaken: Writing as re-vision. Reprinted in Adrienne Rich 1984. *On lies, secrets and silences. Selected Prose 1966-1978.* Essex: Virago.

Stokoe, Elizabeth H. 1998. Talking about gender: The conversational construction of gender categories in academic discourse. *Discourse & Society* 8, 2, 217-240.

Weatherall, Ann 2000. Gender relevance in talk-in-interaction and discourse. *Discourse & Society* 11, 2, 290-292 .

Wetherell, Margaret 1998. Positioning and interpretative repertoires: conversation analysis and post-structuralism in dialogue. *Discourse & Society* 9,3, 387-412.

Transcription notation

[ ]   overlapping speech
<>   pause, less than 1 second
<2>   timed pause
( )   transcriber's comment

How apologies get to be gendered work

Miriam Meyerhoff

University of Hawai'i at Manoa

Two aspects of apologies are examined in this paper. The discussion first focuses on what an apology does in interpersonal and social terms, and this leads to reflections on why apologies are not universally recognised as a speech event, that is, why some cultures do not distinguish apologies from other linguistic practices, as is the case in English, for example. There follows some discussion of the connections between these theoretical and reflexive observations and the empirical findings that show that in cultures where apologies are a *bona fide* speech act, some of their work is probabilistically associated with one sex rather than with another. It is suggested that beliefs about the sexes and beliefs about what constitutes naturally gendered work are expressed through this probabilistic association. The paper constitutes a modest exploration and reflection of the issues raised. The full and final story on apologies (within or across cultures) remains very much open to research and debate.

Transgressive and empathetic apologies

It is useful to begin by drawing a distinction between two major ways in which apologies are used. The canonical or prototypical apology is a familiar concept. Someone does or fails to do something, and attempts to make good. In 1998, much of the western world found itself inordinately fixated on the President of the United States' personal life. Without revisiting the sordid details of the case, it is useful to focus on one of Bill Clinton's early attempts to put the matter to one side. Appearing on national television, he acknowledged having had an improper relationship with an intern and apologised for having caused pain and humiliation to his family. We may assume that his public apology was an analogue of even more heartfelt and effusive apologies he made personally to his wife and daughter. We may assume that this involved his saying 'I'm sorry', and a good deal more besides.

But take another case where the same linguistic formula may be used. Imagine the following situation (taken from life, but with names changed). A man, who we will call Charles, decides to track down an old friend whom he has not spoken to for nearly four years. Let us call her Sue. They exchange the usual gossip: jobs have changed, they have both moved several times. Things have been better, Sue tells him. On her daughter's first birthday last year, her husband announced he had fallen in love with someone else and had been having an affair. Failed attempts at reconciliation had followed, piling further affronteries on Sue's initial indignation, and exacerbating her disgust at the timing of his announcement. At the end of the story, there is little Charles can say other than 'Sue, I'm sorry. I'm just so sorry'.

The first example is probably considered the more typical or basic exemplar of an apology for most people. An act of transgression has occurred and the social order has been disturbed. The function of an apology in these cases is to establish responsibility. However, as a good deal of the previous work on apologies has noted (starting with the still influential ethnographic work of the sociologist Erving Goffman (1971), and more recently developed in Nicholas Tavuchis' (1991) thoughtful monograph on apologies), this is done through a complicated mixture of social and personal factors.

On the one hand, the apology is a social act. This is because an apology openly acknowledges the existence of a social norm which has somehow been threatened or violated. In addition, by acknowledging the importance or value of the social norm, its normativity is reaffirmed and reconstituted. But on the other hand, an exemplary apology is a matter between two individuals. Even apologies from one government to another, or from one group of citizens to another are predicated on and only succeed insofar as there is an accepted metaphorical relationship between individuals. This personal dimension to an apology accounts for why second-hand or mediated apologies are seldom as successful as direct one-to-one apologies. This was made clear in the interpretation and gloss provided of the legal settlement reached in a New Zealand court case between the Honourable Helen Clark and Dr Joseph Brownlee in late 1999. Part of the final (and public) settlement was for an apology to Dr Brownlee to be read in court by Ms Clark's lawyer. As reported in the national media at the time, Dr Brownlee's lawyer took some pains to make clear that mediated or not, a full apology was part of the settlement.

Because of this mixture of personal and social functions, the person offering an apology assumes responsibility of two kinds. First, they assert a responsibility *as a member of a community* to support, not violate, social contracts. This assertion is not just phatic, it is extremely functional, because in asserting this responsibility the apologiser begins to help actively rebuild the structure of social values that might have been endangered by their transgressive act. Second, the apologiser accepts *personal* responsibility for having caused the threat or violation. The functionality of this is a bit more subtle. By accepting this responsibility, it appears that any hurt or anomie that the recipient might have been feeling is no longer perceived to be a burden of the recipient alone. Of course, the distinction made here between personal and social work is a bit idealised. Clearly, both kinds of responsibility work simultaneously at constituting interpersonal relations, and also at constituting social relations.

Janet Holmes (1990) has documented the distribution of these apologies in New Zealand English, looking at both the transgression type and the social characteristics of the apologiser. Although her database has an inherent positive bias (that is to say, only transgressions followed by apologies were recorded; transgressions that go unacknowledged or unrepented were not), some interesting patterns emerge. The majority of apologisers in Holmes' corpus were women. This might suggest that apologies are a strong index (in the sense in which the term is used by Elinor Ochs (1992)) of some characteristic or cultural property that is equally strongly associated with women. However, the indexicality involved was more complicated than this. Holmes also found that when New Zealand men did apologise, they chiefly did so to women. This is an intriguing result and it is not entirely clear what should be made of it. In her article, Ochs stressed the point that the cultural association of some trait or behaviour with women or men is a powerful means by which ideologies of gender are constituted and reconstituted through everyday interaction. Perhaps Holmes' data shows that the process by which apologies acquire status as an index of femininity is a process in which New Zealand men are also fairly actively involved.

The motives for and functions of transgression apologies are remarkably interesting in themselves. For instance, it is tempting to think that certain emotions, such as feeling sorry for some social transgression, are entirely natural human responses, but it is worth noting that the speech act of an apology is by no means universal. Bambi Schieffelin (personal communication) has observed that the Kaluli (in Papua New Guinea) have no corresponding category of speech event. Similarly, Marilyn Strathern's (1968) discussion of the notion of feeling sorry for someone in Hagen (also in Papua New Guinea) suggests that there is again no discretely recognisable speech event analogous to the English/ European apology. We will return to this point below; for the moment it will serve to contextualise further discussion of apologies. The general lesson to be drawn from this ethnographic work, then, might be, as Catherine Lutz very nicely puts it, that emotions are not in some sense *precultural* (that is, universal), instead 'emotional experience is . . . pre*eminently* cultural' (1988: 5).

However the chief purpose of this paper is not to examine transgression apologies. The focus here is on the second kind of apology illustrated at the start of the paper: the empathetic apology. There are several interesting aspects to these apology routines.

First, I consider how a function like the expression of empathy might have emerged from what I take to be the core function of apologies (that is, to acknowledge and redress some transgression). Second, in some cultures at least, the empathetic apology appears to be gendered in ways similar to the transgression apology. During a period of fieldwork in a village community on Malo island in northern Vanuatu, I noticed that empathetic apologies appeared to be women's work, rather than men's. Because women on Malo also generated the bulk of the transgression apologies that were recorded (in a pattern similar to that documented by Holmes for apologetic work in New Zealand English), this further (and more exclusive) asymmetry between women and men's use of empathetic apologies is especially provocative.

How empathetic apologies are used: establishing authority through empathy

Let us be clear about the focus here. We are dealing with the person (only a woman in Malo, as I have noted) who punctuates a tale of woe with variations on 'I'm sorry; I'm so sorry' (*sore* in Bislama), as shown in example 1. It is also the linguistic formula sometimes employed to soothe a crying baby. A female caregiver may snuggle the child and caress it repeating, 'Sorry, sorry, sorry', as shown in example 2.

(1) Lisa (L), Adelin's (A) aunt, is telling a story about an earthquake. The people in the story were so scared that they ran out of their house, forgetting to pick up their baby.

L:	afta tufala i ron olsem ya mama blong pikinini tu	so they both ran like that even the child's mother
A:	**sore**	**oh no**
L:	mama blong pikinini tu i ron afta bebi i stap, ledaon gud	even the child's mother ran and the baby stayed, lying quietly
A:	**awe, sore**	**oh NO**

(2) Lunchtime at Visi (V) and Lolan's (Lo) house. Also present, Susana (S, V's niece), Miriam (M) and baby Lara (La).

S:	hem wetem Bubu Maks	he and Bubu Max
V:	(sam) oli stap (go) aot nao	some people are going to be leaving now
S:	Bubu Maksi	Bubu Maxi
V:	sam oli stap aot sam oli wantem stap mared	some people are leaving some people want to stay married [i.e. they will stay with their families]
M:	mm	mm
La:	*hmhmhmhmhm*	[noises of fussing and distress]
Lo:	{kiss} **aya sore**	**sorry**

This use of the routine *sore* 'sorry' is similar to dubbing someone a 'poor thing' of course, and feeling pity and being sorry for someone else are undoubtedly closely related. Both require some displacement of the speaker's self; both require an attempt to unify or bring more closely together the speaker's and the addressee's experience. One of the things that makes them different, though, is that pity is an emotion that leaves intact a status or power difference between the interlocutors. Being sorry requires no such power differential. For example, I do not pity my husband when he fails to get the job he had been hoping for, but I do pity someone without the means to satisfy their basic daily needs.[1]

Expressing sorrow for someone else does not require such an existing power differential (though it is true that if a tragedy befalls someone that almost inevitably sets up some hierarchy with the fortunate placed above the unfortunate). On the contrary, by co-opting the linguistic formula associated with apologies for transgressions and by introducing it into a domain where it expresses empathy, one actually introduces some such imbalance or asymmetry. The way in which it does this, paradoxically, is through an implication of sameness.

This may seem paradoxical, but the paradox can be unpacked and thereby better understood. It lies at the nexus of the basic, prototypical function of a transgression apology and the dynamics of expressing empathy. Empathy itself is an interesting emotion. It necessarily involves insinuating yourself into someone else's experience. This is supported by ethnographic work in communities in which there is no category of speech event equivalent to an apology. Schieffelin (personal communication) attributes the absence of a category apology in Kaluli to the fact that Kaluli assert that it is impossible to know what another person is thinking or feeling. 'Pity', of course, can be felt for someone else (pity is also discussed in the communities Strathern and Lutz worked in – and interestingly, in all these communities pity is packaged with emotions that may seem non-intuitive partners to Western minds, such as 'love' and 'compassion'), but it seems that these cultures have a place for pity because pity does not require getting inside another person's head.[2]

Of course, having experience in something is not a neutral state. In Anglo-European culture, experience translates fairly directly into authority. I would suggest that expressing empathy with someone else is an indirect means of asserting experience in, or authority over, someone else's affairs. If one person chooses to demonstrate their empathy with someone else's dilemma or misfortune by assuming a posture of having shared the fear or disgust that the addressee actually did experience first-hand, the actor implies some authority in another person's life or experience. In other words, it seems that empathy *may* be, but *need not* be, a guileless stance of altruism.

Now if a means of expressing empathy is needed, and if the covert assertion of experience and authority inherent in empathy is recognised, then the use of an apology as a means of expressing empathy might seem to make more sense. The responsibility prototypically associated with an apology can be readily mapped (metaphorically) into a claim of experience. This may be why some people dislike it so intensely when someone says 'I'm so sorry' as a way of expressing empathetic concern. Any reader has probably heard, as the response to an empathetic apology, variations on: 'It's OK, you don't have to apologise, it's not your fault'. This may be delivered with varying degrees of exasperation. Negative responses along these lines are, on the face of it, rather puzzling. Why should someone care one way or the other if someone else is prepared to assume responsibility for something that happened to them? Undoubtedly, there are a number of motives for rejecting an empathetic apology, but when it actually *annoys* the recipient, a plausible interpretation of the cause of that annoyance is that the recipient resents the implied intrusion of a third-person into their personal experiences or personal affairs. It is similar to expressions of resentment that can be observed when a person who is not an immediate addressee tries to chip into a conversation, e.g. 'I wasn't talking to you'. In the case of the empathetic apology, one conclusion is that the annoyance is caused by the suggestion that there might be someone else out there (worse still, not just out there, but someone you know well enough to be open with), who is suggesting that they might have some responsibility for or authority over the life you are trying to lead. Worst of all, there is the implication that they might even have more control than you yourself do (since the apology will only be directed to someone who has just divulged some information that indicates they can't keep out of trouble's way).

Gendering of expressions of empathy and authority

How might this assist us in understanding why apologies are distributed sex preferentially in New Zealand English and also in Malo? And how might this assist us in understanding why the metaphorical use of an apology to express empathy is particularly so gendered on Malo? At least part of the answer to these questions lies in how women's work is constructed more generally, at least in most of the English-speaking world. If we look at this, it becomes clear that the account presented here about how empathy may implicate authority is not some silent success story ('How the sisterhood subverted the system, and came out looking sweet on top of it').

If apologies assume responsibility for a situation and if women are apologising more than men in New Zealand and Vanuatu, then it can be argued that in the distribution of apologies we see further evidence of the way interpersonal work – the work of the intimate (and perhaps we could even say the domestic?) sphere – is expected to be done by women. That is, responsibility for others' emotional state, and for managing the unfolding of personal disappointments or success is expected to be taken by women.

This is reminiscent of Pamela Fishman's (1983) groundbreaking research. Fishman observed that, in couples, women shouldered a good deal more of the responsibility for interpersonal and emotional work between intimates than their male partner did. In a recent ethnographic critique of the service industry, Deborah Cameron (1999) has pointed out that women are increasingly called upon to exercise similar stereotyped or enculturated interpersonal and emotional skills in the paid workforce. The call centres that Cameron studied have emerged as major employers, and therefore important socioeconomic forces, in the 1990s, and Cameron points out that many speech traits that are stereotypically considered 'feminine' feature prominently in the guidelines used to train and evaluate personnel in these workplaces. She discusses an emphasis on presenting a 'smiling demeanour', well timed and varied minimal responses, active questioning of the interlocutor. It is also striking how often the words 'empathy' and 'empathetic' crop up in the manuals she cites. Cameron argues convincingly that the indexical relation between femininity and paying attention to other's needs or feelings is being actively traded on here (in this case to the disadvantage of men, who are sometimes excluded from these jobs on the grounds that they are inherently less well suited to them). But I think there is another relationship that is being actively constructed and indexed too, and this is the relationship between subservience and attention to others. Since these relationships reflect extremely dynamic social processes, this means femininity is being indirectly constructed in terms of subservience as much as attention to others.

Including subservience in the picture adds a useful dimension to the goal of understanding the distribution of apologies. It could be argued that it makes a good deal of sense, if you are (for one reason or another) already in a subservient position with respect to others, to pay attention to information about the feelings or state of mind of those who enjoy a higher social position than you do. This may explain why we often find an overall tendency for women to pay attention to and to express empathy with men (through such means as apology routines). Of course, this leaves unexplained Holmes' finding that women apologise to other women, and my own observations that in Malo women also use apology routines with children, and even in reference to complete strangers and unknown third parties. In these cases, it is hard to see how a relation of subservience is being indexed. Perhaps the extension of apologies to these domains can be accounted for by referring back to the earlier observation that once the speech act of an apology exists (i.e. once the possibility of getting inside someone else's head is allowed), then speakers are free to exploit whatever opportunities that may open up for them as some kind of hidden bonus.

So the account of empathetic apologies presented here is not, at heart, an especially new one. It is similar to Penelope Eckert's (1989; 1999) account of why young women in the high school groups she studied were generally using more advanced forms of the various sound changes taking place in the Detroit region than their male peers were. Eckert has observed that if some of the more obvious material and social options for claiming status in and out of school are more readily accessed by the boys in these groups, it is probably unsurprising to find that the girls transform linguistic practices into social capital. If girls' participation in or access to other capital-rich practices is restricted, they may unconsciously turn to practices in which they have better access.

Finally, I would like to raise some interesting questions about the association between women, apologies and empathy as avenues for future research. The first is: what does this general association between women, apologies and empathy tell us about the relationship between men and empathy? One implication of the account outlined in this paper is that men are freed up to express empathy in terms that do not assume responsibility. That is, the gendered distribution of apologies in New Zealand English and on Malo puts men in a position of all care and no responsibility. Men can and do make evaluative comments on states of affairs and on other people's behaviour – 'Our hearts go out to everyone in Taiwan in the wake of this terrible natural disaster'; 'We all feel very deeply for the family in what must be a very difficult time for them' – and undoubtedly these evaluative comments are as sincere or insincere as any women's empathetic, 'I'm so sorry'. The crucial difference between expressions of empathy that are (gender-neutral or) gendered male and women's expressions of empathy using an apology, is the degree of responsibility assumed by the empathetic speaker.

Another question raised relates to the role of the recipient. In this discussion, the focus has been almost exclusively on what apologies and empathy mean to the person offering them, and it has touched only briefly on the wide range of responses they elicit in recipients. I believe that the role and actions of recipients are crucial if we are to untangle further the interaction between gender, subservience and attention to others, factors which I have argued here have a place at the centre of an understanding of apologies.

Notes

1   If this is a fair characterisation of pity and being sorry, then it raises as a tangential question (which must be left unanswered here), namely: is it possible that pity stands in functional opposition to envy? You cannot envy someone who is an equal. This seems a promising avenue for future elaboration. The relationship between pity and envy might be an analogue of the functional relationship between an apology and a compliment.

2   Because empathy involves working your way into someone else's experiences, it differs too from sympathy. Where sympathy makes a claim of reciprocality (it

implies: you and I are alike, we share equivalent thoughts, experiences or values), empathy is an asymmetric relation (it implies: I know how you feel – but you may be none the wiser about me).

References

Cameron, Deborah 1999. Styling the worker: Language, gender and emotional labor or 'you don't have to be nice to work here but it helps to pretend'. Unpublished paper presented at Cornell University.

Eckert, Penelope 1989. The whole woman: Sex and gender differences in variation. *Language Variation and Change* 1, 3, 245-267.

Eckert, Penelope 1999. *Language Variation as Social Practice*. Oxford: Basil Blackwell.

Fishman, Pamela 1983. Interaction: The work women do. In Barrie Thorne, Cheris Kramarae & Nancy Henley (eds), *Language, Gender and Society*. Rowley, Mass.: Newbury House, 89-101.

Goffman, Erving 1971. *Relations in Public: Microstudies in the Public Order*. New York: Basic Books.

Holmes, Janet 1990. Apologies in New Zealand English. *Language in Society* 19, 2, 155-199.

Lutz, Catherine A. 1988. *Unnatural Emotions: Everyday Sentiments on a Polynesian Atoll and their Challenge to Western Theory*. Chicago: University of Chicago Press.

Ochs, Elinor 1992. Indexing gender. In Alessandro Duranti & Charles Goodwin (eds), *Rethinking Context: Language as an Interactive Phenomenon*. Cambridge: Cambridge University Press, 335-358.

Strathern, Marilyn 1968. Popokl: The question of morality. *Mankind* 6, 11, 553-562.

Tavuchis, Nichola 1991. *Mea Culpa: A Sociology of Apology and Reconciliation*. Stanford: Stanford University Press.

What 'you' can say in Japanese: gender as a pragmatic factor in Japanese second-person reference through history

Andrew J. Barke

Tohoku University

Introduction[1]

The use of linguistic markers of gender varies across languages. In some languages, such as that used by the Karajá of Brazil, the use of systematic sound differences to indicate speaker gender is found in all contexts. In other languages such as English, speakers may signal their gender identity in some contexts and not in others. Japanese probably lies somewhere between these two poles. Speakers of Japanese may make use of a variety of gender markers such as sentence final particles, interjections, and supra-segmental elements (Ide 1990) as well as second-person singular pronouns. These markers vary in how exclusively they are used by each gender. For example, the feminine rising sentence final particle *wa*, is almost never used by male speakers. Other markers such as the masculine second-person pronoun *kimi*, are mostly found in male speech, but may occasionally be found in female speech as well.

Many authors have noted that gender differences exist in the usage of Japanese personal pronouns (Shibamoto 1985, Ide 1990, Tsujimura 1996, Maynard 1997). This is not a recent phenomenon, but has a long history dating back at least to the 8th century AD. Of the six commonly used second-person singular pronouns in Modern Standard Japanese (*anata, anta, kimi, omae, temee, kisama*), only two (*anata* and *anta*) are found to be frequently used by both male and female speakers, while the remainder *(kimi, omae, temee, kisama)*, are generally limited to male speech. This contrasts with the situation regarding personal pronouns in most European languages in which the gender of the speaker is not a major factor in determining the form of the pronoun.

This paper examines the role of gender as a pragmatic factor affecting the use of Japanese second-person singular pronouns. A survey of 72 past and present forms of second-person singular pronouns in Japanese is undertaken in order to obtain an historical perspective.

Gender and politeness in Japanese

The notion of politeness is highly relevant to any discussion of gender markers in Japanese speech. The maintenance of good interpersonal relations is highly valued in Japanese culture and is achieved to a large degree through the selection and use of appropriate grammatical as well as lexical forms. For example, inflections on verbs are used to indicate politeness, and in many cases, there is a choice of verb form: plain or honorific. In situations where there is no power differential between the interactants (e.g. a close friend or sibling), the plain form of a verb will be used. If a degree of politeness is required by the context (e.g. when talking to a stranger), then the polite –*masu* inflection attached to the stem of the verb will be used. Further politeness can be expressed by using the honorific forms of the verb when speaking of a superior, and plain forms when speaking of oneself. The different politeness-based forms for the verb *iku* 'to go', for example, can be seen in Table 1.

Table 1: Politeness-based forms of the Japanese verb iku *'to go'*

	Plain Form	Polite Form
	iku	*ikimasu*
Honorific Forms	*ikareru*	*ikaremasu*
	irassharu	*irasshaimasu*
	oide ni naru	*oide ni narimasu*
Humble Forms	*ukagau*	*ukagaimasu*
	mairu	*mairimasu*

As with verbs, personal pronouns also vary in accordance with the level of politeness required in a speech context, but this variation differs according to the gender of the speaker. Ide (1979: 43) illustrates the approximate ranges of politeness or formality of five of the six second-person singular pronouns mentioned previously in relation to speaker gender (shown in Figure 1). It should be noted that each has the ability to convey varying degrees of politeness within a certain range depending on factors such as the context of the utterance.

Second-person personal pronouns allow the speaker to make direct reference to the addressee. Therefore, one might expect that they would be commonly used in everyday discourse. However, this is not the case because of the general tendency in Japanese society to avoid directness in order to be polite. In a sense there is a taboo in operation concerning direct speech which has resulted in a range of second-person singular pronominal forms varying in degrees of politeness. New polite forms are usually created through the borrowing of euphemistic expressions from other nominal categories indicating location or direction, or they are created from Chinese compound words that act rather like a title. Many of the latter have politeness embedded within their morphological structure (Barke & Uehara 1999). However, once such new terms become widely used, they lose their indirect/respectful connotation. As politeness in existing forms reduces, new polite expressions need to be introduced resulting in a cycle of borrowing and discarding of terms. A schema showing how the Japanese pronominal taboo works is given in Figure 2 using terms from Modern Japanese as examples. Note the almost complete turnover of terms associated with gender usage. The existence of the politeness requirement for indirectness in Japanese has resulted in the personal pronoun word class being an open class. This goes against the common assumption in linguistics that personal pronouns are so integrated into the grammatical core of a language that they seldom change over time.

Japanese has seen a large number of second-person singular pronouns come and go throughout history. More than 140 forms have been in use since the Nara Period (710-794), an average of at least one new form for every nine years. A selection of 72 forms was made (shown in Table 2) based on work by Suzuki & Hayashi (1963), Miller (1980), and Tsukishima (1982). Reference was also made to the 'Nihon Kokugo

Figure 1: Second-person singular pronouns and gender of speaker (Ide 1979: 43)

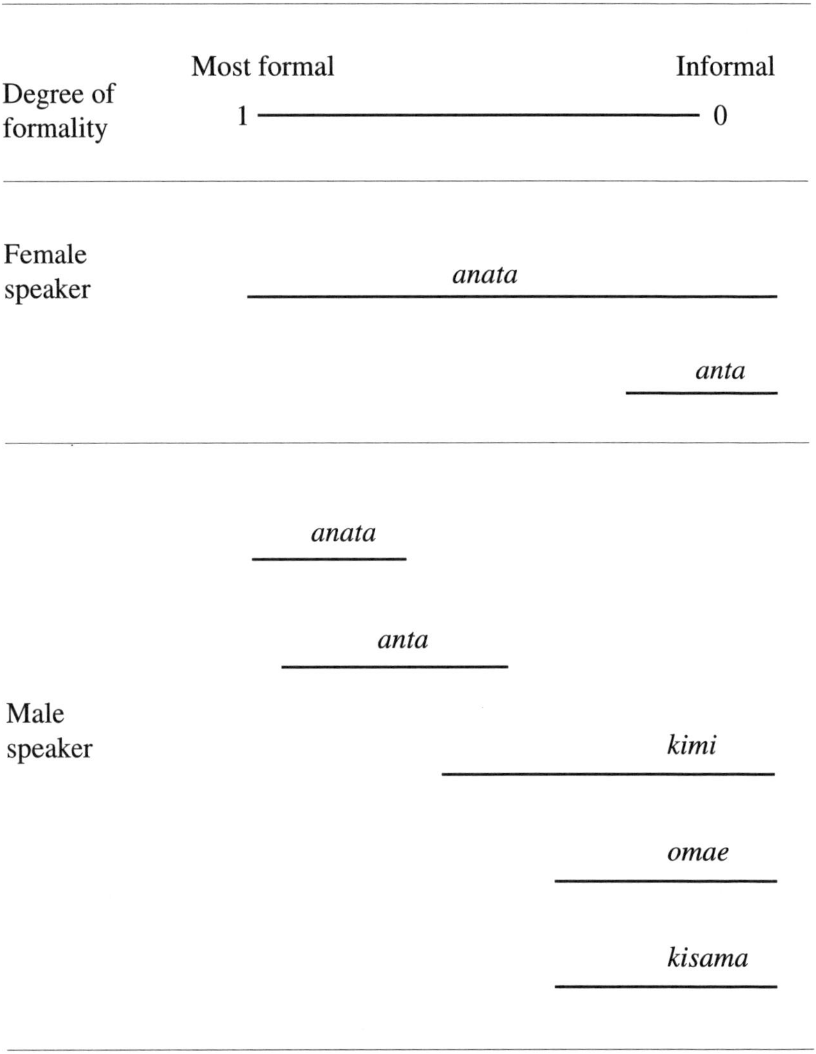

Degree of formality	Most formal 1 ———————————————	Informal 0

| Female speaker | *anata* | |
| | | *anta* |

	anata	
	anta	
Male speaker		*kimi*
		omae
		kisama

Figure 2: The life cycle of Japanese second-person pronouns

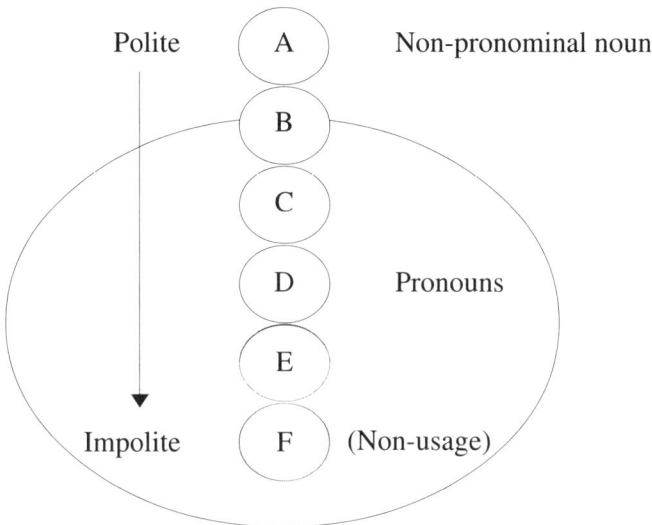

A: A noun/nominal phrase is borrowed as a euphemistic/polite expression to refer to the hearer (e.g. *sochira no hoo* 'in that direction [near you]').

B: While maintaining its nominal meaning and associated euphemistic politeness, pronominal usage of the noun/nominal phrase increases (e.g. *sochira* 'there [near you],' *otaku* 'your home').

C: As the noun/nominal phrase becomes widely used as a pronoun, its nominal meaning and associated politeness diminish (e.g. *anata* 'you,' *omae* 'you').

D: With the reduction in politeness, the contexts in which the term can be used become limited (e.g. *temee* 'you,' *kisama* 'you').

E: Eventually, all associated politeness is lost, and the term falls out of use.

Note: A form does not necessarily go through all stages of the life cycle, as some, for example, may fall out of use before they reach the derogatory stage. Moreover, the above schema does not imply all the forms follow the same linear scale.

Daijiten' (1972), a highly respected 20-volume dictionary of the Japanese language. Of the 72 terms surveyed, at least 27 (37%) of the total had specific gender restrictions (i.e. could be used only by female speakers or by male speakers).

Table 2: Japanese Second-person Singular Pronouns

Old Japanese (Nara Period 710-794)	*agi, i, imashi, **kimi**, mashi, mimashi, na, nanji, nare, nushi, onore, ore*
Late Old Japanese (Heian Period 794-1185)	***gohen**, imashi, **kiden**, kimi, kinji, mashi, nanji, nare, nushi, onore, ore, sokka, soko, sore(ni), wadono, wanushi*
Middle Japanese (Kamakura/Muromachi Periods 1185-1603)	*are, **gohen**, **kiden**, kihen, **kihoo**, kimi, **kishoo**, konata, nanji, nushi, okoto, onmi, onushi, **otemae**, onore, onoshi, **sochi**, sokka, soko, **somoji**, sonata, **sonohoo**, sore(ni), wadono, wagami, wagoryo, wahito, wanushi, ware*
Early Modern Japanese (Edo Period 1603-1868)	***agami**, anata, **anta**, are, arisama, **gohen**, **katasama**, **kiden**, kihen, **kihoo**, **kikoo**, kimi, **kisama**, **kishoo**, konan, **konasa(a)**, **konasama**, **konasan**, konata, **konatasama**, miuchi, nanji, nishi, nushi, okoto, omae, omaesama, omaesan, **omahan**, omee, omeesan, **omi**, omisama, onmi, onore, **onoshi**, onushi, **otemae**, **sochi**, sochira, sochitora, sokka, soko, **sokomoto**, **somoji**, sonata, **sonatasama**, **sonohoo**, sore(ni), **soresama**, **sosama**, sotchi, temae/temee, unu, wadono, wagami, wagoryo, wanushi, ware, waresama, **warisama**, waro*
Present Japanese	*anata, anta, **kimi**, **kisama**, **omae**, **temee***

Note: Forms written in bold indicate terms that had gender related usage.

In this survey, three points of difference between the genders became apparent. The first of these was the fact that there were more cases in which the use of new polite forms began in female speech (13 instances in female speech which was more than double the 6 instances found in male speech). Secondly there was a semantic difference between the forms used by male and female speakers. Many examples first used in male speech were polite Chinese compound words that made direct reference to the addressee, and included the Chinese morpheme *ki* meaning 'honour/respect' (e.g. *kikoo, kisho, kiden*). In contrast, terms originating in female speech tended to be euphemistic expressions indicating the position or direction of the addressee (e.g. *somoji, soresama, konasama*). The third difference noted was that while a number of forms which had originated in female speech were later adopted into male speech, the opposite pattern is almost nonexistent. An example is given in Table 3.

Table 3: Gender-based borrowing and politeness reduction in the Japanese second-person pronoun konasan

Historical Period	Female usage with ...			Male usage with ...		
	Superior	Equal	Inferior	Superior	Equal	Inferior
Early Modern	○					
		○	○···			
		○	○	○	○	
		□	□	□	□	

Note: The arrow indicates a borrowing between female and male usage, and outlined circles show a limited degree of usage. Here the borrowing is made from female speech into male speech.

A possible motivation for female speakers to be leaders in the creation of new polite terms of address in Japanese is found in Ide (1992). In a survey of 200 men and women, regarding politeness levels of the various forms of the verb *iku* 'to go', she found that women gave a lower judgement of a form's politeness than men did. Furthermore, when queried about which forms would be appropriate for use with a specified addressee (such as a spouse, a friend, a workmate etc.), women were found to select politer forms of address than their male counterparts. Ide concludes from her results that in order for women to show the same level of politeness as men, they must use politer forms of language. This sensitivity to politeness found in women's use of Modern Japanese offers an explanation as to why new forms of the second-person singular would appear in female speech. Perhaps women are more sensitive to the loss of indirect/polite connotations of second-person personal pronouns, and so have the need to start using new, more indirect terms before male speakers do.

This group of terms also indicates that gender can affect the choice of second-person singular pronouns in two ways. As discussed above, the gender of the speaker often affects the choice of form. However, the gender of the hearer may also play a role in determining the type of term used. These two dimensions are not mutually exclusive as they may or may not jointly affect the decision making process at any one time. Cross-tabulating the two dimensions, we get numerous combinations for gender-related usage: use by women with women; use by women with men; use by men with women; use by men with men and so on. Further illustration is found in Table 4 which depicts the usage of three terms of address from the Edo period (1603-1867): *somoji, sonatasama,* and *kiden.*

Table 4: Gender restrictions on some Early Modern Japanese second-person pronouns

		Pronoun		
Speaker	Addressee	*somoji*	*sonatasama*	*kiden*
Female	Female	○	*	*
Female	Male	○	○	*
Male	Female	○	*	*
Male	Male	○	*	○
		(if to a child)		

Note: Here we can see an uneven distribution of gender-restrictions on the terms. Use of *somoji* occurs in almost all of the gender combinations except male-male (unless the addressee is a male juvenile), while *sonatasama* and *kiden* are restricted to one combination.

Gender, therefore, can be been seen to play (and to have played) an important role in the selection process of the form of the second-person pronoun in Japanese. If the gender of the speaker and the gender of the hearer are to be taken into account when a pronoun is chosen, the appropriate forms must exist in order to be able to make the necessary distinctions. In other words, the salience of gender in Japanese personal pronouns results in the existence of a large class of words. The open nature of the personal pronoun class of words is not unique to Japanese, and in fact has been reported to occur even in the so-called 'stable' pronoun systems of certain European languages. Braun (1988), for example, describes how the use of polite expressions in these languages occasionally undergoes 'rapid' change. He offers several examples including that of the German language which produced three or four different pronouns of politeness.

Of course, gender is not an independent variable affecting pronoun usage; it interacts with the other pragmatic factors associated with politeness maintenance mentioned earlier. The more factors involved in the equation, the more forms will be needed to accommodate the expression of those factors and their combinations. Thus gender and its interaction with other pragmatic factors leads to a synchronic increase in the number of personal pronoun forms.

Changes over time

If we refer back to Table 2, we can see that there appears to be a steady increase in the number of forms of the second-person singular, peaking in the Early Modern Japanese era. It would be difficult to come to any conclusions regarding this apparent change in numbers, however, as it may merely reflect the availability of written resources from which the examples are taken. More can be said about the sudden drop in numbers between Early Modern Japanese and the present, which is referred to by Mizutani & Mizutani (1987: 1) who state:

> There is a great difference between *keigo* (polite language) before and after World War II, as postwar Japanese society has become highly democratized in language as well as other areas.

The authors note that second-person singular pronouns have been a part of the democratisation of the language, which accounts for the sudden drop in numbers seen in Table 2. Nonetheless gender continues to be an influential factor with regard to second-person pronoun usage in Japanese: 42% (26/62) of the pronouns in Early Modern Japanese showed gender related usage compared with four (66%) of the six most commonly used second-person singular forms in current usage.

Conclusion

In this paper, we have seen that the use of second-person singular pronouns in Japanese conveys information regarding the gender of the speaker and sometimes the listener too. This system is an important aspect of politeness in Japanese language discourse. The historical significance of gender in second-person singular pronouns was shown in a survey of 72 forms which have been in use at least since the eighth century AD. Over this time period, 40% (29) of second-person singular terms have been associated with gender-based usage at some stage. Furthermore, we have seen that the interaction between gender and politeness has led to this class of words being relatively large, with a high turnover. This turnover appears to have been led by Japanese women who appear to be more sensitive to issues of politeness in language.

Notes

1   Nicola Daly assisted with the editing of this paper.

References

Barke, Andrew J. & Satoshi Uehara 1999. T/V or not T/V?: A historical and comparative approach to social deixis in terms of address in Japanese. Paper presented at the 14th International Conference on Historical Linguistics Workshop on Historical Pragmatics, Vancouver, Canada.

Braun, Friederike 1988. *Terms of Address: Problems of Patterns and Usage in Various Languages and Cultures.* Berlin: Mouton de Gruyter.

Ide, Sachiko 1979. *Onna no Kotoba, Otoko no Kotoba* [Women's speech, men's speech]. Tokyo: Nihon Keizai Tsushinsha.

Ide, Sachiko 1990. How and why do women speak more politely in Japanese. In Ide Sachiko & Naomi H. McGloin (eds), *Aspects of Japanese Women's Language.* Tokyo: Kurosio.

Ide, Sachiko 1992. Gender and function of language use: quantitative and qualitative evidence from Japanese. *Pragmatics and Language Learning* 3, 117-129.

Maynard, Senko K. 1997. *Japanese Communication: Language and Thought in Context*. Hawaii: University of Hawaii Press.

Miller, Roy 1980. *The Japanese Language*. Tokyo: Charles E. Tuttle.

Mizutani, Osamu & Nobuko Mizutani 1987. *How to be Polite in Japanese*. Tokyo: The Japan Times.

Nihon Daijiten Publication Committee (ed) 1972. *Nihon Kokugo Daijiten*. [Encyclopaedia of the Japanese Language]. Tokyo: Shogakukan.

Shibamoto, Janet 1985. *Japanese Women's Language*. Orlando: Academic Press.

Suzuki, Kazuhiko & Ooki Hayashi 1963. *Hinshibetsu Nihon Bunpoo Koozoo 2, Meishi/Daimeishi* [Parts of speech – Japanese grammatical structure 2: nouns/pronouns]. Tokyo: Meijishoin.

Tsujimura, Natsuko 1996. *An Introduction to Japanese Linguistics*. Oxford: Blackwell.

Tsukishima, Hiroshi 1982. *Kooza Kokugoshi 4 Bunpooshi* [A course on Japanese language history 4: History of grammar]. Tokyo: Taiseikanshoten.

Violence in the home: intervention, gender and identity

Damian O'Neill

Massey University

Introduction

In New Zealand 30,000 cases of violence are reported to the police each year, 80% of which are family related. Since only a small minority of domestic assaults are reported to the police, it is likely that actual cases of violence are even more numerous. The great majority of these cases involve men assaulting their partners or children (Boyle 1994; Policing Development Group 1994). One in ten New Zealand women are physically assaulted by their partners each year (McMaster and Swain 1989; Leibrich, Paulin & Ransom 1995).

The Manawatu Men Against Violence collective (MMAV) combine an anger management skills-based approach with a feminist analysis of domestic violence in an intervention programme. From 1995-96 I undertook an evaluation of this programme. This paper documents the gender interventions which took place during the ten week programme, and examines some of the shifts in identity which occurred as a consequence of the programme.

To document the interventions, I attended one programme as a participant-observer. I obtained informed consent from the group as a whole, including participants and facilitators, before beginning the observations. Pre- and post-programme interviews, with 13 volunteers from a series of programmes over 1995, provided the basic data for assessing the course's effects.

Gender interventions of the programme

Gender socialisation can be seen as constraining men towards violence in a number of ways, including expectations concerning how they should think, feel and behave. Such expectations can have destructive side-effects, such as limiting the range of emotions men experience and articulate as they try to live up to cultural scripts of being tough and in control. This can lead to emotional numbness coupled with angry and uncontrollably violent outbursts (Marriot 1988). Gender socialisation also creates certain expectations about family roles which can fuel conflict. A traditional man may have certain expectations of his partner which she may not share. He may see himself as *the head of the household* and as *the one who wears the pants*. He may feel justified in using violence as a means of asserting his authority.

One of the most immediately obvious features of the Men Against Violence course was the emphasis placed upon 'male identity'. The group was explicitly encouraged to think of themselves as *men*. To this end the participants were constantly referred to as *men*. For example 'I'd like to ask every man here today to take part in this next exercise'. From this initiating backdrop, the programme moved on to encourage the participants to become aware of, and challenge, their attitudes towards and expectations of masculinity and traditional gender roles. An implicit challenge throughout the course was whether the participants were responsible enough to make intentional changes in their lives based upon their new-found awareness of socialisation and socio-structural constraints.

One exercise the men engaged in during the programme was obviously aimed at raising their consciousness of constraints which surround their gender socialisation. This was a brainstorming session exploring physical, social and emotional stereotypes of what constitutes a 'real man' and a 'real woman'. Suggestions were recorded on a whiteboard by a facilitator and included *brave, messy, disciplines kids, strong, hard, protects,* for 'real men', and *sexy, soft, nice, stroppy, secretary, good cook, understanding,* for 'real women'.

The next task was to replace some of the labels that the men thought were narrow or demeaning with less restrictive suggestions. For example *disciplining* was the first to be removed from the 'real man' description. 'I hate this shit' said one man and replaced it with *good with children*. For the 'real woman' description *manipulative* was replaced by *wise*. In this second round the focus moved from stereotypes to positive and non-sexist characteristics of each sex. The participants were then challenged by the facilitators to assume many of these behaviours.

Another form of intervention in the programme was the definition of violence as *control*. In this strategy the men's accounts of their violence, which usually referred to anger and victim blaming, were re-interpreted in terms of control. Reasons for individual men seeking to 'control' their partners were also discussed. Violence was put in the context of a series of male/patriarchal controlling strategies. Visual models such as the Power and Control Wheel and the contrasting Equality Wheel (Lambourn 1997) were used to emphasise this perspective.

A feminist 'power triangle' model of society (based on McMaster and Swain's 1989 model) was also explained to the men, providing an awareness of the context of their *controlling* relationships. In this model a triangle is used to represent the relationship of the man and the woman. Two key ingredients are identified as determining the nature of the relationship: personalities and socialisation. But other factors, beyond the immediate relationship are also acknowledged. The model includes a second larger triangle which surrounds the first and represents the pressures and expectations of the wider family. An example of such pressures was provided by a man whose father-in-law laughed at him when he helped with the washing. This second triangle suggested to participants that if their wider family accepts violence, this plays a role in supporting a violent relationship.

A third triangle was placed around the other two to represent the influence of society. Male dominated institutions such as the police, law, media, church, and workplace were placed in this context. For example the bible has sometimes been used to justify men's violence and dominion over women. The three layers of this model gave the men an insight into some of the external social forces which have helped to shape their relationships and behaviour, and which have encouraged them to control and justify being violent to their partners.

Through giving and soliciting examples (e.g. one man likes to be the breadwinner) the facilitators were able to obtain group consensus that there was a history to women's oppression and sexism. Finally the participants were challenged to make non-sexist/non-violent choices which would prevent the perpetuation of such patterns.

Aside from these overt challenges to their 'sexist' and 'violent' worldview, the men were also exposed to new ways of relating to each other and to experiencing themselves emotionally. Here interventions were aimed at emotional development to compensate for the constraining effects of masculine socialisation in their lives.

One of the ways in which this was achieved was by each man sharing his personal story with the group. This was a trying and often very sad exercise. The men were encouraged to tell their stories by the facilitators who modelled emotional expressiveness and honesty. They asked questions and encouraged the men to describe how they felt. In this way the men were exposed to new ways of experiencing themselves emotionally, and they were actively encouraged to articulate this *primary* experience. By providing this experience it was hoped that subsequent *secondary anger* could be more readily attended to, before their anger rose to dangerous levels (Dutton 1988).

The men also experimented with another major social taboo, namely caring and being emotionally supportive towards other men. The motivation for this exercise was the belief that if the men were able to engage in emotionally open and supportive talk with each other, their emotional dependence upon their partners could be reduced. Their need for control, which is considered to be a primary motivation for violence, might also be reduced (Stordeur & Stille 1989).

Aside from consciousness raising and emotional development, the course was also designed to teach the men other new skills designed to promote healthier, more fulfilling and equal relationships with their partners. The aim was to impart skills which would complement the consciousness-raising and emotional development of the men by providing new behaviours for them. These skills were outside the norms of masculinity, and included the skills of compromising, listening to and empathising with their partners, and communicating assertively, clearly and respectfully with them.

Outcomes

As mentioned above, I interviewed 13 voluntary participants from various runs of this programme offered by MMAV over the period of a year. One section of the interview dealt with the men's relationships, and this component is here used as a means of gauging the impact of the programme. The fact that the participants self-selected and that all the data was self-reported limits the generalisations which can be derived from these interviews. Acknowledging these limitations, there is nonetheless useful information to be drawn from the interviews which may be used to inform more focused and hypothesis-driven research projects at a later date.

In the following sections I present some of the dominant themes which emerged from the interviews. My definition of 'dominant' is that at least eight of the 13 men brought up and elaborated upon the issues in response to my open-ended questions. Quotations from the interviews will be used to illustrate each theme.

Pre-course themes

Before discussing the men's talk on their relationships, it is worth reviewing how the men accounted for their violence. Typically they used two interweaving stories. One was of blind, overwhelming, blanked-out rage.

> You get wound up so much inside like a spring, and the release of that spring is your arm shooting out with a closed fist. I didn't think about punching, it's just a reflex action (Paul).

The second story involved pathologising themselves and/or their partners, i.e. they blamed their behaviour on their own disposition, or on the problematic behaviour of the others:

> I always knew I had a bit of a problem with my temper. I can certainly do without it as part of my character. When I get angry, I just get physically violent (Chris).

> A lot of pressure, a nagging wife for a start, built up and up and all of a sudden I snapped (Carl).

One component of the interview explored the men's perceptions of the gender structures and social arrangements which existed in their sexually intimate relationships. More specifically, the men were asked to discuss how they felt about being a man, what they liked or disliked about their partners, and the roles they played in their relationships.

The men typically indicated that they did not ordinarily think about 'being a man'. In fact they did not think about themselves as *men* but rather identified themselves as non-gendered persons. Typically the men, prior to the course, took up a liberal humanist position through which their agency was constructed as representing an essential personhood, an underlying and universal self existing independently of gender.

> I've never thought about it, that's what I am. You take it for granted, um, I don't know. I've never really considered it . . . I *am me. The fact that my gender is male is irrelevant* because if I was a female then I would still look at it from the sense of, I am me and this is how I want to be. It's not I am a woman I want to be this way or I am a man I want to be this way. It's I am me, the male or female doesn't matter. I suppose I'm a man but that's beside the point, I am my own man . . . I don't look at it as man or woman. It's what you want to be, *the body is not necessarily the self* (Peter).

When questioned about gender and roles in relationships the men overwhelmingly responded once more from this *liberal* subject position. They maintained that relationships between men and women should be 'equal', with gender being irrelevant to the structural dynamics of the 'partnership'.

> I don't believe that there are *different roles for men and women* in a *partnership* today. We're all *just people. Both sexes* should be treated the *same* (Mike).

This liberal construction of the men's relationships as 'non-sexist' and 'egalitarian' could be found in the men's talk on decision-making, men's role in housework, child care and women's work outside the home.

> I've always thought that the *two partners should share everything.* They should be *equal* and share the *cooking* and the *cleaning.* I like cooking and *I'm into doing my share* of the cleaning. It wouldn't get to the point of me being asked to clean the floor for example because it would be done before it was needed (Robert).

The men were aware that others did not necessarily agree with their personal position. Consequently, they would contrast themselves and their egalitarian attitudes with the gendered expectations of others.

> *I get a bit of shit about it, cooking* tea and all the *washing, cleaning* the house. Oh her father and that . . . *'house husband'* and just a load of stupid shit (Terry).

Although the men universally employed liberal discourse to discuss their relationships, they frequently employed, although implicitly, gender specific assumptions of men and women and their role in the relationship. During their accounts, some of the men implied that there were in fact separate roles for each sex within their relationship.

> I also, you know, I done cooking, washing you name it, vacuuming, *just to help her* . . . *helping out* with the washing and things like that (Sean).

Such phrases revealed that the men were not as 'liberal' as they represented themselves. They were in fact using a gender-specific discourse. From a pro-feminist position this non-liberal, gender-specific discourse can be constructed as sexist. It is possible that other themes in the men's talk about violence are also informed by such a discourse. This may assist in understanding some of the themes in the men's stories, and enable us to consider some of their implications.

When questioned about what they liked and disliked about their partners, the men's positionings of their partners tended once more to slip in and out of the liberal account. Commonly, consistent with the liberal humanism, the women were constructed as good friends, being valued as persons and 'mates' in their own right.

> *Good company.* She's *good to be with* and that (John).

However the men also constructed women using gender stereotyped criteria. Their partners were typically praised for being 'good mothers', 'good cooks', 'family focused' and 'supportive'. Such virtues reflect traditional qualities associated with being a 'good wife'.

> *Excellent mother*, never raises her voice to the children no matter what, I mean she works, she *takes care of the home, excellent cook* and everything, you know the *kids* are never without anything, um just overall *a really good lady* . . . she was an *excellent wife* . . . I never went without anything . . . she *looked after me* in every way, shared everything she had with me, the children (Dave).

Similarly, characteristics of the woman partner constructed by the men as dislikeable were typically traits which conflicted with conventional constructions of the 'good wife' such as 'assertiveness', 'uncleanliness' and 'selfishness'.

> Sometimes she would get incredibly *selfish* and *not care* about the rest of us. I'd just look at her and think what a *bitch*, what am I doing here with you? ... *I don't like her when she's like that* (Robert).

The men thus appeared to slip in and out of their liberal humanist position. While maintaining that they were non-sexist, they constructed their partners favourably when they fulfilled traditional sex role stereotypes, and constructed them negatively when they did not. The implication of this pro-feminist reading of the interviews for understanding the men's violence thus warrants consideration.

When sex role stereotypes are not met by partners, this may cause stress, conflict, tension buildup and a sense of justification of 'angry' feelings. These angry feelings may then 'heat up' or 'explode' in violence. It seem likely that aspects of men's talk concerning their partners are related to some of the accounts of tension building provided by the men when they explained their violence to their partners. In such accounts the woman's 'unreasonable' behaviour was commonly constructed as 'precipitating' the violence by causing high degrees of stress and tension within the man, who was construed as the 'victim' of her unruly behaviour. Such an interpretation of the data suggests that the men's employment of a gender specific discourse may inform their 'pathological' constructions of their partners and thus contribute to their overwhelming 'inner tension'. This is supported by some of the accounts of violence:

> I felt *justified in my anger*. . . I seemed to have lost *my rights as being able to speak out* . . . I mean every argument started off just like how we're talking, um you know in a proper manner, um trying to force my point of view . . . I think I was trying to um, because you felt like that *you found other ways of trying to reinforce your status as a man or so you went over the top in doing it.* I'm somebody. I'm gonna show I'm somebody by enforcing all these rules around here . . . you were in charge of what you implemented and that sort of made you feel a bit more important you know if you want to look at it that way (Sean).

Post-course themes

The follow-up interview to the programme came some eight to ten weeks
following the completion of the course, roughly five months after the
first interview. At the beginning of each interview the men were asked
for feedback on the course. The vast majority of the men reported that
they felt 'woken up' and 'enlightened' by the programme's content. Their
'consciousness' was expanded, placing a 'new light' on things.

> *It enlightened me* to a lot of *different ways of thinking* (David).

Some of this 'enlightenment' concerned the anger management techniques the course offered

> It made me *aware* of the *factors involved in violence,* like where
> you're at and the *buildup to it.* Just to be able to *monitor* sort of like
> where your *tension level* is at and to do something about it before
> you reach *explosion point* (Aaron).

Others appreciated learning to be more sensitive with other people and
to respect their opinions and rights to be different.

> I think I've thought *most about rights* more than anything. Um.
> I've never sort of taken much to, well *I've always sort of thought
> that I was right,* and I never sort of thought about any sense of
> anybody else's, you know. Nowadays *I can accept some one else's
> opinion even if it is a bit different from mine* (Mike).

In the post-course interviews, participants were once again asked to
account for their violence towards to their partners. This was done with
reference to the most recent episode, or if there was no recent episode,
the most vivid case they could recall.

Here there was a noticeable shift in the men's response, with two
dominant themes being shared. It was interesting that a greater amount
of emotional talk occurred in both areas. As with the pre-intervention
stories, the buildup of an overwhelming inner tension prior to violence
was common. What was different however, was the improved ability of
the men to articulate the primary emotions leading to their 'uncontrol-
lable' rage. This was a contrast to the surprised and passive 'victim of
rage' approach presented prior to the course.

A second theme which emerged was one of choice and control. Noticeably absent was the pathologising of the man himself or the woman. The men recognised that they had made a choice to manipulate, intimidate, coerce or punish. There was more talk of choice and under-lying emotions, such as fear and insecurity, being the motivators for control. Sometimes both these themes were apparent in the same man's account:

> I think my anger and violence came out of emotional hurt, just feeling hurt and not heard, it just builds into anger for me . . . it was the grouping together of a whole lot of things, um frustration, feeling annoyed, disappointed with myself . . . Yeah I thought that I sort of had the upper hand and her take that, I've won this round, bugger you (Ray).

Some of the men spoke of learning about the social construction and constraints surrounding men, macho-ness and masculinity. These men took up a more structuralist position as they constructed 'norms' as constraints and rejected them because of their problematic implications for violence. The men's new 'big picture', as one man put it, thus appeared to be informed by the construction of gender structures.

> All this *macho bullshit* doesn't do anyone any good (Steve).

Some of the men maintained the pre-programme story when asked what it meant 'to be a man', rejecting the employment of a gendered identity:

> So long as I'm a good person, I don't really care about, *I'm not a man*, or you know, I've never looked at it as though I'm a man, you're a woman sort of thing. It's just *I'm a person* (Peter).

Most of the men however indicated that the course had prompted them to think about their 'manhood' in a different way. Typically these men employed a feminist account alongside liberal resources when doing so, constructing conventional stereotypes and cultural expectations as being dangerous, and they spoke of choosing to behave outside of these constraints. Traditional masculine traits, such as being 'tough' and 'macho', were rejected, while traditionally feminine characteristics such as 'caregiving', were incorporated into their constructions of manhood. The men had thus become aware of their masculinity as it is socially constructed, and appeared to have consciously decided to reconstruct this in an unconventional manner when forging their (new) identities as men.

> It's changed the *ideals* that I've had, about what a *male and a father's meant to be*. . . a man to me . . . is good with his *family*, um, gives them *time and loving*. It doesn't have to be anything special, *a big hero* or anything (Sean).

The advent of a gendered consciousness in the group with respect to personal identity represents a transformation in the men's self-positioning. From a pro-feminist position this is a positive shift. The men are more likely, following the course, to see themselves and their behaviour as constructed through normative forces, and this provides a space to resist their constraining effects.

With regards to their relationships, the men displayed liberal attitudes. Most of the men indicated that they had changed their sexist ways, while others maintained that they had always been egalitarian and non-sexist.

When asked to comment on the course's emphasis on equal power sharing in relationships, the men unanimously agreed with this liberal position. While some constructed themselves as having been this liberal before the course, others had shifted to this position and typically described their shift through constructing themselves prior to the course as 'old fashioned' and 'dominant'. These men reported that they had been 'enlightened' by the course in this respect.

> Three months ago I would have laughed at you if anybody said I'd be staying home looking after the kids and she was going to work. But now I'm *woken up* if you like, *I've changed* . . . I never cooked anything at all before. I never did the dishes, I wouldn't do the dishes . . . I never touched cooking or nothing cause tea was on the table, she just cooked tea and lunch and that was it. Well *it wasn't my place to do bloody dishes*, it wasn't my scene. I was making the money . . . looking at it now I sort of think that I thought then that *it wasn't the male thing to be* involved in you know . . . It was *a chauvinist bloody thing*, it wasn't my scenario. Not going out with snotty nosed little kids in the bloody supermarket, and I can honestly see that now (Andrew).

When asked about their 'ideal relationships', the men once more took up a liberal position and constructed their ideals as 'egalitarian'; while placing an emphasis on 'communication', 'caring' and 'support'.

> My ideal relationship would be *based on respect* and *involve lots of nurturing and support* (Robert).

These men spoke of shifts occurring in their relationships as a consequence of their new awareness. They reported greater diplomacy and communication with their partners, increases in their input into housework and putting more effort into their children. These changes were reported as being very positive for the men and a reduction in stress and tension was also reported.

> There's been *a change in the way we relate* you know . . . And *I can hear* what she's saying and *she will listen* to my points too. Um. So yeah we talk through things and decide on what to do and *that makes life a lot easier let me tell you* (Carl).

> I feel like, *less stressed* by it when I can *share* it, the *responsibility* I mean (Richard).

In terms of helping to reduce men's violence, this reduction in tension, associated with the various 'shifts' towards an egalitarian lifestyle appear to be a very positive outcome of the programme. Thus this study provides some evidence that interventions promoting gender equality are positive to the extent that they reduce 'inner tension', a commonly hypothesised cause of men's violence (O'Neill 1998).

Conclusion

To summarise the observations and resulting discussion of the programme itself, it appears that the gender interventions to the 'stopping violence' programme work at a number of levels. These include:

- Changing attitudes towards violence through reframing violence as a choice and a patriarchal control strategy.
- Consciousness raising about sex role socialisation constraints.
- Reducing relationship tension, via changing expectations and the provision of new forms of relating.
- Imparting 'primary' emotional awareness.

The present study demonstrates that identity shifts can take place in men over a relatively short period of time. Gender consciousness, imparted in a supportive, challenging and closed group, can encourage new behaviours and ways of being in the world. But these results must be interpreted with caution. They are grounded in the accounts of a small self-selecting sample. Such participants may be a special group of violent men, namely men who want to change, or at least to be seen making the effort to do so, and thus the data may be skewed. Additionally the interview data may be further biased by a motivation on behalf of the participants to inform MMAV of what they think MMAV might want to hear.

Certainly more research needs to be undertaken in this area. However, exploratory research, such as the evaluation study reported here, is useful for uncovering promising themes for future research.

References

Boyle, Allan 1994. *Social Report: June 1994*. Palmerston North: Palmerston North City Council.

Dutton, Donald G. 1988. *The Domestic Assault of Women: Psychological and Criminal Justice Perspectives*. London: Allyn and Bacon.

Lambourn, Barbara 1997. *Community Action to Prevent Family Violence*. Wellington: Safer Community Council.

Leibrich, Julie, Judy Paulin & Robin Ransom 1995. *Hitting Home: Men Speak About Abuse of Women Partners*. Wellington: New Zealand Department of Justice.

Marriot, Allan 1988. *The Prance of Men*. Christchurch: Hazzard Press.

McMaster, Ken & Peter Swain 1989. *A Private Affair? Stopping Men's Violence to Women*. Wellington: Government Print Books.

O'Neill, Damian 1998. A post-structuralist review of the theoretical literature surrounding wife abuse. *Violence Against Women* 4, 457-490.

Policing Development Group 1994. Family violence is 'the cradle for the perpetuation of violence and crime in the community'. *The Roper Report*. Wellington: Policing Development Group.

Stordeur, Richard A. & Richard Stille 1989. *Ending Men's Violence Against Their Partners: One Road to Peace*. London: Sage.

How long have women been leading language change?[1]

Margaret A. Maclagan

University of Canterbury

When sociolinguists first examined the question of language use and gender, they found that women used more standard forms than men did. Chambers and Trudgill state:

> For very many variables, other things being equal, women tend on average to use more higher status variants than men do. Indeed, this is perhaps the most strikingly consistent finding of all to emerge from sociolinguistic dialect studies in the industrialised western world (1998: 61).

This is especially true for women of higher social classes. These women use more standard forms for items that show stable sociolinguistic variation. They also lag behind others in adopting new sound changes. (See Labov 1990; Pauwels 1987; Wolfram & Schilling-Estes 1998; and James 1996 for summaries of research). Part of the female gender role therefore seems to include being guardians of 'good language'. So in 1988, when Elizabeth Gordon and I found that higher class young women in our sample were leading the EAR/AIR merger in New Zealand English (NZE), we reported this result without drawing attention to it (Gordon & Maclagan 1989).

Today, it is accepted that women do use more standard stable prestige forms, but researchers have come to expect that even women from higher social classes may lead non-stigmatised sound changes (Wolfram & Schilling-Estes 1998: 187). Part of women's gender role is now seen as setting new standards for language (Holmes 1997; Milroy & Milroy 1993).

The question can then be asked whether women have changed their behaviour over the last part of this century or whether researchers have changed the way women's behaviour is interpreted. In this paper I suggest that women have not changed their behaviour; they have actually been leading non-stigmatised changes in language for some time. In particular, I suggest that women led the move towards a distinct NZE accent as early as the nineteenth century and that, as they led this movement, so they helped to create the accepted norms of what is now NZE. And therefore the female gender role of creating language standards has been operating for at least a hundred years within New Zealand.

New Zealand social dialectologists are fortunate to have recorded material for almost the entire history of Anglophone speakers in this country. After World War II in 1946-48, the Mobile Disc Recording Unit of the National Broadcasting Corporation of New Zealand toured the country recording, among other things, pioneer reminiscences (Lewis 1996). These recordings are available at the University of Canterbury where they form the Mobile Unit (MU) Archive which is part of the data being analysed in the Origins of New Zealand English Project (ONZE) (Maclagan & Gordon 1999). It includes recordings of first generation New Zealanders born as early as 1850. This paper presents acoustic results for ten speakers, all first generation Anglophone New Zealanders born between 1864 and 1886, and shows that women born in the nineteenth century were already in the lead in the movement towards what has become modern NZE.

Data

The speakers in the Mobile Unit Archive come from both the North and the South Islands of New Zealand, and from different types of settlements (rural, militia and gold mining). The ten speakers who are analysed in this paper are selected to match as closely as possible the overall balance of speakers in the Archive. There are five men and five women of similar ages and similar places of origin. Table 1 provides some social inform-ation on the ten speakers.

Because the archive consists of interviews with the speakers, the words analysed were isolated from continuous speech. Deterding (1997) indicated that, although the vowel quadrilateral shrinks when vowels from connected speech are analysed, the relative positions of the vowels remain constant. Rastatter & Jacques (1990) and Rastatter, McGuire, Kalinowski & Stuart (1997) demonstrated that older speakers produce more centralised vowels, but that their vowel patterns do not change markedly. We can thus be reasonably confident that the vowel patterns obtained from connected speech for these older speakers give a valid representation of their speech.

Table 1. Details of the speakers

Speaker	Sex	DoB	Home Region	Type of Town
SH	F	1864	Coromandel, NI	Gold
MT	F	1875	Waikato, NI	Rural
EC	F	1876	Waikato, NI	Militia
AH	F	1877	Central Otago, SI	Gold
CD	F	1886	Central Otago, SI	Gold
WD	M	1865	Coromandel, NI	Gold
PM	M	1873	Otago, SI	Non Gold
JE	M	1874	Coromandel, NI	Gold
JMcK	M	1875	Central Otago, SI	Gold
FB	M	1879	Waikato, NI	Militia

One of the major characteristics of the MU data is its variability. Peter Trudgill, who carried out impressionistic analysis on the data, noted that individual speakers have combinations of realisations for phonemes that would never have occurred in Britain (Trudgill, Gordon, Lewis & Maclagan in press). Because of this variability, and because the data are extracted from continuous speech, a minimum of 20 tokens for each vowel or diphthong were analysed, and more for the sounds which have been particularly noted as characteristic of NZE. Only words which receive sentence stress were chosen for analysis. Close to 4,000 tokens were analysed across the ten speakers.

Analysis

The words to be analysed were digitised using Sound Sampler at 22.05 kHz. Acoustic analysis was carried out on Soundscope 16 (a Macintosh acoustic analysis program). Three formants were measured at the vowel target for monophthongs and at each of the targets for diphthongs. The formants were measured using the LPC analysis window and the default settings (14 coefficients, and 20 ms frame advance).

The vowels were normalised using Lobanov's technique (see Disner 1980), but this made little difference. The spread of the tokens for the individual vowels was reduced, but the relative positions of the vowel centroids did not change. Questions have been raised about the advisability of normalising results, especially when the data show marked variation (Disner 1980). Because of the variability in the present data, the non-normalised data will be presented in this paper. Data are not presented for individual speakers, rather the results are averaged across all five men and across all five women

Results

Figure 1 presents non-normalised acoustic plots for modern NZE (after Maclagan 1982) based on 25 men and 25 women. The patterns for the men and the women are similar. They both have high DRESS and TRAP vowels,[2] central GOOSE vowels, lowered STRUT vowels, raised NURSE vowels, and raised LOT and THOUGHT vowels, so that there is a relatively straight line across the top of the quadrilateral (THOUGHT, GOOSE, FLEECE). And both the men and the women have central and somewhat lowered KIT vowels. A recent acoustic study by Watson, Harrington & Evans (1998) shows the same patterns for NZE.

When the variables of age and social class are not constant, differences appear between men and women's vowels (see Maclagan, Gordon & Lewis 1999). The data on which Figure 1 is based were selected to involve as little social variation as possible. All speakers were of similar ages (approximately 20 years) and social classes and all spoke the General variety of New Zealand English. When these variables are kept constant, there is remarkably little variation in the vowel patterns of the two genders. Women and men are doing 'being New Zealanders' rather than marking gender differences.

Figure 2 presents the pure vowel charts for the ten early New Zealand speakers. Again there are more similarities than differences in the male and female patterns. And the overall patterns are very different from modern NZE as shown in Figure 1. Considering first the overall patterns,

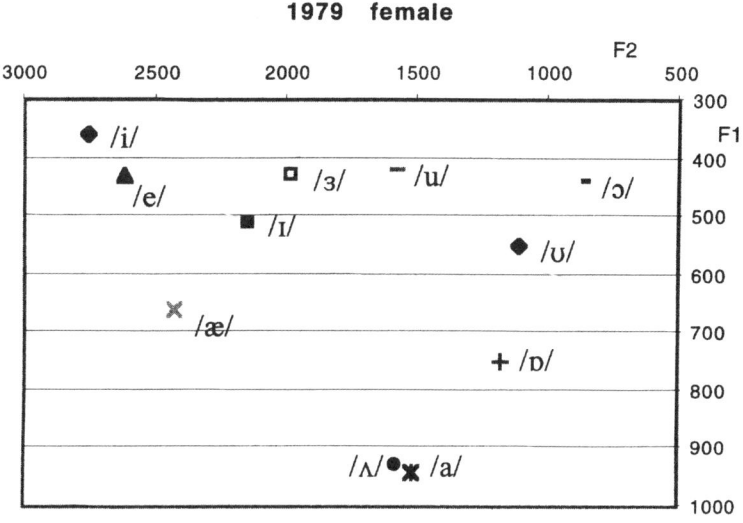

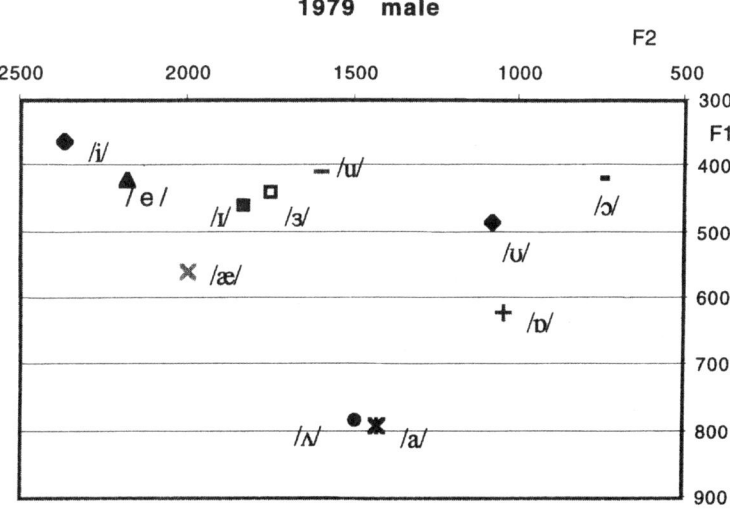

The scales are different on the two graphs to help compensate for the differences in size between male and female vocal tracts.

Figure 1. Acoustic plots for Modern NZE pure vowels

MARGARET A. MACLAGAN

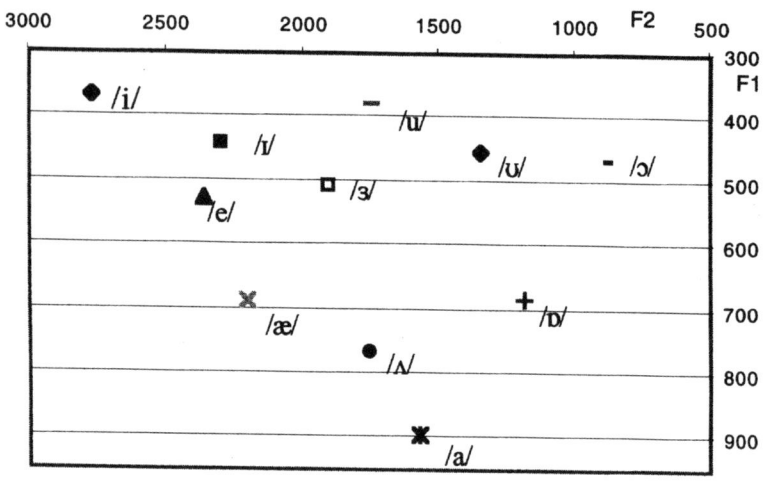

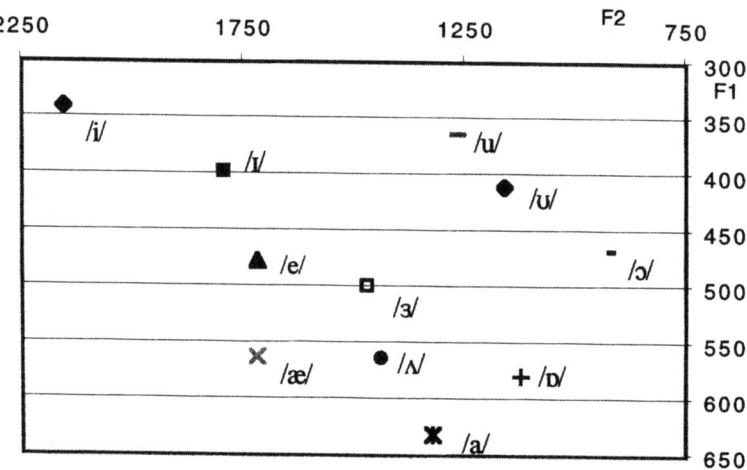

The scale is different on the two graphs to help compensate for the differences in size between male and female vocal tracts

Figure 2. Acoustic plots for Mobile Unit speakers, pure vowels

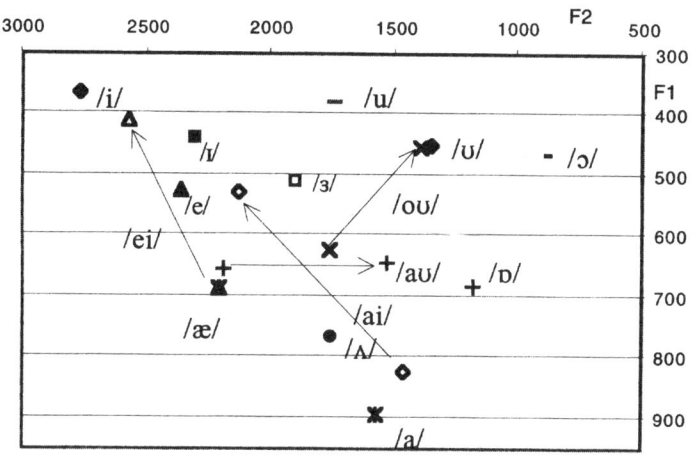

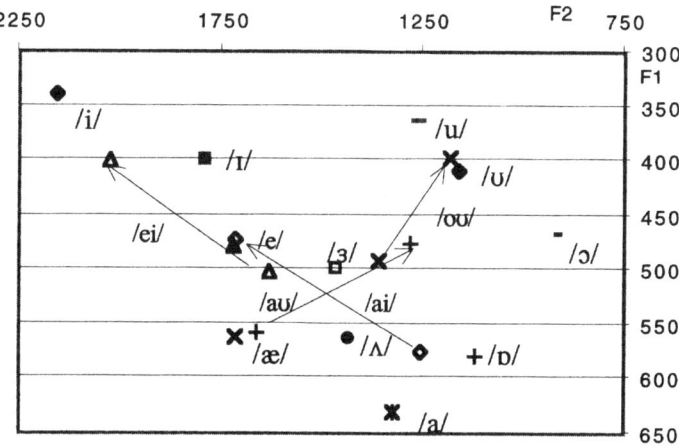

The scale is different on the two graphs to help compensate for the difference in size between male and female vocal tracts.

Figure 3. Acoustic plots for Mobile Unit speakers, diphthongs

it can be seen that the DRESS and TRAP vowels are not nearly as high as in Modern NZE, and the STRUT vowel has not yet lowered. The GOOSE vowel has centralised so that it is as central as the START vowel, but the LOT and THOUGHT vowels are not yet raised, and the NURSE vowel is still relatively open. The KIT vowel is still higher than the DRESS vowel. There is no sign of the modern NZE centralised KIT vowel for these early speakers of NZE.

Considering next the differences between the male and female vowel pattern, it can be seen that the women's GOOSE vowel has centralised more than the men's. GOOSE is more fronted than START for the women, but not for the men. The LOT and THOUGHT vowels have started to raise for the women, but they are not yet as high as in modern NZE, so there is not yet a straight line across the top of the quadrilateral. The women's DRESS and TRAP vowels are relatively more raised, and although the KIT vowel is still higher than the DRESS vowel for the women, it has begun to centralise. A check of the phonetic context does not show any consistent contextual effects that would explain the women's different pronunciations. The difference between the positions of the KIT vowel for the men and women suggests that the NZE front vowel movement is a pull chain (Maclagan, Gordon & Lewis 1999), not a push chain, as has been previously proposed (see Bauer 1979).

It therefore appears that the five women have moved farther in the direction of modern NZE than the five men.

Figure 3 presents the diphthong charts for the five men and women. When people first started to comment negatively on a NZE accent, the diphthongs PRICE and MOUTH were among the first sounds to be singled out (Gordon 1998; Maclagan, Gordon & Lewis 1999). Impressionistic analysis of speakers in the Mobile Unit archive, shows that the MOUTH diphthong has moved most, followed by PRICE then GOAT and FACE. From the acoustic analysis, the women can again be seen to have moved farther towards modern NZE than the men. Considering first the FACE diphthong, it can be seen that the women start on their TRAP vowel. The men, by contrast, still have a relatively short FACE diphthong which starts just below their DRESS vowel. The GOAT diphthong has a fronter start for the women than for the men (as central as their STRUT vowel), but there is the least difference between the men and the women for the GOAT diphthong.

The PRICE diphthong starts in a more open position for the women than for the men, being below their STRUT vowel. It has not yet moved farther back towards the modern NZE [prɔis] for either men or women. It is a longer glide for the women because it still moves towards the DRESS vowel even though DRESS has raised. MOUTH is the diphthong that shows the greatest movement. Its starting point is related to the TRAP vowel for both men and women, and it has followed TRAP as TRAP has raised. Figure 3 also shows that the women are starting to demonstrate the very short glide for MOUTH which is characteristic of modern NZE. The men still produce tokens that end with [ʊ] whereas the women are moving towards the modern NZE version of [mɛəθ] with its very centralised second element.

Woods (1997) carried out an impressionistic analysis of ten MU speakers and ten related speakers from the next generation. As in the present study, she found that the older women produced tokens of MOUTH with higher first targets than the older men's tokens. When she considered the next generation, she found that the men had continued to raise the starting point for MOUTH but that the women had reversed the trend and were using a more open starting point. This would indicate that higher starting points for MOUTH were not yet stigmatised for the early women described in the present paper, but that they had become stigmatised by the next generation (see Maclagan, Gordon, & Lewis 1999). Woods' finding and the results of the present paper are consistent with women leading in non-stigmatised sound changes.

Discussion

The interesting question is why the women's vowels are more advanced than the men's. Why were women as early as the 19th century adopting what we now consider to be a female gender role and leading in language change?

In the ONZE project we use Peter Trudgill's theory of koinéisation (Trudgill 1986; Trudgill, Gordon, Lewis & Maclagan in press) to partly explain the formation of NZE. This theory states that there are three stages in the formation of a new dialect in a dialect contact situation: accommodation, levelling and focussing. Accommodation occurs in face to face situations as people adapt to the differences between their idiolects. For NZE, some accommodation must have happened on the ships as people sailed to the new country. Levelling occurs as features specific to different dialects are levelled out so that any features which are too marked or too closely associated with one particular dialect disappear (Trudgill et al, in press). This stage can last for a considerable time as more and more features are levelled out. During the levelling stage, many different features can co-occur, leading to the variability which is characteristic of the MU data. In the final stage of focussing, the new dialect stabilises and develops its own set of features.

The ten men and women analysed here are somewhere in the stages of levelling and focussing. There is still variation within their particular idiolects. For example, one of the women, CD, has a relatively open variant of TRAP and an extremely close one that does not seem to be phonetically conditioned. So the different variants of the phonemes have not yet settled down and levelled out for the individual speakers. Nevertheless, a focussing trend can be seen towards what is known today as the NZE accent. The women have moved farther along this focussing continuum than the men have.

Parental influence is not the cause of this difference between the men and the women. One of the intriguing features of the ONZE corpus is that the speakers often do not show dialect features that would be expected from the information that is available about their background. In a dialect contact situation like NZE in the 19th century, there is no stable surrounding dialect for children to learn, and it is hard to predict precisely which varieties of sounds they will learn. The exceptions to this are individuals who grew up in extreme isolation and whose speech was therefore largely based on that of their parents, a situation that is not true for any of the ten speakers analysed here.

As women's speech has been analysed, a salient female gender characteristic is the extent to which women pay attention to positive politeness and accommodate their speech to the speech of the people with whom they are speaking (see Giles & Powesland 1975). I suggest this is what happened in the 19th century. In the very volatile dialect contact situation in which they found themselves, the women followed this female gender pattern and accommodated to the speech around them by levelling their own regional features in the interests of facilitating communication.

Another female gender characteristic is the way in which women's usage may actually set the standard for the language (Milroy & Milroy

1993; Holmes 1997). As the women analysed here accommodated their speech to the general direction of the focussing that produced NZE, so their speech would have become accepted as the 'standard' for the new dialect. The women were both more sensitive to the way in which the new dialect was developing, and then, by their own speech, helped to steer the dialect farther in this direction.

To return to the question in the title of this paper, 'For how long have women been leading language change?' From the New Zealand data analysed here, the answer is that women seem to have been leading language change for more than 100 years. We cannot necessarily generalise from this NZE data across other varieties of English or across other languages because the social situations will differ, but this answer certainly holds for New Zealand.

Note

1   The work reported here was supported by grants from the Foundation for Science Research and Technology and by the University of Canterbury. I would like to express my appreciation to Elizabeth Gordon and Peter Trudgill for their support and comments.
2   I follow John Wells' 1982 convention of referring to the various vowel phonemes by means of keywords.

References

Bauer, Laurie 1979. The second great vowel shift? *Journal of the International Phonetic Association* 9, 57-66.

Chambers, J.C. & Peter Trudgill (eds) 1998. *Dialectology* (2ed). Cambridge: Cambridge University Press.

Deterding, David 1997. The formants of monophthong vowels in standard Southern British English pronunciation. *Journal of the International Phonetic Association* 27, 47-55.

Disner, Sandra F. 1980. Evaluation of vowel normalisation procedures. *Journal of the Acoustical Society of America* 67, 253-261.

Giles, Howard & Peter Powesland 1975. *Speech Style and Social Evaluation*. London: Academic Press.

Gordon, Elizabeth 1998. The origins of New Zealand Speech: the limits of recovering historical information from written records. *English World-Wide* 19, 61-85.

Gordon, Elizabeth & Margaret A. Maclagan 1989. *Beer* and *Bear, Cheer* and *Chair*: A longitudinal study of the *ear/air* contrast in New Zealand English. *Australian Journal of Linguistics* 9, 203-220.

Holmes, Janet 1997. Setting new standards: Sound change and gender in New Zealand English. *English World-Wide* 18, 107-142.

James, Deborah 1996. Women, men and prestige speech forms: a critical review. In Victoria L. Bergvall, Janet M. Bing, & Alice Freed (eds), *Rethinking Language and Gender Research: Theory and Practice*. London: Longman, 98-125.

Labov, William 1990. The intersection of sex and social class in the course of linguistic change. *Language Variation and Change* 2, 205-251.

Lewis, Gillian 1996. The origins of New Zealand English: A report on work in progress. *New Zealand English Journal* 10, 25-30.

Maclagan, Margaret 1982. An acoustic study of New Zealand English vowels. *The New Zealand Speech Therapists Journal* 37, 20-26.

Maclagan, Margaret & Elizabeth Gordon 1999. Data for New Zealand social dialectology: The Canterbury Corpus. *New Zealand English Journal* 13, 50-58.

Maclagan, Margaret A., Elizabeth Gordon, & Gillian Lewis 1999. Women and sound change: Conservative and innovative behaviour by the same speakers. *Language Variation and Change* 10, 19-41.

Milroy, James & Lesley Milroy 1993. Mechanisms of change in urban dialects: the role of class, social network and gender. *International Journal of Applied Linguistics* 3, 57-77.

Pauwels, Anne 1987. Women and language in Australian society. In Anne Pauwels (ed), *Women and Language in Australian and New Zealand Society*. Sydney: Australian Professional Publications, 7-31.

Rastatter, Michael P. & Richard D. Jacques 1990. Formant frequency structure of the ageing male and female vocal tract. *Folia Phoniatrica* 42, 312-319.

Rastatter, Michael P., Richard A. McGuire, Joseph Kalinowski & Andrew Stuart 1997. Formant frequency characteristics of elderly speakers in contextual speech. *Folia Phoniatrica et Logopaedica* 49, 1-8.

Trudgill, Peter 1986. *Dialects in Contact*. Oxford: Blackwell.

Trudgill, Peter, Elizabeth Gordon, Gillian Lewis & Margaret Maclagan. Determinism in new-dialect formation and the genesis of New Zealand English. *Journal of Linguistics* in press.

Watson, Catherine, Jonathan Harrington & Zoe Evans 1998. An acoustic comparison between New Zealand and Australian English vowels. *Australian Journal of Linguistics* 18, 185-207.

Wells, John C. 1982. *Accents of English*. Cambridge: Cambridge University Press.

Wolfram, Walt & Natalie Schilling-Estes 1998. *American English*. Malden, MS: Blackwell Publishers.

Woods, Nicola 1997. The formation and development of New Zealand English: Interaction of gender-related variation and linguistic change. *Journal of Sociolinguistics* 1, 95-125.

Sex as a factor in rises in New Zealand English

Paul Warren and Nicola Daly

Victoria University of Wellington

Introduction[1]

Speaker sex stereotypes involving intonation refer to female speech as 'high-pitched', 'shrill', 'over-emotional' and 'swoopy' (Henton 1989). Less emotively, female speech is described as having 'a relatively wide pitch range with frequent and rapid long glides' (McConnell-Ginet 1978: 549). In our study of New Zealand English intonation (Daly & Warren 2001), we investigated two global acoustic measures corresponding to these stereotypes: the overall pitch range used by speakers, and the dynamic nature of their pitch contours. Our analysis confirmed both a greater range of pitch and greater dynamism in pitch use in female speech. Since male and female speech is in any case distinguished by anatomically determined differences in pitch levels (women have higher-pitched voices than men), we argued that these additional differences in range and dynamism indicated that pitch parameters may serve as sociophonetic indicators of sex and/or gender differences.[2] Our finding of such additional differences contradicted a previous review of studies of American and British English and of Swedish (Henton 1989). Reanalysing the reviewed studies using a semitone pitch scale, perceptually more relevant than the original physical Hertz scale, Henton concluded that there was no consistent difference between female and male pitch ranges. However, research on Dutch by Haan & van Heuven (1999) has resulted in findings similar to our own as far as overall pitch range is concerned, with a larger range in female speech in a variety of utterance forms, including statements and questions both in reading tasks and in natural dialogue. Our findings also contradicted a further study by Henton (1995), which found no difference between the sexes in pitch dynamism, i.e. in the rate of change in pitch over an utterance.

Our previous discussion of this body of research highlighted two crucial differences between the more recent studies (ie. Haan & van Heuven 1999; Daly & Warren 2001) and the earlier studies. One is the use of a perceptually more relevant transformation of the raw acoustic frequency values from the Hertz scale to an ERB scale, more closely reflecting the frequency selectivity of the human auditory system, rather than to the semitone scale used by Henton (see Hermes & van Gestel 1991 for a discussion of these scales). Another is that the more recent studies included dialogue tasks. Since one of the claims often made about female speech is that it shows greater orientation towards the addressee than is found in male speech (Coates 1996; Fishman 1983; Holmes 1993), and since dialogue tasks give a clearer opportunity for addressee-orientation, it can be argued that such tasks make the detection of differences between the sexes more likely. Indeed, of the studies reviewed by Henton (1989) that contained speaker sex contrasts, the only one which included dialogue (Graddol & Swann 1983) was also the only one to show evidence of a greater semitone pitch range for females, and specifically only in the dialogue task.[3] Note though that both Haan & van Heuven (1999) and Daly & Warren (2001) found a greater ERB pitch range for females not only in dialogues, but also in sentence reading tasks. Yet the earlier studies using reading tasks showed a numerically greater range for men when the Hertz values were re-expressed on a semitone scale (Henton 1989), and gave inconsistent results when the values were converted to the ERB scale (Daly & Warren 2001). Daly and Warren argue that the crucial difference between these later reading tasks and the earlier ones is the presence of questions, which create a reading situation which is more like dialogue than the declarative reading passages used in the other studies. Haan and van Heuven compare the recording situation for their subjects to that of actors in a radio play, and claim that their female speakers may have been better actors. Certainly, questions are an important part of interaction, and form a significant proportion of dialogue turns (for instance, Stenström 1994: 3 reminds us that questions and answers form the 'backbone' of conversation).

It can be argued that questions themselves are more likely to reveal sex differences in pitch use. This is principally because most question forms use a rising intonation, at least in languages such as English and Dutch, if not more widely (Cruttenden 1997: 163, though see Ladd 1996: 113ff for a more cautious view). Since most speakers normally use the bottom third of their pitch range when speaking (Cruttenden 1997: 124), there is greater scope for increasing the range of a rising pitch movement than that of a falling movement (since to take the latter too low results in creaky voice, effectively in a breakdown of voicing). It is therefore not surprising that if sex differences in range are to be found, then they will be found on utterances that typically involve movement outside this bottom third of the range, as will be the case with many question types. Interestingly, however, both Haan & van Heuven (1999) and Daly & Warren (2001) found that the increase in global pitch range was a trait not only of female questions, but also of female statements. Since other studies using only statements had failed to observe such sex differences, we concluded that the key factor contributing to the presence of such differences is actually the presence of questions in the reading task, leading to a dialogue-type setting.

Many question intonation forms are distinguished from a statement intonation not simply by an overall rising vs falling pitch, but by a marked rise – in contrast to a falling or level pitch – on the last pitch accent or nucleus of an intonation group. Haan & van Heuven (1999) studied some of the detail of such pitch accents in their sentence materials, and found that the overall sex difference in pitch range was reflected in greater final falls in statements and rises in questions. That is, the final pitch movements in the utterances were more marked for women. For the statements, this appears to be achieved by a greater anticipatory resetting of pitch for the nuclear fall by the women, whereas the starting point of the final pitch accent for the men continues a general downward trend, and is lower than the starting point of the preceding pitch accent (Haan & van Heuven 1999: Fig. 1). For questions, the final rise starts at a comparable position in the pitch range of both men and women, but rises further for the women. These more dramatic local movements clearly add to the dynamic intonation that is characteristic of female utterances. This may be found in other languages too. Thus in a study of French, Ryalls, Le Dorze, Lever, Ouellet and Larfeuil (1994) calculated the difference between the average pitch in the final syllable of questions and that of the final syllable of statements for each of 40 speakers, and found a greater difference for women than men. While this measure does not in itself mean that women use larger rises, it does at least show that they differentiate more between questions and statements. However, this result should be treated with caution, since the data use the linear Hertz scale rather than a perceptual scale such as ERB.

One of the objectives of the current study is to investigate the size of final pitch movements in the New Zealand English data reported in our previous study. We will focus our study on questions, and indeed on questions realised only by intonational means, i.e. questions that have a word order that is entirely compatible with statements. We will not be considering the rising intonation on declarative utterances that is frequently associated with antipodean English, the High Rising Terminal (see Warren & Britain, 2000 for a discussion of aspects of the usage of this intonation in New Zealand English). Our data do include instances of this, which are compared with question rises in a separate paper (Warren & Daly in prep).

In addition to the size of the rises, we are also interested in exploring the local dynamics of these utterances, by considering the rate of change of pitch during these final inflections. This exploration relates to the possibility that greater expression is achieved by a more dramatic or rapid execution of an inflection. As noted above, Henton (1995) did not find a speaker sex difference in overall pitch dynamism for her American English informants, whereas our own ERB data for New Zealand English (Daly & Warren 2001) did show greater dynamism for females. In earlier studies, Takefuta, Jancosek & Brunt (1972) found, for American English, that both rising and falling melodies had movements that were twice as rapid for women as for men, and Terango (1966) found that rate of pitch change was higher for effeminate than for masculine male speech. While it is beyond the scope of this paper to explore the relation-ship between notions such as masculinity, gender and sex, we cite Terango's research along with that of Takefuta et al as examples that show a sociophonetic difference in pitch range. Again, though, such studies must be treated with caution because of the use of the physical Hertz scale rather than a perceptual scale. Note also that they deal with global aspects of pitch changes. As far as we are aware there are no studies that explicitly investigate sociophonetic differences in the dynamism of single pitch movements such as the rises we focus on here.

Our research questions relate then to the size of the final pitch movement, and to its dynamic nature. A third aspect concerns the alignment of the pitch movement or tone with regard to the segmental aspects of the utterances. That is, does the pitch movement always begin on the accented syllable with which it is associated, or can it start earlier or later, and does this depend on speaker sex? Again, to our knowledge there is no previous research that investigates sex-related differences in the alignment of tones. It would appear though that some languages show at least dialectal variation in alignment, for instance Swedish (Bruce & Gårding 1978) and British English (Nolan & Farrar 1999).

Experimental studies

Hypotheses

On the basis of the literature reviewed above, and on the basis of our own analysis of New Zealand English intonation (Daly and Warren 2001), we predict that our New Zealand English speakers will show speaker sex differences not only in the global measures of intonation discussed there, but also in the local attributes of final rises. Focussing specifically on the final rises in intonation-only questions, we hypothesise that a more expressive use of intonation by women in the dialogue or dialogue-like settings of our recordings will mean that:

1. women will exhibit greater final rises than men, on the perceptual ERB scale, this difference being consistent with the previously noted trend for a greater overall pitch range;
2. similarly, just as the overall pitch dynamism of these female informants has been shown to be greater than that of the men, so their final rises will be more rapid;
3. additionally, women will start their rises later, relative to the segmental material, than the men, in order to achieve the greatest possible impact.

Note that for each of these hypotheses we focus on inter-sex differences. While there may be differences between speakers within each group, this is not of primary interest here.

Methodology

Two studies were conducted. Study 1 is a closer examination of the speech data reported in Daly and Warren (2001) and considers in detail the size, rate and alignment of final rises in intonation-only questions in sentence reading and dialogue tasks. Study 2 is a follow-up investigation of possible semantic differences in the questions realised by women and men. Differences in the methodology used in this second study will be described after the results for Study 1.

The speakers and materials for the first study were the same as those used in Daly and Warren (2001). Our informants were New Zealand English speakers, six female and five male, all Pakeha (New Zealanders of European descent) and aged between16 and19 years. They were recorded performing a battery of speech tasks, originally developed by Grabe, Nolan & Farrar (1998) for a comparative study of British English varieties. The two sets of data reported here are from a sentence reading task and a map-based dialogue task. In the latter task, pairs of subjects were each given a simple map. The two maps differed slightly, with different locations marked on each, and with some differences in the names used for common locations. One subject's map had a route marked on it, which (s)he had to describe to the other subject. The differences between the maps resulted in many questions and information-seeking turns as well as directives. The utterances selected for analysis were intonation-only questions with a final nuclear rise, i.e. a rise which was associated with the last accented item in the intonation group. Three intonation-only questions (in fact members of pairs of statements and questions using the same word strings and distinguished only by intonation) were taken from the sentence lists recorded by each speaker. Since not all of these were realised with rises, we obtained a total of 29 intonation-only questions from the reading task, 15 for females and 14 for males. 67 intonation-only questions were extracted from the map task recordings, 50 from females and 17 from males.

Pitch tracks were generated for each sentence using the auto-correlation method of the software package PRAAT (Boersma & Weenink 1998), giving Hertz fundamental frequency values every 10 milliseconds during voiced speech. These values were then hand-corrected for sampling errors. The Hertz measurements were then converted to the perceptual ERB scale, using the formula ERB=16.7*log10(1+X/165.4), where X is the frequency in Hertz. Measurement points for the final rises were determined as follows: the beginning of a rise was an elbow point at which the pitch track turned upwards for the final rise, from either a falling, level or gently rising contour to that point; the finish of the rise was a point at which pitch levelled off, or if it continued to rise then the finish point was the final pitch value obtained in the analysis. The size of the final pitch rise used by speakers was computed from the ERB values at these points, and the rate of change of the rise was measured in ERB per second. In addition, the alignment of the beginning of the pitch rises was noted. This was expressed relative to the syllable in which it occurred, i.e. was coded as being in the syllable with which the pitch accent is associated, or *n* syllables earlier or later than this. Further detail was noted as to where in a syllable the rise started, i.e. in the syllable's onset, nucleus or coda. This type of analysis was chosen rather than using a measure of temporal displacement from e.g. the beginning of the accented syllable, since a temporal measure would depend on the segmental make-up of the syllables in question, which would be variable in the case of unscripted speech such as in the map task.

Results

Sentence list data

The rise and rate-of-change values for each sentence were entered into one-way analyses of variance with speaker sex as the factor. These analyses provided weak and only marginally significant support for our hypotheses: the female speakers produced rises which were slightly larger (2.83 ERB vs 2.31 ERB; $F[1,27]=3.17$, $0.05<p<0.10$) and slightly more rapid (10.78 ERB/sec vs 8.35 ERB/sec; $F[1,27]=3.03$, $0.05<p<0.10$).

The alignment data provided stronger support for the hypothesis that females would realise their rises later. All the final accented words in the sentence list questions were bisyllables with stress on the first syllable. Most (77%) of the male rises started on this stressed syllable, i.e. the pitch movement was aligned with the accented syllable, whereas most (71%) of the female rises started on the following unstressed syllable (this speaker sex difference in alignment was significant in a chi-square analysis: $\chi^2=4.52$, $df=1$, $p<0.05$).

Map task data

The size and rate of rises for each intonation-only question from the map task were also entered into analyses of variance, again with sex as a variable. The analysis for rise size provided strong support for our hypothesis of greater rises for females (2.02 ERB vs 0.91 ERB; $F[1,65]=21.74$, $p< 0.001$). There was no significant sex effect for rate of change (females: 20.00 ERB/sec, males: 15.58 ERB/sec; $F[1,65]<1$).

Alignment of the rises was very much more variable for this set than for the reading list, largely since the size of the accent units containing the rise was not limited to bisyllables with initial stress, and in fact included a large number of monosyllables. Nonetheless, rise alignments again appeared to be later for females (42% of their rises started after the syllable associated with the accent, compared with 24% for the males). However, the inherent variability in this spontaneous data meant that this difference was not statistically reliable.

Discussion

The data for this first study give some support for our hypotheses that females produce larger and more rapid final rises in intonation-only questions. Although the sentence reading task did not provide traditionally significant differences for either of these measures, the trends were in the expected direction. What is more, the alignment measure showed clear evidence that the women were initiating their rises later. For the map task, where the length of the final accent unit was not as tightly controlled, there was greater variation in the alignment of the rise for both sets of speakers. However, the women executed significantly larger rises than the men in this map task.

An analysis of the combined rise size data from the two tasks revealed main effects of both task ($F[1,92]=32.21$, $p<0.001$) and sex ($F[1,92]=17.76$, $p<0.001$), with larger rises in the sentence reading task and for females. There was no interaction of these factors. In the equivalent comparisons for the rate of change data, there was a significant effect only of task ($F[1,92]=5.72$, $p<0.05$), with faster rises in the map task. These task effects suggest smaller but more rapid rises in the map task. Overall there were also more rises aligned with the accented syllable in the map task (67% vs 53%), though this difference was not significant.

The difference is most likely a reflection of the presence of monosyllabic accent units in the map data, in which the rise can be aligned no later than the accented syllable. This factor may also have contributed to the differences in rise size and speed, since rises on monosyllables may need to be executed more rapidly, and may not reach such high pitch levels.

The two tasks together support a difference between female and male speech, with females using larger and more rapid rises, aligned later with respect to the text. Before concluding that these data demonstrate a realisational or sociophonetic difference in the rises produced by females and males, we need to consider an alternative interpretation of our findings, which is that females and males are signalling different meanings with their different rises. Although intonational meanings are difficult to characterise, a possible difference that is compatible with the data presented thus far is that the female tokens, with their later rises, are expressing 'polite insistence', whereas the male tokens, with an early rise, could be more contrastive in nature (see Pierrehumbert & Hirschberg, 1990 for discussion of such intonational meanings). While such an interpretation of our results still supports a difference between the sexes, this is a sex difference in approach to the task, rather than a difference in more direct sociophonetic markers of speaker sex.

To investigate this possibility more closely, we designed a second study, in which female and male speakers were required to read sentences that explicitly compared neutral and contrastive questions. In addition, this second study contained balanced sets of accent units of three different lengths (single words of 1-, 2- and 3-syllables, all with primary stress on the first syllable). The main purpose of this variation in accent unit size was to explore a further aspect of final rises in New Zealand English, namely whether in a short accent unit a rise is compressed (i.e. the same rise is realised over a shorter time span) or truncated (the rise trajectory remains the same but a smaller rise is achieved), relative to longer ones (see Grabe, Post, Nolan & Farrar, to appear, for evidence that some British dialects differ from one another in this respect). This aspect of the data will not be discussed here. Finally, this second study included a larger number of relevant sentences than the reading task in Study 1, to provide a more robust test of the sex differences outlined there.

Study 2

This study used 15 pairs of intonation-only questions such as *You want to watch the judo?* Each question was accompanied by a scene-setting context. The two questions in each pair had exactly the same wording, but were distinguished by their context. One in each pair (the 'neutral' reading) was a question simply asking for information, the other (the 'contrastive' reading) was placed in a context that led to a surprised and contrastive questioning of the final lexical item, i.e. of the word in nuclear position. These two contexts were felt to typify the probable semantic differences between late- and early-rise versions of the questions in the sentence lists in Study 1. Examples of the two contexts are given in Appendix B.

The final word in each sentence used mainly voiced segments, to ensure continuous pitch tracks. For five sentence pairs this final word had one syllable (*bowls, dill, jam, Jane, wine*), five had bisyllabic words (*ginger, jelly, judo, lager, Mary*), and five had three syllables (*badminton, Budweiser, marmalade, vinegar, Vivien*). In each case lexical stress (and therefore the association point for the rising accent) was on the first syllable of the word.

Five female and four male Pakeha speakers of New Zealand English, all in their early twenties, recorded the 15 pairs of sentences. They were different speakers from those used in Study 1, and so the results for the two studies cannot be directly compared. Pitch data were obtained using the same procedures as outlined above for Study 1.

Hypothesis

Our main hypothesis for this second study was that if the results for Study 1 showed a genuine sociophonetic difference between female and male speakers, then the effects of speaker sex on the rise variables should be found in this study too. The alternative hypothesis was that the differences found in Study 1 were semantic differences resulting largely from different approaches taken to the recording task by females and males, and that the contexts introduced for this study would remove such differences.

Results

The first thing to note about the results for this study is that the difference between neutral and contrastive questions is marked not by differences in alignment, as would be predicted if the sex difference in Study 1 was due to a semantic difference between these types of question, but by a difference between a simple rise and a rising-falling tune. Some 93% of the neutral questions had simple rises (i.e. 98 of the 105 neutral question utterances). The remainder mainly had falls, some of which had a slight rise over the last few analysis frames. Of the contrastive questions, a clear majority (75%) had a rising-falling tune, with the remainder having simple rises. This distribution of tune types did not differ for women and men. Since our interest here is in the realisation of final rises, we will have little more to say about the other types of utterance. It does seem though that the use of an early rise to mark contrast, which was suggested as a possible meaning-related difference between males and females in Study 1, is not a typical contrastive question intonation for this variety.

The size and rate of the rising nuclei were entered into analyses of variance with speaker sex and context (neutral vs contrastive) as factors. For rise size, neither of the main effects nor their interaction were statistically significant. While it is unclear whether such small differences could be perceptually relevant, it is noteworthy that the trends in the data are in the predicted direction. That is, female rises were slightly larger than male (1.73 ERB vs 1.61 ERB) and rises in the contrastive context were slightly larger than rises in the neutral context (1.89 ERB vs 1.62 ERB). For rate, there was a significant main effect of speaker sex (female mean: 14.38 ERB/sec, male mean 9.23 ERB/sec; $F[1,156]=9.83$, $p<0.01$), but no other effects.

The alignment patterns for neutral and contrastive questions do not support the notion that early rises are associated with contrastiveness, since the rises on the contrastive utterances started on average later than those for the neutral utterances, although this difference was not statistically reliable in the chi-square test.

There was a clear tendency for women to start rising later. Figure 1 gives an overall indication of where rises started, pooling data for words of differing length, for neutral rises only. In this figure the cumulative probability of a rise starting is expressed as a function of syllable position in accented and post-accented syllables, for women and for men. This figure shows that the majority of male rises are started within the accented syllable, but that fewer than half of the female ones have been started by the time this accented syllable has been completed. Given that a third of the utterances had monosyllabic accents, these figures for the first syllable are somewhat inflated, but the sex difference is still clear. Looking only at words of more than one syllable, we find that while 62% of the male rises start on the accented syllable, only 23% of the female rises do, with the remainder starting on one of the following syllables. This pattern – which is similar to that found in the sentence reading task in Study 1 – was significant in a chi-square test (χ^2=11.82, df=1, p<0.001).

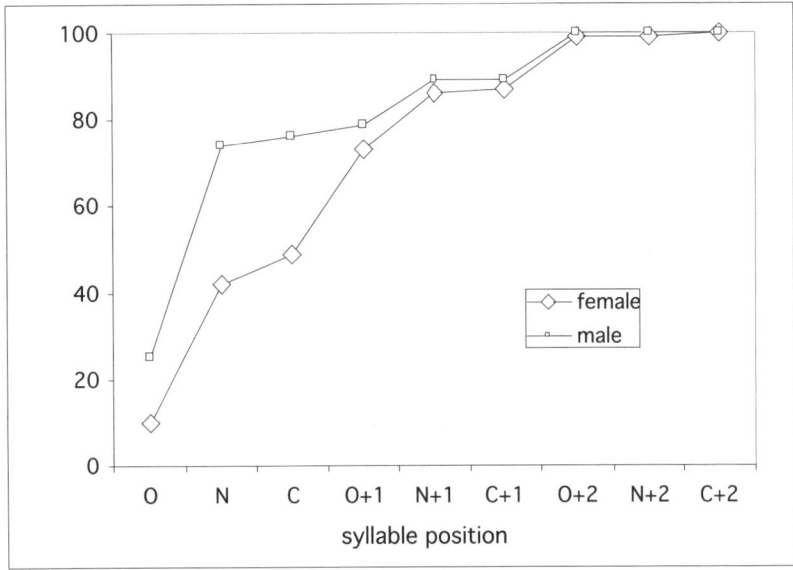

Figure 1. Cumulative percentage or rise onsets in neutral context questions in Study 2, showing speaker sex differences in the alignment of rises with the text. 'O', 'N' and 'C' indicate the onset, nucleus and coda of syllables respectively. '+1' and '+2' refer to the first and second syllable after the accented syllable.

Discussion

The results for Study 2 reinforce the findings from Study 1 of sex-related differences in the realisation of final rises. Females produced faster rises, and started them later. The overall size of the rise did not differ for females and males, suggesting that the major cause of the sex difference resides in the tune-text alignment of the rises. Since the alignment point is later for the females, they must rise more rapidly in order to achieve an equivalent size of rise. This is represented schematically in Figure 2.

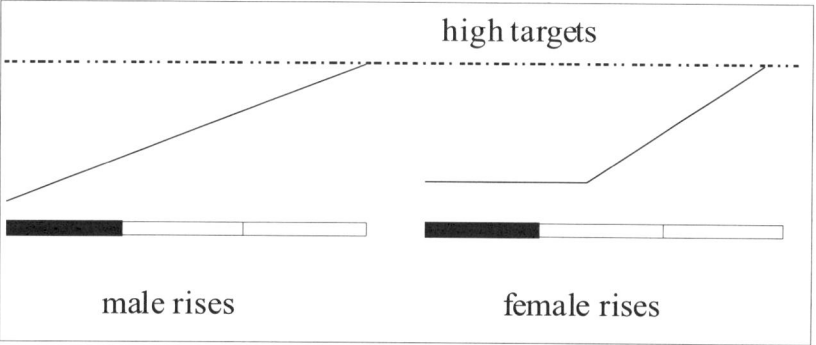

Figure 2. Schematic representation of male and female rises, showing the interrelationship of rise size, speed and alignment. The oblongs represent syllables; the filled one is accented. The dotted line indicates the target pitch value for the rise. The solid lines show the realisations of the rise for males and females.

These data indicate that the speaker sex differences found in the sentence list and map task were most likely also differences of phonetic realisation rather than the results of expressing different meanings.

General Discussion

In summary, the results of our two studies show consistent effects of speaker sex on the realisation of final nuclear rises in intonation-only questions. In every case there was at least a numerical difference in the direction predicted in our initial hypotheses: females used larger rises, they rose more rapidly, and they started rising later. The relative strengths of these differences appeared to vary according to task. For the dialogue task, the main difference involved the size of the rise. In the reading tasks in both studies there was a significant difference in rise alignment. In addition the rate of the rise was greater for females in the neutral questions in Study 2, and marginally so in the questions in Study 1, where there was also a marginal effect of the size of the rise. Our most consistent finding was of a later rise in the female speech. The difference in speed may simply be a reflection of having to rise faster if you rise late. The larger rise, most evident in the dialogue task, may further enhance the salience of a rise.

Study 2 addressed the possibility, arising from discussion of the first study, that male and female speakers are taking different approaches to the tasks involved, and that the differences in their intonation might reflect differences in the meanings being expressed, with early low rises for the males expressing contrast. The use of utterance contexts in this second study were an attempt to control quite explicitly the meanings being realised. While it is still possible that different meanings or nuances are being signaled by men and women, the use of different intonation patterns for the contrastive utterances suggests that the males in Study 1 were not expressing contrast. The persistence of the sex difference in the neutral yes/no intonation-only questions is a strong indicator that different realisational means are being used by women and men.

It has been widely claimed that an overriding motivation for female speakers when they communicate is to produce speech which is closely tailored to the needs of their conversational partners (Holmes 1993). This has repeatedly been observed in studies of New Zealand English interviews and conversations. For example, previous studies have shown that female interactants interrupted less, used more minimum feedback, used more tag questions to encourage interaction from their conversational partner and used and accepted more compliments. In these ways, Holmes (1993) surmised, New Zealand women are highly attentive to the needs of their conversational partners. Elsewhere (Daly and Warren 2001) suggest that the use of a wider pitch range and more dynamic pitch is evidence of female speakers making an effort to attract and maintain the interest of their conversational partners. It is possible that the magnitude, speed and lateness of the final rise used by female speakers in the present study can similarly be explained in terms of some communicative advantage. The kinds of rise used by the female speakers may enhance the clarity of their speech. Pitch movements at the beginning or the end of an utterance may be more perceptually salient than movements within an utterance. By placing their pitch rise closer to the end of their utterances, female speakers are increasing the clarity of the function of their utterance. By making the final rise more prominent in this and other ways, such as by the size of the rise, the function of the utterance (i.e. question) is more clearly signaled. There is also some suggestion from early research by Uldall (1972) that higher rises may express a more 'pleasant' attitude in the speaker. Uldall used a range of synthesised intonation contours on different grammatical sentence types to obtain subjective judgements of speaker characteristics on a range of parameters. Using factor analysis, she found that high rises (including high rising elements of fall-rise contours) featured regularly at the positive end of a pleasant/unpleasant dimension.

In conclusion, it is apparent that final rises in intonation-only questions are another aspect of intonation in which there are clear differences between the sexes, at least for our Pakeha speakers of New Zealand English. Further research is needed in order to investigate the details of when and how such sex-related differences are exploited by speakers as indicators of gender identity.

Notes

1   We would like to thank Janet Fletcher for her comments made on an earlier draft of this paper. This research was made possible by a grant to the first author from the Marsden Fund of the Royal Society of New Zealand (contract VUW604) and by a research fellowship to the second author from the Victoria University of Wellington Strategic Development Fund (grant 212).

2   Note that we use "speaker sex" to refer to the biological sex of our informants, and make no claims about possible relationships between our findings and the use of pitch cues to mark sexual orientation or gender identity.

3   In Warren and Daly (2001) we reanalyse the Hertz values using the ERB scale, and find in fact that all but one of the six speaker sex comparisons reviewed by Henton show a numerically greater range for females, including all three tasks – dialogue, reading, sustained vowels – used by Graddol and Swann.

References

Boersma, Paul and David Weenink 1998. *Praat 3.8β. A System for Doing Phonetics by Computer.* [Computer software]. Institute of Phonetic Sciences: University of Amsterdam.

Bruce Gösta & Eva Gårding 1978. A prosodic typology for Swedish dialects. In E. Gårding, G. Bruce, & R. Bannert (eds), *Nordic Prosody.* Gleerup, 219-228.

Coates, Jennifer 1996. *Women Talk.* Oxford: Blackwell.

Cruttenden, Alan 1997. *Intonation.* Second Edition. Cambridge: Cambridge University Press.

Daly, Nicola & Paul Warren (2001). Pitching it differently in New Zealand English: speaker sex and intonation patterns. *Journal of Sociolinguistics.*

Fishman, Pamela M. 1983. Interaction: the work women do. In Barrie Thorne, Cheris Kramarae, & Nancy Henley (eds), *Language, Gender and Society.* Rowley, MA: Newbury House Publishers, 89-101.

Grabe, Esther, Brechtje Post, Francis Nolan & Kimberley Farrar (to appear). Pitch accent realisation in four varieties of British English. *Journal of Phonetics.*

Grabe, Esther, Francis Nolan & Kimberley Farrar 1998. IViE-a comparative transcription system for intonational variation in English. *Fifth International Conference on Spoken Language Processing.* Sydney, Australia.

Graddol, David & Joan Swann 1983. Speaking fundamental frequency: Some physical and social correlates, *Language and Speech* 26, 351-366.

Haan, Judith & Vincent J. van Heuven 1999. Male vs female pitch range in Dutch questions. *Proceedings of 14th International Congress of Phonetic Sciences.* San Francisco, 1581-1584.

Henton, Caroline 1989. Fact and fiction in the description of female and male speech. *Language and Communication* 9, 299-311.

Henton, Caroline 1995. Pitch dynamism in female and male speech, *Language and Communication* 15, 43-61.

Hermes, Dik. J. & Joost C. van Gestel 1991. The frequency scale of speech intonation. *Journal of the Acoustical Society of America* 90, 97-103.

Holmes, Janet 1993. 'New Zealand women are good to talk to': an analysis of politeness strategies in interaction. *Journal of Pragmatics* 20, 91-116.

Ladd, D, Robert 1996. *Intonational Phonology.* Cambridge: Cambridge University Press.

McConnell-Ginet, Sally 1978. Intonation in a man's world. *Signs: Journal of Women in Culture and Society* 3, 541-559.

Nolan, Francis & Kimberley Farrar 1999. Timing of F0 peaks and peak lag. *Proceedings of 14th International Congress of Phonetic Sciences.* San Francisco, 961-964.

Pierrehumbert, Janet & Julia Hirschberg 1990. The meaning of intonational contours in the interpretation of discourse. In P.R. Cohen, J. Morgan & M.E. Pollack (eds), *Intentions in Communication*. Cambridge, MA: MIT Press, 271-311.

Ryalls, John, Guylaine Le Dorze, Nathalie Lever, Lisa Ouellet & Céline Larfeuil 1994. The effects of age and sex on speech intonation and duration for matched statements and questions in French. *Journal of the Acoustical Society of America* 94, 2274-2276.

Stenström, Anna-Brita 1994. *An Introduction to Spoken Interaction*. London: Longman.

Takefuta, Yukio, Elizabeth G. Jancosek & Michael Brunt 1972. A statistical analysis of melody curves in the intonation of American English. In Andre Rigault & Rene Charbonneau (eds), *Proceedings of the Seventh International Congress of Phonetic Sciences*. The Hague: Mouton, 1035-1039.

Terango, Larry 1966. Pitch and duration characteristics of the oral reading of males on a masculinity-femininity dimension. *Journal of Speech and Hearing Research* 9, 590-595.

Uldall, Elizabeth 1972. Dimensions of meaning in intonation. In Dwight Bolinger (ed), *Intonation*. Harmondsworth: Penguin.

Warren, Paul & David Britain 2000. Intonation and prosody in New Zealand English. In Allan Bell & Koenraad Kuiper (eds), *New Zealand English*. Wellington: Victoria University Press, 146-172.

Warren, Paul & Nicola Daly (in prep). When and why do women rise late in New Zealand English?

Appendix A

Sentence list material used in Study 1
1. He is on the lilo?
2. You live in Ealing?
3. You remembered the lilies?

Appendix B

Examples of contexts and questions used in Study 2.
Neutral context
Your friend has come over for the afternoon. The TV is on and the judo championships are being broadcast. You wonder if she wants to watch them. You ask her by saying: 'You want to watch the judo?'
Contrastive context
You're planning a TV evening with your friend. She says she wants to watch the judo. You're surprised because you thought she'd want to watch the movie. You ask her: 'You want to watch the judo?'

Panel Discussion: How can language and gender research be best used in the workplace?

Chair: Janet Holmes, *Victoria University of Wellington*

Panel participants:

Jennifer Coates, *Roehampton Institute, University of Surrey*
Vicky Noble, *Associate Nurse Executive at Capital Coast Health, Wellington*
Anne Pauwels, *University of Wollongong*
Sally McConnell-Ginet, *Cornell University*
Judy Lawrence, *Chief Executive Officer, Ministry of Women's Affairs*

Introduction

One of the highlights of the 1999 Language and Gender Symposium was a panel discussion which brought together the Plenary speakers, three academics with interests in language, gender, and workplace research, Jennifer Coates, Sally McConnell-Ginet, and Anne Pauwels, and two workplace practitioners, Judy Lawrence, the Chief Executive Officer of the Ministry of Women's Affairs, and Vicky Noble, a senior New Zealand nurse. Each panel member was invited to provide some information on their own workplace experience, as well as their reflections on the panel topic, 'How can language and gender research be best used in the workplace?'

Jennifer Coates commented on the implications of research on women's ways of talking and interacting in professional contexts in the public sphere. Vicky Noble discussed the changes in the discourse of the medical sphere which have been brought about by a dramatic increase in the extent to which the medical profession has become client-centred. Anne Pauwels drew attention to the importance and implications of research on sexist language in the workplace. Sally McConnell-Ginet showed how language and gender research highlights the spurious reasons produced to justify the failure to promote able academic women, and she also pointed to the danger that this research may be misused to support such rationalisations. Judy Lawrence reflected on her own experience as a woman working in a predominantly male professional world, and identified a number of discourse patterns which disadvantage women which she had observed, and which she felt worthy of further research.

Jennifer Coates

Jennifer Coates is Professor of Linguistics at Roehampton Institute at the University of Surrey. Her books on language and gender have been set texts in language and gender courses for many years. Women, Men and Language *has been through two editions and a third edition is due out soon, clear evidence of its popularity. Her most recent book,* Language and Gender, *a book of fascinating papers, is set to oust her previous book only because impecunious students cannot afford to buy two textbooks. It is a wonderful collection of focal articles in this area. Professor Coates has also written specifically about women in the professions, and her contribution draws on her expertise in this area.*

I will begin by drawing attention to historical precedent, the historical factors in language and gender research. In the early nineteenth century, work and the home became separated so two spheres were established: the public sphere and the private sphere. Women were associated with the private sphere and men with the public sphere, and thus began a pattern which is obviously still in place. This means that in the public sphere we have had the establishment of androcentric norms, including androcentric linguistic norms.

The question facing women, as more and more women enter the public workplace, is 'will the linguistic resources that women bring, the linguistic patterns that women prefer, will these be accepted in the workplace, or will women be forced to adopt the androcentric norms of the public sphere?'

There is evidence that in some areas women's ways of talking are, if not accepted, at least used, and are being seen to be extremely effective. One of the problems is that where women do succeed in using linguistic patterns that they feel comfortable with, and which can be seen to have good outcomes in terms of their profession's goals, the powers that be do not always recognise these good outcomes. I will give just three brief examples.

One is Sue Fisher's work on nurse practitioners in the United States. This is a relatively new profession and Fisher looked at their use of questions. Questions are multi-functional, like all linguistic forms, and there's been quite a lot of evidence, such as Janet Holmes' work on tag questions, which has shown that, while many people think of questions as information seeking devices, questions can do many other things. Questions are very good, for example, in keeping discourse going, pulling in the other person or persons present. Sue Fisher found that nurse practitioners used questions as a way of facilitating conversation, as a way of opening up the discussion and making the person with the illness or the problem feel there were open-ended ways of answering. By contrast the medical doctor asked questions that closed down information, making it very difficult for a patient to really talk about the whole issue that was bothering them.

Secondly Candace West researched GPs in health centres in the United States, extending Marjorie Goodwin's work on directives. Majorie Goodwin had shown that twelve-year-old kids on the street in Philadelphia used directives differently depending on gender. The boys she studied typically used more aggravated directives, that is forms that got someone to do something, such as bare imperatives, and that this constructed a very hierarchical group. Girls, on the other hand, were more likely to use inclusive forms such as 'let's' or to use modal expressions like 'can' and 'could' to persuade other girls to do things: eg. 'we could do x'. Astonishingly, West found similarities between the behaviour of the black kids in Philadelphia and the white doctors in a medical practice. She compared the men and the women's practice in terms of how they got patients to do things such as taking their trousers off, or agreeing to take a certain number of tablets. She found that the women doctors were far more likely to use forms such as 'lets' in their directives and other forms that included pronouns such as 'we' rather than 'you', and that they used modals such as 'can' and 'could' or forms such as 'perhaps', e.g. 'perhaps we could do so and so'. This was very nice research because she looked at the outcomes. This was videoed evidence and so if they said 'could you take your trousers off please', she would then be able to see whether they took their trousers off or not. The evidence was that the women doctors were far more successful in gaining patients' compliance. Patients' compliance with what they were asked to do was far higher for the women doctors than for the male doctors. It was a very small sample, and West warns that one shouldn't over-generalise from her research, but it does seem to indicate a trend where women using a particular set of forms were highly successful in doing presumably what the doctors were aiming to do, so it is a very interesting piece of evidence.

The final piece of research I'd like to bring to your attention is some work done in Cardiff. I'm sure you all know of Nikolas and Justine Coupland's work on inter-generational talk. There is a whole group of postgraduate students in Cardiff doing research on talk with the elderly. Karen Atkinson examined interactions between home helps and elderly persons. These are often interactions that involve just women, because the vast majority of the elderly are women and most home helps are women. In this context one would expect asymmetrical talk because of the age difference and the status difference between the younger professional home help and the elderly patient, the person in need of help. But they have gender in common. And Karen Atkinson noticed there was a large amount of co-operative, overlapping speech. They did not interrupt each other. Rather it was as if they were singing the same tune, expressing the same things together. She felt that what was happening was that the home help made gender more salient than age and status. So this conversational practice of supportive overlapping speech, a sort of polyphonic talk, which I have found in the conversations of women friends, seems to be a very common feature of women's talk when they're relaxed and talking spontaneously

What all these examples show is that women professionals seem to be using language in ways that minimise status differences and reduce asymmetry, whereas many male professionals seem to have adopted linguistic practices which accomplish power and status, and which therefore maintain or even increase asymmetry. I sometimes adopt rose-coloured spectacles and think it would be great if some of the linguistic practices that seem to be typical of women in the private sphere could be brought into the workplace where they can clearly function effectively, and be of benefit to everybody. But in this discussion I want to end on a pessimistic note. If you look at the work of feminist historians, people who have charted the struggles in terms of the definition of gender, and the definitions of masculinity and femininity through the last two centuries, people like Lenora Davidoff and Catherine Hall, what they argue is that where gender boundaries are pushed, where people try to change things, there is always resistance, and resistance will be met with sanctions which range from ridicule right up to the extreme of violence. So, however much I would like to see these practices brought into the workplace there's a bit of me that is pessimistic and despairs of it ever happening.

Judy Lawrence

Judy Lawrence has more than 25 years' experience in government public policy and in social policy in New Zealand, Australia and internationally. She is currently Chief Executive of the Ministry of Women's Affairs, a position she has held since April 1995. Over the last 5 years, she has led the Ministry on work in mainstream gender analysis, and provided policy advice on childcare, retirement savings, matrimonial property legislation and disparities in the labour market. She has also contributed to the public sector Equal Employment Opportunities policy and the career development of Maori policy analysts in the public sector.

I have been asked to provide a workplace practitioner's perspective on language in the workplace, and, in particular, to highlight some of the issues that I have experienced with the use of language in the workplace. These may prove fruitful areas for further research. The Ministry of Women's Affairs has itself been the subject of research by participating in the Victoria University Language in the Workplace project, led by Professor Janet Holmes. This research has provided very useful insights into the way in which our organisation uses language.

The Ministry of Women's Affairs includes a diverse group: the majority are women with just one man, and a number of cultures, with a predominance of Maori and non-Maori (which include Pacific Island, Sri Lankan and Caucasian New Zealanders). The experience of participating in the Language in the Workplace project highlighted communication issues across cultures, which has assisted us in better managing our staff, and staff understanding where others are coming from when involved in project work. This has valuably informed our work, and especially assisted us in our listening. In addition, we operate with other groups across the public sector, and with other sector groups outside government, as well as other non-government organisations. All of these have their own particular cultures. Those different cultural values and influences, whether they be ethnic or organisational, have a very large part to play in the way in which we communicate and thus inform the way in which we use language. This is another area which could be further explored through research.

From a personal perspective I have had experience working in New Zealand, Australia and The Netherlands, and have also travelled to a number of countries and worked with a wide range of people from different cultural backgrounds. These experiences have taught me the importance of verbal communication, both written and spoken. They have also taught me how important non-verbal communication is, in the way we negotiate, the way we seek agreement, and the way we attempt to understand others' perspectives.

I have lived through some significant changes within the New Zealand Public Service. My first job in the public service was as the first female policy adviser in an almost 100 percent male engineering environment, working both in the field and in the office. I experienced the significant changes in EEO practice that took place during the 1980s, both before and after the State Sector Reforms. I have served Cabinets with a critical mass of female Ministers through to total male Ministers' groups, and I also served the first female Prime Minister as my Minister. I have worked with a range of groups as Chief Executive from predomi-nantly male through to predominantly female. These experiences have reinforced my view that organisations and cultures, and the critical mass of a dominant culture, have a very significant impact on language, and thus hearing, learning, decision-making and the implementing of Government's decisions.

Another conclusion that I have drawn from these experiences is that language is but one manifestation of the socially prescribed roles of men and women, the dominant power relationships, the changes in those power relationships as more women have entered the workforce, and the changing approaches to public management that have evolved within New Zealand and overseas.

I have a few observations to make based on these experiences. One of the first gender distinctions in language that I can recall in the public sector that raised much debate was the use of the masculine pronoun in statutes, and the suggestion by female MPs that this should change. It took some time for material to be re-written to avoid the use of the masculine pronoun as a pseudo-generic; the adoption of *he/she* initially created all sorts of jokes and ridicule.

From drawing attention to sexist language, we moved into an apparently gender-neutral phase which, in some respects, served to hide some of the real differences between women and men, and led to accusations of merely politically correct behaviour around the use of gender language. In my view this has had a negative effect on many considerations of gender issues. It is only very recently that we have moved beyond that phase as more data about women has become available in the policy environment.

Naming is another important area where the use of language in the workplace can affect how people feel and operate. How you choose to address someone is important, and their personal preferences are crucial. Some people insist on using an individual's full given name – in my case 'Judith' – rather than their preferred name. There are a number of men, usually older men, who find it very difficult to use my chosen name 'Judy', and will still refer to me as 'Judith'. Their reasons are respectful – they do not wish to appear too familiar, and they are expressing respect for my current position. Nevertheless, by ignoring my preference, they hook in to older associations of the address term 'Judith' which has associations for me of marginalisation and dismissal.

Another change I have noted relates to the use of address terms such as 'dear', 'love' and 'honey'. Out in the research field, especially in Australia in the 1970s, such terms were commonly addressed to women scientists by men. They would not be tolerated in New Zealand today. But it is interesting that these words are now sometimes used by women in all-women interactions as jokey terms of endearment.

As a senior adviser over several years, there have been those who have welcomed my advice as a woman, and who have actively encouraged me, whereas others have manifested a number of non-inclusive body language behaviours, such as avoiding eye contact. These non-inclusive communication strategies close down opportunities to contribute in formal or even informal situations. Informal situations are often also punctuated by jokes that exclude women.

Working as the Chief Executive in the Ministry of Women's Affairs, I have experienced another set of behaviours that is often manifest through language, namely, the 'shoot the messenger' syndrome. This is most commonly found in dominantly male groups that have little to do with women's issues, or who hold very stereotypical views about women. I recall a particular incident where the Ministry was leading the way in the public sector in family friendly work practices. In opposing the creative developments we were suggesting for our particular workforce, the opposition produced emotive, challenging statements, reinforced by ridicule which was manifest in the tone of delivery. The women presenting our case, by contrast, used persuasion, logic and reason during the discussion and retained their cool.

It is tempting at times to mimic the language and behaviours of the male dominant group. However, when I have observed this kind of mimicry in other women, the purpose of the language and the communication often completely falls apart, and the messenger becomes the butt of the discussion, rather than the message that is being delivered. This is a no-win situation. Women can be damned if they adopt male behaviours, yet regarded as ineffective if they don't.

I have also observed some stereotypical female behaviours in meetings, such as tantrums. I have to say, though, that such tactics are not exclusively used by women. And the net result is, generally, that while such behaviour may be successful in the short-term, it often blocks the important message and reduces the chances of achieving the long-term goals.

In my experience, women often pick up a range of subtleties that men completely miss in the discussion when these issues are subsequently raised. Women tend to ask clarifying questions, whilst men make statements. These differences are often not observed by men. Body language is also picked up more often by women than by men in these situations.

My experience working in a balanced male/female management team environment was that some men would pick up a female comment made at an earlier point and re-state it, and then the Chair would develop the point. The woman would be left reflecting 'I raised that point several minutes ago and it wasn't heard or picked up'. Interruption, on the other hand, is common amongst both male and female groups, and in mixed groups as well.

These observations are all anecdotal. Research and its translation to the workplace would enhance communication within and between organisations. Workshops could be a good way to effectively transfer research results within and between organisations.

I would like to congratulate Janet Holmes' initiative in undertaking research in this area since I believe the rigour with which that research is carried out gives a robustness to the findings that can then be more readily used in the work situations to understand relationships and group dynamics.

Sally McConnell-Ginet

Sally McConnell-Ginet is Professor of Linguistics and Director of Women's Studies at Cornell University. She has been very active in the Linguistic Society of America (LSA), directing the prestigious LSA Linguistic Institute in 1997, and she is currently the Secretary-Treasurer of the Association. Professor McConnell-Ginet is a fully qualified mathematician and philosopher, as well as a linguist, and her work in formal semantics and pragmatics is very widely known and respected. Her contribution to this panel, however, draws on her position as one of the leading international researchers in language and gender. Her work with Penelope Eckert, on the role of language in constructing, maintaining, and challenging gender identities and relations, has been tremendously influential in shaping the direction of current work in this area.

My own research has not dealt explicitly with language used in work settings, but I do have a practitioner's knowledge of a particular kind of workplace – namely, a research university – and particular roles in that workplace – namely, those of academic teaching and research staff. Language and gender research does provide some insight into the experience of the increasing numbers of women in such roles, and some suggestion that women may actually be well positioned to benefit from changes in the university environment. At the same time, this research needs to be handled with caution and presented with considerable sensitivity if it is not to end up supporting rather than challenging disadvantage for women in academic positions.

I'll start with the positive. Like the health-care field, educational institutions have in a variety of ways begun to pay more attention to those who are supposed to be the direct beneficiaries of what we do. Students are often described as our 'customers,' or 'clients', and many American universities have become more student-centered in their aims and in their policies. In particular, there is an increased focus on the importance of effective teaching, at least in the rhetoric of university officials. Some research suggests that instructional techniques that actively engage students in exploring and testing new ideas produce better results than the more traditional methods, in which students passively listen to the authoritative pronouncements of the erudite scholar, who dispenses his [this pronoun is not generic!] nuggets of wisdom from on high for their eager young minds to absorb. And at least some language and gender research suggests that the kinds of communicative skills needed for the new student-centered approach to teaching are precisely those at which women tend to excel in conversation – facilitating others' contributions to an exchange by asking open questions, responding in encouraging ways, expanding helpfully on what others say, and generally supporting others in their talk. So it might seem that women go into classrooms better prepared than their male colleagues for the shift to student-centered teaching methods. At my own university, both women and men are recognized for outstanding teaching, but women have in fact gotten a somewhat higher proportion of such awards than men in comparison to their numbers among the teaching staff.

There are some down sides, however. In particular, although research universities claim to value teaching 'equally' with research, it continues to be the case that someone whose research is deemed outstanding will be promoted and given tenure even if the teaching is pretty mediocre, whereas an outstanding teacher whose research is deemed only average (it may be pronounced quite good or 'competent', but simply not 'brilliant') will not be promoted and tenured. For a number of reasons, more women than men seem to lose out in this teaching vs. research weighting. There are separate issues, of course, as to how the research is evaluated, and whether what gets called 'competent' if Mary does it , might merit 'brilliant' if John is responsible, but we can put these questions aside for the moment. An authoritative mode of self-present-ation may enhance the impression John makes, whereas if Mary is focused on getting others to understand for themselves, then her own mental acuity may get somewhat obliterated. Such observations have led many to suggest the usefulness of coaching women in more self-affirming ways of talking, especially in contexts like academic confer-ences. But even if we set those matters of evaluation of research quality aside, there is the continuing problem of the relatively lesser weight put on effective teaching in assessing academic staff.

And there is another problem that language-gender research may indeed exacerbate. To the extent that our research supports the already popular stereotype that facilitative styles are gendered 'feminine' and that authoritative styles are gendered 'masculine', women who do not excel at facilitation (and thus at the teaching and advising functions of their job) will be seen as deficient. Women may be given more teaching and advising responsibilities (after all, they're supposed to be good at that) and fewer opportunities to display their scholarly credentials (again, it being supposed that women do not relish displaying their own abilities and achievements). Given the bias of research universities towards research achievements, this cannot ultimately help women advance. There may be many independent reasons why we would like to see more credit given for teaching/advising skills. At the same time, I am reluctant to see us perpetuate a view of women's 'natural' role as facilitative and helpful, and thus hold all women to a higher standard in such arenas, while being less apt to recognize and reward those women whose emphasis might be on their research agendas. (The consumer-isation of universities also has implications for kinds of research, with legislative bodies and others in the public domain wanting to see research with immediate practical implications. I can't pursue here this tension between applied and theoretical work, but it too has important gendered dimensions.)

Su Olsson's stories of women's struggles in corporate workplaces suggest that the major issue is not differences in women's and men's competency – including their communicative competency. The big problem is people's attitudes towards women and men, their sharply differentiated expectations that lead, as psychologist Virginia Valian puts it, to persisting under-evaluation of women's work and over-evaluation of men's.

How can we use language and gender research in the workplace? With great caution, emphasizing the critical importance not only of what people say, and how they say it, but also of how others interpret and evaluate what they say.

Vicky Noble

At the time of this presentation Vicky Noble was the Associate Nurse Executive at Capital Coast Health, Wellington. She has worked in the USA, Britain, China and Australia as well as in New Zealand, including the infamous Greenlane Hospital. She has very wide experience in a range of spheres, including providing advice on nursing policy, playing an educational role for nurses, and teaching interpersonal relations in a medical context. Most recently, she has worked as a Clinical Nurse Consultant in the surgery area, and as a Clinical Nurse Specialist in Gynaecology at Hutt Valley Health. During 1998 and 1999, Ms Noble worked with Chief Nurse Executive, Anita Bamford to develop and strengthen nursing practice at Capital Coast Health. Since she made this presentation, she has moved with her family to Jakarta.

Language and gender are topics that we talk about a lot in my workplace, but we talk about them in different contexts. To remove them from the context of our workplace, and to put them in a different setting within another discipline, actually triggers and stimulates a different type of discussion. In this presentation I draw on conversations with colleagues about language and gender in our workplace. I will also talk about the triangular relationship between the patient, the doctor and the nurse, and how that triangular relationship – which has its own power base – has changed and altered in the last twenty years since I have been in nursing practice. I will consider these questions raised by my colleagues: what has driven the change in those power bases? Is it is a result of social change affecting many gender relationships within the workplace, or is it peculiar to relationships in the hospital setting?

When I came back to New Zealand after having been in China for five years, the job that I came to in New Zealand was at Hutt Valley Health. I remember thinking on my first morning, after reading a tray full of papers, that I really had missed out on something. Hutt Valley Health was a 'CHE' and was contracting with the 'RHA' for various 'buckets' of 'DIG's to 'deliver best possible outcomes for its clients'. Since my move to Capital Coast Health two years ago, those 'CHE's have become 'HSs' before our 'RHA's became the 'THA' and more recently the 'HFA'. I think that's interesting because nursing has had to find its own place within this accountancy-based jargon. I think it also underpins the strategic direction of healthcare, not only in this country but in many other countries of the world, which has been based on 'containing costs' or, as you or I might refer to it, saving money.

What effect have the health reforms had on the way we work and how we communicate with each other? Let's first take a look at how it was when I trained as a nurse twenty years ago. Hospital culture stood firmly in a rigid hierarchical structure: the chief nurse, the matron, and the chief doctor, the medical superintendent, were in control. They co-existed, each relying on their own power base to maintain the status quo supporting the dominant ideology, which was male, medical, technical, and controlling. Patients remained neatly and tightly secure in their beds: they did not go anywhere quickly. Doctors pronounced diagnoses and gave instructions. Nurses not only did their duty, but they also did what they were told. Both the nurses and patients were silenced. This silence meant that few instructions were queried and that, for patients, their illness remained quite a mystery. Nurses took on the role to translate the meaning of this diagnosis, but most patients did not want to know. There were elements of fear about what their illness meant because none of the language was accessible. What has changed? The triangular relationship between nurse, patient and doctor has been turned upside down: the locus of power and control has shifted not from the doctor to the nurse as we would like, perhaps, but from the doctor to the patient. And what has driven this shift in power and control? I think in different countries there may be different answers to that question, but for us here in New Zealand it has largely been driven by a model of healthcare which we now call being 'patient focussed'. Whilst over the last three to five years we paid lip service to the notion of patient focussed healthcare, I think we are starting to see some of the results and some of the changing nature of that power base.

How is this shift illustrated? We talk about the responsibility of getting well lying with the patient now: 'It's up to you.' The information that we give patients to help them get better is meant to be easily accessible. Instead of talking about arteries being 'occluded', we talk about them being 'blocked'. Instead of talking about 'prophylaxsis', we talk about 'prevention'. So we do make attempts to make patients' problems more accessible to them. In New Zealand I think the Health and Disability Commissioner and the Code of Rights have made a real impact, and have brought about some of the more significant changes to the power base. We have patient satisfaction surveys where patients are encouraged in their own words to describe or criticise their own experience; patients have access to information on the internet; we have consumer groups; we have consumer participation on our own boards. Patients have a right to know and they have a right to make an informed choice based on the best available evidence. The patient is encouraged to have expectations and make demands. So, in terms of language, patients are encouraged to ask questions, and options are discussed. Patients are addressed by their titles, particularly the elderly, instead of their first names, and that is a significant change. Doctors are less patronising in their tone in some cases.

How has the situation changed for doctors? Doctors have had to change the way that they function within the healthcare setting, though within the public healthcare setting more than the private setting. Doctors are bound by contracts, there are parameters and boundaries attached to their practice. The choice of pharmaceuticals which they have available in their treatments is reduced, and there is now an expectation of responsibility to an organisation. On the other hand, whilst there have been changes, there is still some way to go. In the last week, for example, we have had very short-notice cancellation of clinics because doctors are unable to make it, but forget to let the management team know. Doctors go on study leave or annual leave providing very little notice to the management team. So there remain areas for improvement,

Nurses are challenging treatment choices. This has come about through the idea of evidence-based practice, which has had a significant effect on the way that nurses and doctors now communicate. A nurse is able to present to a doctor what she believes to be the best possible evidence, as identified in the literature, to contest and to challenge some of the treatment options which are prescribed for the patients. If there is an independent source of best evidence on the way that a patient is being treated, a nurse is not coming from a position of necessarily criticising or personally undermining a doctor. This has been a very empowering process for nurses: as a result doctors are now heard asking nurses, 'What do you think?' When doctors come into the wards and units they are now asking the nurses who are managing or who are key in the care of patients about their progress, and I think that is a great improvement. Doctors also engage in gossip and small talk with nurses, and that is an improvement too.

Nurses have moved from a principally gender-based model of nursing, seen by many to be about performing what is essentially women's work, to a professional model where we are now expected to articulate very clearly what it is we do, what we contribute to the process, and what difference we make. This move has really challenged the nursing profession and there is a good deal of literature and research identifying and formalising nursing's own body of knowledge. So for nurses there are a lot of specific ways that people are communicating differently, and these have changed relationships in the workplace. This change is seen in the loss of the handmaiden role. Doctors actually clean up after themselves now. Moreover, nurses do not have to ask them to clean up they do it spontaneously! In many cases there is a shared objective in getting the best possible outcome for patients and I think that has been significant.

In conclusion, however, I have some pessimistic views on the future, but it is a short-term pessimism rather than a long-term one. It is really about moving to the next generation because, whilst there are pockets of excellence and pockets of great change, especially within Wellington hospital, there are still areas – wards and units – bound by a very strong patriarchal model, where nurses continue to be silent and are silenced by very strong medical practices and professionals who refuse to change. So my pessimism is short-term because this generation will move on. I welcome younger medical colleagues into the nursing workplace, with the refreshingly different approaches to communication that I have outlined in this presentation.

Anne Pauwels

Currently Dean of Arts at the University of Wollongong, formerly Chair of Linguistics at University of New England, Armidale, Professor Anne Pauwels also worked for many years at Monash University. Her areas of expertise include language maintenance and shift, and cross-cultural miscommunication, including the implications of cross cultural work for a variety of different professional contexts. She is the leading Australian researcher in the language and gender area, and especially in sexist language.

I am still very optimistic about a range of areas in feminist linguistics, especially if we look back and see what we have been able to achieve in a relatively short period of time. If I were to express a cautionary note it would be that we cannot take any progress for granted. There will always be times when our achievements and changes are yet again questioned or unravelled. However, I believe that an increasing number of women, and some men, are willing to become activist about gender-inclusive language in the workplace. Indeed I find it encouraging that many younger women who while at university, were appreciative of the previous generation's linguistic activism, but who could not see the point of continuing with it, often change their attitudes once they enter the workplace. In the work context they notice that what they took for granted at university is not at all obvious in their new environment.

I will focus on issues of gender inclusive language reform in the workplace. My paper (this volume) deals with issues of non-sexist usage or feminist language reform, including questions about the kinds of reform needed, and the processes involved in the adoption of reforms. Perhaps more than any other area, this area of feminist language research has had a very strong connection with the workplace right from the start. I would even claim that in this case linguists and language professionals have lagged behind women in the professions who have put sexist language and the need for reform on the table. For example a German linguist who was active in the women's movement was alerted by her non-linguist sisters about the language issue. 'You're a linguist why aren't you involved in this issue?' they asked her. She replied 'I'm a feminist, yes, and I believe in stopping wife-beating, but language? what's the problem with language?' She rapidly realised that women in the workplace were very aware of the problems around the use of sexist language, and they expected linguists and language professionals to address them.

I believe that at least in English language countries the adoption of linguistic reform in the workplace has been relatively successful. There is certainly substantial evidence that *forms* have changed, and also that some of the meanings have changed, but it is not automatic, and we still cannot be confident that a person who uses the term 'chairperson' really intends to include both women and men.

Another important achievement, especially for the workplace, is the increased power women have to name themselves rather than being named. In my workplace I hear women (both academic women and women in general staff positions) say that they are very proud of being able to name themselves: 'I can call myself *Ms* even if the entire world is against it'. Feminist language reform has given more women, especially in the workplace, the confidence to name themselves, rather than simply being named, and that is a powerful resource.

The workplace has also been the prime area for the adoption of non-sexist language reform as promoted in language guidelines, at least in English language countries. Unfortunately to date the adoption of linguistic reform has been mainly restricted to the replacement of words and phrases considered discriminatory. The current work undertaken by feminist linguists in the workplace will move us beyond this word replacement approach. Current research in the workplace, such as the work undertaken by Janet Holmes and her colleagues, is about critically analysing the forms of discourse in the workplace, how we interact with each other and how power is expressed in, and exerted through, ways of speaking. The results of this kind of work will move linguistic reform forward in the workplace.

However, it is with regard to the application of these results that I would like to sound a warning note. There is the danger of appropriation, and especially misappropriation, of these findings by a growing communications industry which is not really interested in cautious academic statements about gender and discourse behaviour in the workplace. The translation of academic findings for training packages in communication skills has often been disastrous. Discourse patterns observed in specific contexts have not only been lifted out of context but have also become prescribed discourse strategies for success. Deborah Cameron has documented this thoroughly and insightfully in her book *Verbal Hygiene.*

It is clear that what sells in the communications training industry is firm advice – 'say this and do this'. I have been very disappointed with some leading feminists who seem to know very little about the linguistic research into these issues, and who have embraced the misleading, but seductively simple, clear-cut divisions and strategies promoted by the communications industry. Clearly, the next major challenge for linguistic researchers is to find ways of presenting significant research findings, while minimising the potential for this kind of total misappropriation.

Inclusive language is good business: gender, language and equality in the workplace

Anne Pauwels

University of Wollongong

Introduction

At the turn of the new millennium, taking stock and looking back at past achievements and problems have become common practice: such a momentous occasion indeed prompts reflection. Scholars active in the field of gender and communication are no exception: in recent times there have been a series of 'state of the art' overviews critically surveying and discussing the achievements in more than a quarter century of gender and communication research (e.g. Bergvall 1999; Bergvall, Bing & Freed 1996; Cameron 1998). The main achievements and advances have been summarised in Table 1 below:

Table 1: Achievements in language and gender research

• Wealth of data on gender and communication across speech events, languages and speech communities.
• Unraveling many myths and stereotypes about women and men as language users and about women's and men's communication practices, behaviour and skills.
• Exposing the complexities of the interaction and relationship between gender and language.
• Moving away from an essentialist notion of gender to a social constructionist one: gender is viewed as a dynamic socio-cultural construct that is historically, culturally, situationally and interactionally constituted and negotiated.

Women as language users

An important result emanating from 25 years of research is the versatility of both women and men as language users and communicators. This finding was especially significant for women whose linguistic behaviour and communicative practices had been described both in popular and scholarly literature as conservative, as frivolous, as well as lacking in creativity, and devoid of authority. The deficit model of women's speech and language behaviour was still dominant in the 1970s and even 1980s. Although research confirmed that in some contexts (e.g. immigrant communities and in rural communities) women's language use was more conservative or traditional than that of men (see, for example, Burton, Dyson & Ardener 1994; Holmes 1993), research also indicated that women were leading language change and were the linguistic innovators in some speech communities (e.g. Cheshire & Gardner-Chloros 1998; Coates & Cameron 1988; Eckert 1989; Eckert & McConnell-Ginet 1999; Holmes & Meyerhoff 1999). Similarly the long held view of women as lacking authority in language matters (i.e. norm creators) was successfully challenged by showing that women, in some cases deliberately, undertook to break norms and to create their own norms (e.g. in the case of non-sexist language use). The advances thus lie in uncovering the multiple and versatile roles women and men have played as language users, rather than in exchanging one role for another (i.e. women as linguistic innovators rather than linguistic conservatives). See Table 2 for a summary.

Table 2: The multiple roles of women as language users

• Women as linguistic conservatives • Women as linguistic innovators and creators • Women as linguistic consumers • Women as norm followers • Women as norm enforcers • Women as norm breakers • Women as norm makers and creators

Authority in language: women as linguistic innovators

This paper focusses on women as linguistic innovators who have challenged the alleged authority of men as norm makers and creators of language. This is demonstrated through an examination of the phenomenon of gender-inclusive language (also known as non-sexist language) in the Australian (English) speech community. In particular I highlight how women challenged the sexist portrayal of the sexes in language, and how they promoted change. Finally I also make some comments on which changes are occurring and by whom these changes are adopted. It is in the *workplace* that issues surrounding gender-inclusive language use and non-discriminatory communication practices have been raised most prominently – women in the classroom, at the news desk, in the publishing house, in the boardroom, in the union meeting room as well as the courtroom have been at the forefront of raising and acting upon gender and linguistic discrimination issues.

Women and the workplace

It is not surprising that the workplace has been and continues to be the primary locus for women's linguistic activism. Women's participation in the paid workforce has not only dramatically increased over the past 25 years (at least in western nations) but women have also entered and are entering a greater variety of workplace and work environments: male-exclusive bastions in the work and professional arena are getting scarcer although they certainly have not completely disappeared. Indeed despite many equal employment initiatives and objectives women still experience difficulties in gaining access to certain professions and workplaces. There are many obstacles and barriers, including pay equity, promotion opportunities, work conditions and benefits, as well as coping with a work environment unaccustomed, if not hostile, to women's participation. Especially women in executive positions and leadership roles have commented on the (perceived) tensions between power and being female. Some have labeled this tension the 'double bind' situation that women find themselves in: if they act in a feminine way, they are perceived as lacking power and authority. Acting in a way perceived as masculine may provide power and authority to a woman, but at the cost of her femininity ('a ball breaker').

Women and workplace communication

These difficulties and tensions are also experienced by women at the level of language and communicative practices and norms. Women (and men) as communicators in the workplace have been constrained by powerful stereotyped views of what constitutes effective and appropriate communication in the workplace.

In many workplaces ideas of effective and appropriate communication are still equated with the ways in which men (allegedly) communicate. This is especially the case in work environments traditionally seen as the province of the white-collar male professional – the boardroom, the newsroom, the news desk, the bench, the pulpit, the parliament. In these workplaces women's communication patterns and practices are perceived as deficient: they are considered to be in need of communication and linguistic training which equips them with the (supposedly) appropriate communication skills for their workplace. These include: linguistic assertiveness training, public speaking, forceful meeting routines, voice training, changes in proxemic and kinesic behaviour. Given the increased 'linguicisation' of the workplace (Fairclough 1985) as a result of the increase in the services industry, companies are investing massively in the communication training of their staff. This has given rise to an explosive growth in the communication skills training industry ranging from popular self-help manuals to blue ribbon communication training retreats. Unfortunately many of these still propagate a view of gender and communication based on a deficit model, as Cameron (1995) has convincingly shown in her book *Verbal Hygiene*.

In other workplaces women are seen to be more skilled communicators. This applies primarily to work environments associated with the 'helping' professions in which the objective is care of people: teaching, counseling, nursing (see Jennifer Coates's contribution to the panel discussion elsewhere in this volume). Unfortunately these 'findings' are also appropriated by the communications industry to further perpetuate the stereotype of women as person-oriented and the stereotype of men as goal-driven and outcome-oriented, and thus establish women and men as fundamentally different communicators.

Irrespective of the value (positive or negative) attached to women's speaking styles in private or public spheres, women are seldom, if ever, credited with being linguistic innovators or agents of change in the literature promoted by this communications industry. In fact, as mentioned earlier, until the 1970s most linguistic work (sociolinguistic, dialectological, anthropological) similarly accorded women a conservative status as language users. More recent work in these fields provides convincing evidence to the contrary, with adolescent girls and also women emerging as 'movers and shakers' and leaders in language change. Here I would like to focus on one prominent example of women as 'movers and shakers' of *language use rules, practices* and indeed *established norms.*

Women as linguistic innovators: inclusive language

Women's role as innovators in relation to the inclusive language debate can be broken into 3 main areas:
- Exposing gender-bias in language use
- Debating solutions to gender-bias and proposing change
- Promoting and leading change

Exposing gender-bias in language use

The first area, that of *'exposing gender bias'* is well-known and has been described and discussed at length for many languages and speech communities (for references see Pauwels 1998). I will therefore limit myself to the 'bare' essentials. These are summarised in Table 3.

The second wave of the women's movement inspired many women to examine critically the role of language in women's oppression and women's liberation. From the mid-1970s, feminist language professionals in western, post-industrial societies engaged in exposing gender-bias in language use: sexism was found to pervade many aspects of language, including the lexicon and grammar. Elaborate descriptions of linguistic sexism and gender-stereotyping exist especially for English, German, French, Dutch and Spanish. A cross-linguistic comparison of linguistic sexism reveals the following common features:
- Male as norm
- Female as a deviation from the male norm
- Female as dependent on or a derivative of the male
- Female linguistic invisibility
- Gender-stereotyping

Table 3: Exposing gender bias in language use

'... men are defined in terms of what they do in the world, women in terms of the men with whom they are associated' Lakoff (1975: 30).

'The practice of labeling women as married or single also serves supremely sexist ends. There is tension between the representation of women as sex objects and the male ownership rights over women and this has been resolved by an explicit and most visible device designating the married status of women.' Spender (1980: 27).

'De man is the standaarduitvoering, terwijl het lichaam van de vrouw extra wordt benadrukt – *Man is the standard whilst the body of woman is particularly emphasised.*' Brouwer (1991: 30).

'Again and again in the history of language, one finds that a perfectly innocent term designating a girl or a woman may begin with neutral or even positive connotations, but that gradually it acquires negative implications, at first only slightly disparaging, but after a period of time becoming abusive and ending as a sexual slur.' Schulz (1975: 64).

'Le droit de nommer est une prérogative du groupe dominant sur le groupe dominé. Ainsi les hommes ont-ils des milliers de mots pour désigner les femmes, don't l'immense majorité sont péjoratifs. L'inverse n'est pas vrai. – *The right to name is a prerogative of the dominant group over the dominated group. That is why men have thousands of words for designating women, of which the majority is pejorative. The opposite is not true.*' Yaguello (1978: 150)

To date the focus of most examinations has been on lexical, semantic, morphological and grammatical asymmetries which exemplify that language use has a bias towards MAN (Male as Norm).

Debating solutions to gender bias – proposing change

Many feminists, at least in western societies, not only engaged in exposing gender-bias in language use and practices but also expressed a desire to change the patriarchal and sexist 'nature' of language. But this shared belief in the need for changing linguistic forms and discourse did not result in a uniform approach to linguistic reform (see Pauwels 1998). The social, cultural, political and philosophical diversity which characterises the feminist movement is also reflected in the approaches to and aims for feminist language reform. For example, not all forms of feminism interpret women's liberation as a question of achieving mere equality of the sexes. Similarly, not all linguistic reform proposals have as their main aim the achievement of linguistic equality of the sexes. Some reform initiatives aim primarily at exposing the sexist nature of 'patriarchal' language by causing *linguistic disruptions*. In Mary Daly's words:

> . . . breaking the rules of the games, breaking the names of the games, . . . letting out the bunnies, the bitches, the squirrels, the cows, the foxy ladies, the chicks, the pussy cats, the old bats and biddies so we can at least start naming ourselves (Daly 1978: 3).

The strategies used to achieve linguistic disruption frequently involve experimentation and creativity with all parts of speech. The word 'herstory' to refer to history which is not only about men, is an example of linguistic disruption: a morphological boundary <history > has been reconstituted to <his> + <story> on semantic grounds. *Creating a woman-centred language* capable of expressing reality from a female perspective is another prominent objective of some forms of feminist language planning. Proposed changes range from the creation of new women-centred meanings for words like *witch, hag* and neologisms such as *malestream, femocrat,* graphemic innovations including *womyn* or *wimmin,* to developing women-focussed discourses and even creating an entirely new language. An example of the latter is the Láadan language created by the science-fiction writer and linguist, Suzette Haden Elgin 'for the specific purpose of expressing the perceptions of women' (Elgin 1988: 1).

Despite this diversity in reform initiatives and objectives for feminist language planning, it is the *'linguistic equality of the sexes'* approach which has become synonymous with feminist language planning in the eyes of the wider community. This is in part due to the prominence of liberal feminist approaches in the public arena which focus on achieving sex/gender equality. Linguistic discrimination is seen as a form of sex discrimination which can be addressed in ways similar to other forms of sex discrimination (e.g. in employment). In fact the question of gender bias in occupational nomenclature is directly linked to gender discrimination in the employment arena (see Lenk's paper this volume). The prominence of the linguistic equality approach is also due to the media's attention to non-sexist language guidelines, the main instrument of promoting this type of feminist language reform.

Advocates of the linguistic equality approach use the strategies of gender-neutralisation (sometimes gender abstraction) and/or gender-specification (feminisation) to attain their goal of creating a language system which allows for a balanced representation of the sexes. *Gender-neutralisation* involves minimising or eliminating gender-specific expressions and constructions. It entails 'that any morphosyntactic and lexical features marking human agent nouns and pronouns (or other parts of speech) as masculine or feminine are 'neutralised' for gender, especially in generic contexts' (Pauwels 1998: 109). Examples for English include the elimination of gender-suffixes of *-ess, -ette, -(tr)ix,* in relation to human agent nouns (e.g. *hostess, aviatrix, usherette*), the creation of compound nouns involving *-person* (e.g. *chairperson, tradesperson*), and the avoidance of generic 'he'. *Gender-specification* (also known as feminisation) is a strategy used to achieve linguistic equality by making the 'invisible sex' (in most cases, women) visible in language through systematic and symmetrical marking of gender. Although English does not use this strategy much (it is found more often in languages with grammatical gender), the use of 'he or she', and of phrases such as 'policewomen and men', 'actors and actresses' in generic contexts exemplifies the gender-specification strategy. Underlying the linguistic equality approach to reform is a belief that making changes to linguistic *forms* will contribute significantly to the promotion of non-sexist *meanings*.

Promoting and leading change

Women have also been at the forefront of promoting change to inclusive language. They have used and are using a range of strategies to get their message across including promoting change through role models. Leading feminist activists, thinkers, writers and scholars as well as others whose language practices are gender-inclusive act as role models for other language users (mainly women) to follow in their footsteps. In some cases, the feminist role models explicitly appealed to other women to adopt women-friendly language and communication practices (e.g. Daly 1978). Another way of promoting non-sexist language use is through the 'solidarity' strategy: this involves appeal to the notion of a feminist 'sisterhood'. The promotion of change through language guidelines is a form of linguistic activism. To date there has been little systematic work to examine specifically the impact of these strategies on promoting as well as on the spread of feminist linguistic change throughout a speech community.

Although there is plenty of anecdotal evidence of change, this needs to be complemented and confirmed by research evidence. To date this research is still in its infancy, partly due to the fact that feminist language reform is a relatively recent phenomenon. Early findings from research (mainly based in North America) reveal trends of variation and even change in favour of non-sexist language use. Here I discuss findings from recent work on feminist language reform in the Australian speech community which focuses on which changes are occurring and who is making them.

Which changes?

Given the prominence of the 'linguistic equality' strategy, I focus on changes relating to this approach for the Australian speech community.

Generic nouns: occupational terms, titles and agent nouns

In 1996 I undertook a study of approximately 2000 job advertisements from ten Australian newspapers ranging from those with a national distribution (1), to a state-wide (7), and a regional/local (2) distribution (Pauwels 1997). Advertisements were selected at random from the following areas of employment: general positions, hospitality, public service, computing and health. The database yielded 128 different occupational terms ranging from *accountant, aromatherapist, cleaning lady* to *gardener, secretary* and *waitperson*. Only 5.4% of the ads used sex-exclusive terms. These comprised mainly – *man* compounds and a few *–ess* words. Although the potential for sex-exclusive occupational terms is much lower in English than in some other languages, the very low incidence of sex-exclusive terms can be read as marking change. In fact, with the exception of the terms *chairman* and *handyman*, all other – *man* compounds occurred less than their inclusive counterparts as illustrated in the table below. Furthermore there were no instances of *barman, draftsman, salesman* or *storeman*.

Table 4: Use of -man words and their alternatives

-man compound	*-person* compound	Other
chairman (55%)	chairperson (45%)	—
draftsman (0%)	draftsperson (55%)	drafter (45%)
foreman (19%)	foreperson (81%)	—
groundsman (50%)	groundsperson (50%)	—
handyman (55%)	handyperson (45%)	—
salesman (0%)	salesperson (84%)	salespeople (16%)
storeman (0%)	storeperson (100%)	—
tradesman (5%)	tradesperson (90 %)	tradespeople (5%)

The same investigation also revealed that the (already) few female-exclusive terms had been abandoned in favour of gender-neutral ones. For example, there were no *air hostesses* only *flight attendants*, no *salesgirls, saleswomen* or *salesladies*, only *salesperson(s)* or *salespeople*, no *barmaids* or *bar ladies*, only *bartenders*.

In a more recent study (Pauwels 1999) I analysed the use of non-sexist alternatives for *-man* compounds in generic contexts in a corpus of 200,000 words taken from two national Australian newspapers. The overall incidence of generically used nouns in sections other than job advertisements is very low (less than 0.5% – a total of 783 nouns) and the use of *-person, -woman, -man* compounds is even lower (a total of 166), in both generic and specific contexts. The number of occurrences of *chairman, chairwoman, chair* and *chairperson* revealed that *chairman* is used more than the other terms, although a breakdown of the numbers according to referents showed that *chairman* was predominantly used to refer to male referents. The few occurrences of *chairperson* and *chair* (see Table 5) do not allow for an interpretation of emerging trends. In the case of *chairman*, I would have to agree with Holmes' (in press) comment that its continuing, frequent use reflects the fact that far more men than women continue to occupy these positions. It should also be said that newspaper articles are not an ideal source to establish generic uses of this term, as most references to the position specify the incumbent. The same can be said for the frequent use of the word *cameraman* which appeared 23 times – the possible non-sexist alternatives, *camera operator* or *camera person*, did not appear at all.

In the case of *spokesman/spokeswoman/spokesperson* a more substantial change can be noted: although 38 instances of *spokesman* were recorded, *spokesperson* appeared 32 times. A breakdown in terms of referents showed that 47% of *spokesman* uses referred to a male, and that *spokesman* was never used to refer specifically to a female. Most uses of *spokesperson* had no specific referent. There is also some indication that *spokesperson* is being used in connection with male as well as female referents, contradicting the trend noted by Ehrlich & King (1992) that the *-person* compound is used as a mere substitute for the *–woman* compound. Other terms included *tradesman* (5 instances) and *tradesperson* (2), *clergyman* (2), *foreman* (2), *foreperson* (2), *ombudsman* (7), *ombudswoman* (1), *ombudsperson* (3).

This Australian investigation further revealed a low incidence of asymmetrical gender constructions of the sort *driver* vs *woman driver* or *nurse* vs *male nurse*. A total of 7 instances of asymmetrical use were found: they included *female judge* (1), *woman engineer*(2), *woman politician*(2), *woman publican* (1) and *lady taxi driver* (1).

Generic pronouns: he, she, he or she and they

Another prominent feature of the non-sexist language campaign is the elimination of the masculine pseudo-generic pronoun *he*: proposed alternatives have included the dual pronoun *he or she* and its many variations, singular *they*, the generic use of *she*, the use of *it*, and the creation of a new pronoun (for discussions on these alternatives see

Table 5: -man compounds and their alternatives

Term	Frequency	Referent unknown	Male referent	Female referent
cameraman	23	5	17	0
chairman	33	4	28	1
chairwoman	4	0	0	4
chairperson	1	0	0	1
chair	3	1	1	1
clergyman	2	1	1	0
foreman	2	1	1	1
foreperson	2	2	0	0
ombudsman	7	2	4	1
ombudswoman	1	0	0	1
ombudsperson	3	3	0	0
spokesman	38	20	18	0
spokeswoman	8	0	0	8
spokesperson	32	21	8	3
tradesman	5	2	3	0
tradesperson	2	2	0	0

Baron 1986; Bodine 1975; Mackay 1980, 1983; Martyna 1978; Moulton, Robinson & Elias 1978; Soto, Halon, Florio & Cole 1975 and Wilson & Ng 1988).

In a small-scale longitudinal study between 1986 and 1988 (Pauwels 1989, 1998), I recorded the pronoun use patterns of ten university students, as reflected in their written work (approximately 35,000 words per student). The overall findings of this small-scale study included:

- with one exception, all students used non-sexist generic pronouns in their written work most of the time. In fact, the writing of five students (all female) showed no signs of generic masculine generic pronoun use.

- the dual pronoun *he or she* (and its variations *s/he, she or he*) was the preferred alternative to masculine generic *he,* although 'singular' *they* also appeared sometimes. Generic *she* or a new pronoun did not appear at all in the students' writing.

• Between 1986 and 1988 a decrease in masculine generic pronoun use was noted for most students.

In the study on job classified adverts (Pauwels 1997), pronominalisation for anaphoric reference was minimal: the general tendency in this corpus of classifieds was to resort to such agent nouns as *person/ persons* (55.8%), *applicant/applicants* (34.8%), *candidate/candidates* (6.7%), *individual/individuals* (2.4%) and *appointee* (0.3%). Only 2.3% job classifieds recorded pronouns: mainly *he or she*. There was no use of masculine generic *he*.

The first results of a large scale project investigating the adoption of feminist language change in *spoken language* (with a focus on public speech) suggest that 'singular' *they* is the preferred generic pronoun in public speech: 45 radio interviews (approx. 196000 words and involving 14 interviewers and 199 guests) yielded 422 cases of pronominalisation of generic nouns. Dominating the pronoun stakes by a large margin is 'singular' *they* which was used 281 times (67%). This was followed by 72 cases in which the generic noun was repeated (17%). There were still 50 cases of the use of masculine generic *he* (12%). The dual pronoun strategy, i.e. use of *he or she* only occurred 8 times (1.5%) and the generic use of *she* only 3 times (0.5%).

Titles for women: Ms, Mrs or Miss?

Another prominent issue in the feminist language reform debate concerns the asymmetry in titles of address for women and men. The title *Ms* was advanced to restore this imbalance between the female (*Mrs* and *Miss*) and male (*Mr*) honorific titles. Despite its many pitfalls (see Pauwels 1987, 1996, 1997), the title *Ms* is gaining currency amongst female users in many English speaking communities, although reliable figures are not available (e.g. Atkinson 1987; Ehrlich & King 1992; Graddol & Swann 1989; Jacobson & Insko 1984; Holmes in press; Milne 1991; Pauwels 1987, 1996, in press). Small-scale surveys and studies have established that the use of *Ms* ranges from 20% to almost 50% amongst the female population in these communities.

In 1986 and 1996 I undertook surveys involving approximately 500 women in Australian cities and regional towns to examine the acceptance and use of *Ms* (Pauwels 1987, 1996, in press). The study involved short interviews with women in which they were questioned about their familiarity with, understanding of as well as use of the title *Ms*. The interviews in 1996 also collected socio-demographic information, including age, educational background and marital status. The interviews took place in public spaces (e.g. banks, post-offices, insurance offices), and lasted on average about 5 to 10 minutes.

Although familiarity with the actual title was very high in both 1986 and 1996, there is still confusion about its exact meaning. In 1986, 64% of polled women were conversant with the promoted/propagated meaning of *Ms* whereas in 1996 this had risen to almost 75%. The others thought that *Ms* had any of the following meanings: a title for separated, or divorced or professional or feminist women.

In terms of actual personal usage, approximately 37% indicated that they were users of *Ms* in 1996 compared to almost 20% in 1986. This is a remarkable increase over a period of ten years.

Who changes?

The previous sections have established that women have been the initiators and prime promoters of feminist language reform. Given their prominent role as linguistic reformers it can be expected that women will also be leaders of change (i.e. the adoption of proposed changes). To date there is little direct evidence to confirm this, mainly because research has largely focused on examining written language for signs of feminist language change: establishing authorship for media texts or public documents is very difficult as such texts are often handled by a variety of people. Indeed written language is not the ideal medium to undertake a sociolinguistic investigation of language variation and change.

The results of attitudinal studies on sexist and non-sexist language use suggest women favour change more than men do. Furthermore, one could infer from the prominence with which non-sexist language is used in feminist publications that women lead the use of non-sexist language. The small-scale case study of students' pronoun use mentioned above also points in the direction of women leading the change (Pauwels 1998). The scarcity of data on this matter prompted me to embark on the project entitled 'Investigating feminist language change in speech' (funded by

the Australian Research Council). Among its main aims is the construction of a sociolinguistic and sociodemographic profile of those adopting
change, as well as the examination of the process of the spread of feminist
linguistic change throughout the community. To date the preliminary
results from 45 radio interviews reveal that women are leading change
in the adoption of non-sexist generic nouns and pronouns, although only
by a small margin. For example, women's use of the masculine generic
he was down to 6%, whereas men's use of this masculine generic
amounted to 16%. One female interviewer used generic *she*. So far the
radio interviews have involved mainly educated professionals (lawyers,
doctors, academics, musicians, judges, scientists, psychologists, etc) so
no conclusions should be drawn about linguistic change in the wider
community.

The fieldwork on *Ms* conducted in 1996, however, allowed for a
first insight into the socio-demographic profile of the most likely users
(Pauwels in press). The most significant factor in determining title use
is education: women with tertiary education formed the main *Ms* -using
group. Age is also significant but because of the large age groupings
used in the study, it is not possible to pinpoint the most significant age
group for *Ms*. The prime users were found in the age groups <25–40>
(40.5%) and <41– 65> (37.8%). The distribution of *Ms* with regard to
age currently resembles a bell shaped curve. The low usage rate amongst
65+ year-olds may be attributable in part to the relative recency of the
title. The correlation between the factor of 'marital status' and title use
shows that *Ms* is being adopted first by those who fall 'outside' the
traditional categories of 'married' and 'single/unmarried'. But *Ms* use
is also found increasingly among the latter: 60.8 % of *Ms* users identified
themselves as living in heterosexual 'de facto' relationships, 44.8% of
Ms users were divorced or separated, 39.6 % described themselves as
single, 31.4% of *Ms* users were married and 14.3 % were widowed.
This study also revealed that women who were non-users of *Ms* were
far more willing than men to accommodate to the desires of other women
to be addressed by *Ms*.

Concluding remarks

In this paper I have shown that women, especially those operating in
the paid workforce, are linguistic innovators. Their role as *linguistic*

activists who expose gender-bias and promote gender-inclusive alternatives by breaking established norms and creating new norms is beyond doubt. The small-scale Australian studies indicate that women's linguistic activism is beginning to have a substantial impact on language use. To what extent the observed tendencies towards non-sexist language use are indicative of change rather than of variation is yet to be determined. Some alternatives have not only caused instability in 'traditional' usage patterns, but have reached the status of tolerated, and in some cases, preferred use in particular contexts (e.g. the use of non-sexist generic pronouns in radio interviews). What remains to be seen is to what extent this adoption and change can be considered successful. There are some indications that non-sexist or feminist alternatives are being used in a sexist or gender-biased way. Unfortunately this is a major problem associated with the linguistic equality approach which relies heavily on the form replacement strategy to effect meaning change: but changing forms is no guarantee of effecting a change in meaning and in usage patterns.

To establish to what extent women also lead feminist language change (i.e. adoption of feminist linguistic alternatives) we need to undertake further work. However, to date, there are signs that women will indeed emerge as leaders of feminist language change.

References

Atkinson, Donna L. 1987. Names and titles: maiden name retention and the use of *Ms*. *Women and Language* 10, 37.

Baron, Dennis 1986. *Grammar and Gender*. New Haven: Yale University Press.

Bergvall, Victoria 1999. An agenda for language and gender research for the start of the new millennium. *Linguistik Online*: http: //www.viadrina.euv-frankfurt-o.de/ wjournal/1_99/bergvall.htm.

Bergvall, Victoria, Janet M. Bing & Alice F. Freed (eds) 1996. *Rethinking Language and Gender Research: Theory and Practice*. New York: Longman.

Brouwer, Dédé 1991. *Vrouwentaal*. Bloemendaal: Aramith.

Bodine, Ann 1975. Androcentrism in prescriptive grammar: singular 'they', sex-indefinite 'he', and 'he or she'. *Language in Society* 4, 129-46.

Burton, Pauline, Katherine Dyson & Shirley Ardener (eds) 1994. *Bilingual Women, Anthropological Approaches to Second Language Use*. Oxford: Berg.

Cameron, Deborah 1995. *Verbal Hygiene*. London: Routledge.

Cameron, Deborah 1998. Gender, language, and discourse: a review essay. *Signs* 23, 4, 945- 975.

Cheshire, Jenny & Penelope Gardner-Chloros 1998. Code-switching and the sociolinguistic gender pattern. *International Journal of the Sociology of Language* 129, 5-34.

Coates, Jennifer & Deborah Cameron (eds) 1988. *Women in their Speech Communities*. London: Longman.

Daly, Mary 1978. *Gyn/Ecology: The Metaethics of Radical Feminism*. Boston: Beacon Press.

Eckert, Penelope 1989. The whole woman: sex and gender differences in variation. *Language Variation and Change* 1, 245-268.

Eckert, Penelope & Sally McConnell-Ginet 1999. New generalizations and explanations in language and gender research. *Language in Society* 28, 2, 185-201.

Ehrlich, Susan & Ruth King 1992. Gender-based language reform and the social construction of meaning. *Discourse and Society* 3, 2, 151-66.

Elgin, Suzette Haden 1988. *A First Dictionary and Grammar of Láadan*. Madison, (revised edition).

Fairclough, Norman 1985. *Language and Power.* London: Longman.

Graddol, David & Joan Swann 1989. *Gender Voices*. Oxford: Blackwell.

Holmes, Janet 1993. Immigrant women and language maintenance in Australia and New Zealand. *International Journal of Applied Linguistics* 3, 159-179.

Holmes, Janet (in press). Gender identity in New Zealand English. To appear in Marlis Hellinger & Hadumod Bussmann (eds), *Gender Across Languages: International Perspectives of Language Variation and Change*. Amsterdam: Benjamins.

Holmes, Janet & Miriam Meyerhoff 1999. The Community of Practice: theories and methodologies in language and gender research. *Language in Society* 28, 2, 173-183.

Jacobson, M. & W. Insko 1985. On the relationship between feminism and the use of 'Ms'. *Psychological Reports* 54, 388-90.

Lakoff, Robin 1975. *Language and Woman's Place*. New York: Harper.

Mackay, Donald 1980. Psychology, prescriptive grammar and the pronoun problem. *American Psychologist* 35, 444-9.

Mackay, Donald 1983. Prescriptive grammar and the pronoun problem. In Barrie Thorne, Cheris Kramarae & Nancy Henley (eds), *Language, Gender and Society*. Rowley, MS: Newbury House, 38-53.

Martyna, Wendy 1978. What does 'he' mean? Use of the generic masculine. *Journal of Communication* 28, 1, 130-9.

Milne, Brian 1991. *Ms-usage in the Public Service*. Unpublished terms paper.

Moulton, Janice, George M. Robinson & Cherin Elias 1978. Sex bias in language use: neutral pronouns that aren't. *American Psychologist* 33, 1032-6.

Pauwels, Anne 1987. Language in transition: a study of the title 'Ms' in contemporary Australian society. In Anne Pauwels (ed), *Women and Language in Australian and New Zealand Society*. Sydney: APP, 129-54.

Pauwels, Anne 1989. *Feminist language change in Australia: changes in generic pronoun use*. Paper presented at the Tagung der deutschen Gesellschaft für Sprachwissenschaft, University of Osnabrück, February 1989.

Pauwels, Anne 1996. Feminist language planning and titles for women: some crosslinguistic perspectives. In Ulrich Ammon & Marlis Hellinger (eds), *Contrastive Sociolinguistics*. Berlin: De Gruyter, 251-69.

Pauwels, Anne 1997. Of handymen and waitpersons: a linguistic evaluation of job classifieds. *Australian Journal of Communication* 24, 1, 58-69.

Pauwels, Anne 1998. *Women Changing Language*. London: Longman.

Pauwels, Anne 1999. Feminist language planning: Has it been worthwhile? *Linguistik Online*: http: //www.viadrina.euv-frankfurt-o.de/~wjournal/1_99/pauwels.htm.

Pauwels, Anne (in press). Spreading the feminist word? A sociolinguistic study of feminist language change in Australian English: The case of the new courtesy title 'Ms'. To appear in Marlis Hellinger & Hadumod Bussmann (eds), *Gender Across Languages. International Perspectives of Language Variation and Change*. Amsterdam: Benjamins.

Schulz, Muriel 1975. The semantic derogation of woman. In Barrie Thorne & Nancy Henley (eds), *Language and Sex*. Rowley, MS: Newbury House, 64-73.

Soto, Debbie, Forslund Halon, Evelyn Florio & Claudia Cole 1975. *Alternatives to using masculine pronouns when referring to the species*. Paper presented at the Western Speech Communication Association, San Francisco, CA, 1975.

Spender, Dale 1980. *Man Made Language*. London: Kegan & Paul.

Wilson, Elizabeth & Sik H. Ng 1988. Sex bias in visuals evoked by generics: a New Zealand study. *Sex Roles,* 159-68.

Yaguello, Marina 1978. *Les Mots et les Femmes*. Paris: Payot.

'The masculine is not what it used to be'?: German job advertisements after 30 years of feminist linguistic criticism

Uta Lenk

University of Augsburg

Introduction[1]

In an article reviewing 30 years of the Women's Liberation Movement in Germany published in 1998, Luise Pusch claimed that 'the masculine is not what it used to be'. Pusch has been an eminent commentator and protagonist for the demasculinisation and feminisation of the German language during this time period. She claims that it is no longer possible in public German discourse to use generic masculines to mean 'all humans' including women.

Languages with grammatical gender have been at the centre of attention since feminist criticism of language began. Although the problem of the generic masculine does not only appear in languages with grammatical gender, it is most notable in such a context. German, with three grammatical genders, four cases, and its multitude of obligatory inflectional endings is a notoriously difficult language in which to achieve non-sexist language use, even when speakers are perfectly willing. For many speakers, trying to speak German in a non-discriminatory manner threatens fluent speech production.

With the exception of a few plural nouns that do not have a singular form, every noun in German has a grammatical gender which prescribes the use of appropriate determiners, adjectives, noun endings and pronouns, and makes it virtually impossible to use a noun with a truly generic meaning. Similarly, a noun's grammatical gender cannot be altered by simply changing a pronoun or determiner; in many cases the gender of a noun also requires morphological changes (e.g. *der Arzt (m), die Ärztin (f)*, 'doctor').

The grammatical gender of nouns denoting occupations often reflect societal expectations from the pre-feminism era. Most established job denotations use a masculine form, such as *der Lehrer, der Bäcker, der Arzt, der Abt* ('teacher', 'baker', 'doctor', 'abbot'). The feminine equivalents are usually achieved through feminine derivative endings being added to the masculine nouns (i.e. *die Lehrerin, die Bäckerin, die Ärztin, die Äbtissin*). Feminine job denotations that are not derivatives of a masculine job denotation typically appear in specific areas. Often these jobs are menial and low-paid occupations as in *die Amme* ('wetnurse') which has no masculine equivalent, or in areas of domestic service *die Putzfrau* ('cleaning woman') which were not traditionally filled by men.

Discussion concerning the equal linguistic representation of women and men in German has flourished recently (e.g. Burkhardt 1984; Guentherodt, Hellinger, Pusch & Trömel-Plötz 1980; Kargl, Wetschanow & Wodak 1997; Leisi 1992; Leiss 1994; Linke 1993; Lorenz 1991; Lutjeharms 1987; Schmidt 1990; Ulrich 1988). However it is not the purpose of this paper to summarise nor expand upon this discussion, nor do I attempt to discuss whether gender and sex in language have anything to do with each other (see Cameron 1985 for a discussion of this area). The purpose of this paper is to describe current usage of a specific aspect of gender in the German language. After a brief description of the various morphological and lexical possibilities in German for naming occupations without a gender bias, I consider the use of these forms in a corpus of over 3,000 present-day job advertisements. Comparisons are made with a reference corpus of 900 job advertisements from 1969.[2]

Morphological and lexical possibilities of equal linguistic representation of women and men in German

Double formulations, *Beidnennungen*

Braun (1996: 58) suggests that the most straightforward means of achieving equal linguistic representation for women and men is by mentioning both masculine and feminine forms fully as in '*Liebe Wählerinnen und Wähler!*' ('Dear voters-fem and voters-masc') or *Linguistinnen und Linguisten treffen sich im Rahmen einer Konferenz, um über das Problem der sprachlichen Gleichbehandlung der Geschlechter zu diskutieren* ('Linguists-fem and linguists-masc are meeting at a conference to discuss the problem of equal linguistic representation of the sexes.'). This is known as *Beidnennungen* or 'Double Formulations'. This possibility has frequently met with the objection that it results in awkward, clumsy or unwieldy formulations, makes for uncomfortable reading and presents a severe threat to the coherence and comprehensibility of texts.[3]

Economic formulations, Sparformeln

Another strategy is the use of 'Economic Formulations' (*Sparformeln*) which aim to avoid the complications and repetitions of the Double Formulations. By orthographically indicating morphological boundaries, masculine and feminine forms are visually separated. This can be done in various ways: *Student/inn/en, Student-inn-en, Student(inn)en, StudentInnen, StudentInNen*. Objections to this approach include the claim that the resulting forms are not easy to read out loud, or they voice resistance towards the unorthodox use of a capital letter in the middle of a word.[4] Additional difficulties with this orthographic approach arise when articles and adjectives also need to be de-genderized,[5] and the complexity of applying this strategy in the case of compounds that have a generic masculine as their first element, as in *Lehrerzimmer* ('teacher's lounge'), *Rednerpult* ('lectern') or *Schülerrhetorik* ('students' rhetoric').[6]

Gender neutral references

German does have several neutral and/or non-sexist means of referring to people, however. For example, the grammatically female but semantically neutral noun *Person* can be used to generically refer to either males or females. In reality, words ending in *-person* are usually restricted to female referents; conscious reference to a male using a *-person* suffix would appear odd.

Generic derivational morphemes

Several generic derivational morphemes also exist in German. These affixes may be used to denote a group of people without specifying the gender of the members of that particular group: examples of such derivational suffixes include -*leute* (as in *die Kaufleute*, 'merchants')[7] and -*personal* (*Küchenpersonal*, 'kitchen personnel'). The singular derivational morpheme -*kraft* ('person power', as in *Lehrkraft*, 'teaching person', and *Arbeitskraft*, 'working person') and the abstract derivational morpheme -*dienst* ('service', as in *Fahrdienst*, 'driving service') are further examples of this strategy. However, there are words to which these affixes may not be added (e.g. *Lehrdienst, 'teaching service', and *Lehrleute, 'teaching people'). Another problem is that the meanings of these affixes may change in some combinations (e.g. *Küchendienst*, 'kitchen duty', or *Kaufkraft*, 'buying power'). Similarly, the often-used present participle *Studierende* ('those who are studying'), *Lehrende* ('those who are teaching') is only applicable for some, not all job-denotations and entails semantic differences to the traditional masculine/ generic nouns.

Masculine, feminine and generic forms in German job advertisements

All of these possibilities complicate language use, and not all of them are equally accepted in public. However, in the early eighties, legislation was passed regulating an advertiser's obligation to advertise any open position in a manner that indicated equal prospects for female and male applications, unless a person's sex was an indispensable necessity for that job.[8] Thus the use of gender inclusive terms in job advertisements may be interpreted as signaling different degress of employer commit-ment to equal employment opportunities.

The corpora: job advertisements from 1999 and 1969

The advertisements on which this study is based were collected in a rather random manner during the first half of the year 1999. Several issues of one nationwide weekly paper which includes a large employ-ment section (DIE ZEIT) and a Saturday issue of one nationwide daily paper (*Süddeutsche Zeitung*) from the month of February 1999 were analysed. For comparison, and in order to include advertisements that would be directed toward a less intellectual or academic clientele, several Saturday issues of several more local daily newspapers from all over Germany were collected on June 5, 1999 and included in the corpus,[9] which consisted of a total of approximately 3,000 job advertisements. A reference corpus, representing the wording and format of job advertise-ments from 30 years ago, was also used. This consisted of one copy of the *Süddeutsche Zeitung* and one month's copies of DIE ZEIT from the month of June, 1969. The reference corpus consists of approximately 900 advertisements.[10]

Before analysing the content of these advertisements, there is an interesting point of difference in layout between the two corpora which deserves comment. Thirty years ago job advertisement sections were divided into separate sections for men and for women, with a third mixed section that included advertisements of jobs for which both men and women could apply. The mixed sections also contained advertisements by firms which offered several positions, where the high-ranking positions were frequently advertised with generic/masculine nouns, while lower-ranking positions made use of feminine endings. Today, the sectioning, if present at all, is organized not according to gender but according to the fields in which the jobs are being offered, such as 'academic', 'banking', 'software-related', and 'social work'.

Analysis of gendered language in German advertisements 1999 and 1969

Thirty years ago, only jobs advertised in the women's section of the papers included feminine forms of job denotations, and only a few of the jobs advertised in the 'mixed' section made use of feminine forms (see above), with the rest of the mixed advertisements usually using a masculine/generic form. By 1999, this had changed noticeably.[11] Several of the different strategies described in Section 2 above are employed to indicate that both women and men can apply for the position advertised. Some of the advertisements make use of one strategy, while others use a combination of several of the strategies. However, a number of advertisements still do not fulfill the legal requirements described above. Indeed in some cases there is an implication that women are not encouraged to apply.

Strategies used to achieve gender-neutral job advertisements

From the corpus of current job advertisements, six different categories of strategies may be identified. They include:

1) the avoidance of reference to gender, often through use of second-person pronouns
2) the use of gender-neutral plural nouns or semantically neutral derivational morphemes
3) the inclusion of the feminine ending *–in*
4) the Internal I (*Binnen-I*)
5) an addendum which is known as a *Frauenzusatz* ('women special hiring clause') such as 'women are specifically encouraged to apply'
6) the use of the English language.

These strategies will be illustrated with examples below.

Use of second-person pronouns

One way of advertising a job in a gender-neutral manner is to directly address the reader (i.e. the possible applicant). For example, 'you are . . .'. This strategy is effective in avoiding generic nouns or third-person personal pronouns (Figure 1, p. 158).

Such a use of second-person pronouns for the job description is often accompanied by some reference to 'm/f' (abbreviation for *männlich /weiblich* – 'male/female'), indicating that the position is open to applications from women and men. Usually, this indication will appear in a prominent place in the advertisement, such as immediately adjacent to (or at least close to) the job's title.

Gender-neutral plural nouns or derivational morphemes

The grammatically well-established and unproblematic way of referring to mixed groups of people (i.e. applicants) via gender-neutral plural nouns or derivational morphemes appears infrequently in advertisements. This may be because plural nouns or derivational morphemes may only be used to advertise several openings at once. The following example (Figure 2) is advertising for shipping merchants (*Schiffahrtskaufleute*), and makes use of the gender-neutral derivational suffix *-leute*. Formerly, there existed no single word with a generic meaning for shipping merchant, but nowadays there are three forms available: *-kaufleute* (plural generic), the traditional masculine singular form *-kaufmann* and a feminine form *-kauffrau*. This advertisement also uses second-

Figure 1: *Mainpost*, June 5, 1999[12]

Figure 2: *Frankfurter Rundschau*, June 5, 1999

person pronouns (*Sie werden...*, *Sie sollten...*, *Wenn Sie sich...*; 'You will...*, you should..., If you are...*') thus avoiding any reference to gender. This advertisement is quite remarkable in its use of gender-neutral language because of the traditionally male domain of shipping.

Feminine /-in-endings

A widespread means of indicating that applications are open to women and men is the inclusion of *Double Formulations* in which both masculine and feminine job denotations are given fully, and *Economic Formulations* in which the feminine ending is indicated orthographically. These may be adhered to throughout the entire text as in Figure 3, which uses feminine endings in several places in the text: *Netzwerk-Administrator/in, Mitarbeiter/in, PC-Benutzer/innen, eine/n innovative/n, kommunikative/n und teamfähige/n Mitarbeiter/in.*

Warum PFIZER?
„Weil bei uns Team und Technik stimmen!"

Als weltweit führendes Unternehmen der pharmazeutischen Industrie sind wir mit unseren Präparaten in vielen Gebieten Impulsgeber und Schrittmacher. Diesen Anspruch wollen wir auch im IT-Bereich umsetzen. Auch Sie können schon bald – zunächst auf zwei Jahre befristet – in einer der nachfolgenden Positionen dabei sein:

Netzwerk-Administrator/in

Innerhalb der IT-Abteilung verstärken Sie den Bereich Netzwerk-Administration. Sie betreuen unser Netzwerk, das ca. 800 PCs, UNIX-, Netware- und NT-Server umfaßt und sorgen für einen kontinuierlichen Ausbau des Netzes. Wir erwarten fundierte Kenntnisse in allen Aspekten eines heterogenen Netzwerkes. Wichtig sind vor allem praktische Erfahrung mit Novell Netware, Windows NT und aktiven Netzwerkkomponenten wie Router, und Switches. Kenntnisse auf dem Gebiet TCP/IP sind Voraussetzung.

Mitarbeiter/in PC-Support

H.Häffner
Leiter PC-Benutzerservice

Mit Fachwissen, Rat und Tat unterstützen Sie alle PC-Benutzer/innen der Pfizer-Zentrale. Die zu betreuenden Anwendungen basieren auf den Betriebssystemen Windows 95 und Windows NT. Ihre Aufgabenschwerpunkte bestehen im wesentlichen in der Betreuung, Anpassung und Optimierung dieser Systeme und der PC-Arbeitsplätze. Sie befassen sich mit unserer zukünftigen Kommunikationssoftware und der gesamten Client-Software. Grundsatzaufgaben im Zusammenhang mit der neuen Mailtechnologie MS Exchange ergänzen ebenso wie die Handhabung unseres elektronischen Software Delivery Systems Ihr Tätigkeitsfeld. Für diese Funktion stellen wir uns eine/n innovative/n, kommunikative/n und teamfähige/n Mitarbeiter/in mit Erfahrung auf dem Gebiet der Informationstechnik und Supportbetreuung vor. Wir erwarten praktische Erfahrung mit Microsoft-Produkten, eine Zertifizierung als MCSE ist von Vorteil.

Zum zweiten Mal in Folge nimmt Pfizer Inc. nach dem Ranking des US-Wirtschaftsmagazins Fortune (Oktober 1998) den ersten Platz der „most admired companies" im Bereich Pharmaceutical/Health Care ein – und ist somit weltweit das angesehenste Unternehmen auf diesem Sektor.

Für beide Positionen gilt: Ob Einsteiger/in oder berufserfahrene/r Praktiker/in - in der PC-Welt fühlen Sie sich zu Hause, ganz gleich, ob es um Hard- oder Software geht. Ihre Serviceorientierung beweisen Sie durch Ihren Ehrgeiz, wirklich jedes Problem Ihrer internen Kunden optimal zu lösen. Grundkenntnisse der englischen Sprache sind aufgrund unserer internationalen Kontakte unabdingbar. Finden Sie sich in diesem Profil wieder? Passen Sie zu uns und wir zu Ihnen? Dann freuen wir uns auf Ihre Bewerbung, die Sie bitte an nachstehende Adresse senden.

PFIZER GmbH · Personalabteilung · Postfach 4949 · 76032 Karlsruhe · tscheg@pfizer.com
Weitere Informationen finden Sie auf unserer Homepage http://www.pfizer.de

Figure 3: *Badische Neueste Nachrichten*, June 5, 1999

In other cases the feminine endings only appear with the job denotation, with the rest of the text kept in generic formulations, as in one example from the *Frankfurter Rundschau* (June 5, 1999), searching for software developers (*Software-Entwickler/innen*). Applicants are subsequently referred to using generic-masculine forms such as *Hochschulabsolventen* and *Berufsanfänger* ('university graduates', 'newcomers to the job').

Binnen-I – the internal 'I'

The orthographically most unconventional means of advertising a job in a non-discriminatory way is the *Binnen-I* ('internal I'), where the morphological boundary between the masculine/generic form and the feminine ending within the word is signalled by a capitalized 'I'.[13] This strategy indicates that both the masculine and the feminine denotations of the word are meant to be activated. Occurrences of the *Binnen-I* in advertisements are few, probably due to the fact that this strategy has met with the strongest opposition in traditional prescriptive circles. Its use has a marked political connotation (see Braun 1996, Grabrucker 1993 and Schoenthal 1998a for a discussion of the political dimensions of the use of *Binnen-I*). The use of *Binnen-I* is illustrated in Figures 4 and 5.[14]

Other strategies used in the advertisement in Figure 4 are the use of disambiguated definite determiners (e.g. *den/die LeiterIn*, 'director'), gender-neutral nouns (*Führungspersönlichkeit*, 'person with leadership qualities') and direct address using second-person pronouns (*Ihre wissenschaftliche Qualifikation*, 'your scientific qualification'). Generics/masculines only appear with reference to the company as an institution (*Erzeuger, Anbieter, Problemlöser*, 'producers, distributors, service providers') and to the customers (*Kunden*).

Figure 4: Die ZEIT, Feb. 11, 1999

The advertisement in Figure 5 offers three different kinds of jobs with a *Binnen-I* in all of the job denotations, at least one of which is a traditionally male occupation (*BauingenieurIn*, 'construction engineer'). The parts of the text that concern the potential applicants are all disambiguated for gender (e.g. *eine/r der ersten AnsprechpartnerInnen*, 'one of the first contacts') and use direct second-person pronouns (e.g. *Sie nehmen Aufträge entgegen . . ., verfügen Sie . . ., leben Sie unsere Unternehmenskultur . . .*, 'you accept customer orders . . ., you have . . ., you live our company philosophy . . .') or double formulations (*Wir suchen daher jetzt Mitarbeiterinnen und Mitarbeiter*, 'we are now searching for colleagues-fem and colleagues-masc'). Only references to the personnel already with the company (*mit mehr als 65,000 Mitarbeitern*, 'with more than 65,000 personnel') and to the customers (*unserer Kunden*) appear with generic/masculine nouns.

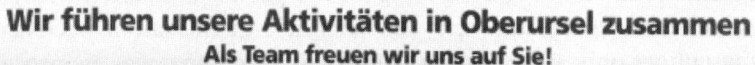

Figure 5: *Frankfurter Rundschau*, June 5, 1999

The Frauenzusatz ('women special hiring clause')

One wide-spread strategy is the inclusion of a clause somewhere in the advertisement that the advertising institution has a policy of hiring women, and that women are specifically encouraged to apply. The *Frauenzusatz* can appear combined with the masculine/generic job denotation as in an advertisement by Kienbaum Executive Consultants searching for a director for development of leadership qualities and human resources (*Leiter Führungskräfteentwicklung und Personalrekrutierung*), and a human resources manager (*Personalreferent*), which adds the following clause at the end of the advertisement: 'Ladies and Gentlemen interested can contact . . .' (*Interessierte Damen und Herren können einen ersten vertraulichen Kontakt . . . aufnehmen* in the *Frankfurter Rundschau*, June 5, 1999).

In an advertisement by a real-estate firm looking for a Specialist Real Estate Agent (*Maklerpersönlichkeit*), it is stated early in the piece that 'the position can likewise be filled by a lady' (*Die Position kann gleichermaßen von einer Dame besetzt werden*, Schwäbisch Hall Immobilien, *Süddeutsche Zeitung*, Feb. 13/14, 1999).

An attempt at humorously dealing with the problem is illustrated in Figure 6, where the pseudo-generic *-fachmann* (literally: 'expert-man') is used. After the masculine-sounding suffix *-mann* a comment is added in parentheses, 'naturally *-man* can be a woman as well' (. . . *natürlich kann -mann auch eine Frau sein!*).

The *Frauenzusatz* seems to be the preferred form for advertisements of academic positions. Frequently abstract terms, such as *Professur* ('professorship') will function centrally in the advertisement, sometimes combined with disambiguation through the inclusion of feminine articles and/or feminine *-in* endings in the text, and a *Frauenzusatz* will then state the university's intention to increase the proportion of women in teaching and research, often in connection with a similar reference to disabled persons as well.[15]

English language advertisements

Another strategy for avoiding the pitfalls of gender-specific German is resorting to English as the language of advertising. An increasing number of advertisements were found that used English either only for the job-

Figure 6: *Hannoversche Allgemeine Zeitung*, June 5, 1999

denotations, or for the entire advertisement. Choosing an English term for the job denotation only, however, does not avoid the problem of gender reference in the entire text. However, running an entire advertisement in English discriminates against people who are not fluent in English, although English advertisements are usually only used when the position advertised requires knowledge of several languages.

Openly or subtly discriminatory advertisements

The strategies mentioned above can all be considered to be an indicator that the advertisers are at least aware of the problem of equal linguistic representation of women and men in German job advertisements. However, quite a few advertisements are still published which do not abide by the legal requirements, and thus signal more or less openly that only male applicants need apply.

Specific sex requested openly

Advertisements that openly request male gender are rare and usually mention heavy physical labor in warehouses or the like. There are also advertisements which explicitly request female applicants for positions directly concerned with women's issues, such as an ombudsperson for women's issues (*die Frauenbeauftragte*),[16] or a managing director of a battered women's shelter. However, advertisements for the position of secretary, especially in areas that are not highly paid, still overwhelmingly use the feminine form *Sekretärin* ('secretary').[17] Secretarial positions with a higher income are slightly more likely to be de-gendered through the use of abstract nouns such as *Assistenz der Geschäftsleitung* ('assistant to the director'), or with a masculine/generic with the feminine ending *Assistent/in*.

Some specific requests for female applicants may use euphemisms to cover discriminatory tendencies. In the following example, the term *Praxismanagerin* ('manager of the practice') is exposed through the addition of *Gute Fee* ('good fairy'),[18] which has a distinctively sexist tone and seems to indicate that really a *Mädchen für alles* ('maid-of-all-work') is what is wanted here.

Gute Fee in Neustadt gesucht...

Wir suchen zur Ausweitung des Praxisteams für eine
Zahnarztpraxis in Neustadt eine engagierte und motivierte
Mitarbeiterin als

Praxismanagerin.

Neben einer hohen fachlichen Qualifikation – insbesondere in
den Bereichen Abrechnung und Organisation – sollten Sie vor
allem Spaß am Umgang mit Menschen haben und diese auch
begeistern können.
Ein sicheres Auftreten sollte Ihr Markenzeichen sein.

Wenn Sie sich angesprochen fühlen, freuen wir uns auf Ihre
kompletten Bewerbungsunterlagen.

New Image Dental
Agentur für Praxismarketing
Herrn Tafuro – Jahnstraße 18
55270 Zornheim – Tel. (0 61 36) 95 55 00

Figure 7: *Hannoversche Allgemeine Zeitung*, June 5, 1999

Subtle indications of sex specificity

Given the number of accessible forms of gender-inclusive language in German, the non-application of any of these in advertisements is quite noticeable. Resistance towards using these forms becomes a marked statement. Employers who do not make use of gender-inclusive language seem to be clearly indicating that they do not consider the establishment of equal opportunities for women and men in their company a high priority. Advertisements that use only masculine/generic nouns or masculine pronouns and male references, and that do not give a single indicator of good-will concerning non-discriminatory language use, indirectly relay the message that 'women are not encouraged to apply'.

Top-Adresse Versicherungswirtschaft

Als eine der ersten Adressen der Versicherungswirtschaft gehören wir zu den führenden Versicherungsgruppen. Zur Stärkung und zum Ausbau unseres Vertriebsweges Makler/ Mehrfachagenten suchen wir den überzeugenden und hochmotivierten Direktionsbeauftragten für die Region Hannover als

Vertriebsleiter
Makler/Mehrfachagenten

In dieser Position berichten Sie an den zuständigen Gebietsdirektor und sind verantwortlich für die Betreuung/Führung und optimale Einbindung der Vertriebspartner in Ihrem Bezirk. Neugewinnung, Produkteinweisung und Fachschulung der Vertriebspartner gehören ebenso zu Ihren Aufgaben wie die eigenverantwortliche Steuerung des Bestandwachstums. Durch die räumliche Nähe zu den Vertriebspartnern minimieren Sie Ihre Reisezeiten und können so einen optimalen Verkaufsservice bieten.

Mit dieser anspruchsvollen Vertriebsaufgabe, die weitere interessante Entwicklungsmöglichkeiten bietet, wenden wir uns an den versierten Versicherungsprofi, der durch seine praktische Erfahrung und Kenntnisse in allen Versicherungssparten Kompetenz ausstrahlt. Ihr hohes Maß an Selbständigkeit, die Bereitschaft zur Übernahme von Verantwortung sowie Ihre ausgeprägte Kontaktfähigkeit und Motivationsstärke runden Ihr Profil ab.

Wenn Sie diese hochinteressante und entwicklungsfähige Position, in der Sie mit Ihrer Leistung Ihren nächsten Karrierestart selbst bestimmen, ansprucht, bitten wir um Ihre vollständigen Bewerbungsunterlagen an die von uns beauftragte Personalberatung BISANZ Management Consultants GmbH, Uerdinger Straße 541, 47800 Krefeld. Herr Dipl.-Kfm. R. Bisanz steht Ihnen für telefonische Vorabauskünfte unter der Rufnummer 0 21 51 /5 07 30-0 zur Verfügung.

BISANZ
Management Consultants GmbH

Figure 8: *Hannoversche Allgemeine Zeitung*, June 5, 1999[19]

Advertisements that use a masculine/generic noun with direct address to the potential applicant but solely masculine pronouns, or even without masculine pronouns as in Figure 8, appear not to address women as potential applicants.

In a few instances, however, the message is even more clearly formulated. Even today advertisements exist using language which we might have expected in the 'mixed' advertisements section thirty years ago. One particular example that appeared in the *Augsburger Allgemeine Zeitung* was an advertisement by a large supermarket chain. In this advertisement, positions on three hierarchical levels were advertised, namely the positions of assistant store manager, cashiers and salespersons. The high-ranking full-time position of assistant store manager was advertised with masculine/generic(?) form, *Marktleiter-Stellvertreter*, while the lower-ranking (full- or part-time) positions were explicitly marked with feminine endings, *Kassierer/innen* ('cashiers'), *Verkäuferinnen* ('saleswomen'). It is interesting to note the different treatment of these two job denotations with regards to the slash for the two different kinds of positions! Such wording differences between the job denotation for the manager and the saleswomen clearly signals that a woman's application for the higher-ranking position would not stand a chance in the selection process. This interpretation is backed by the fact that the management of the chain refused permission to reprint the advertisement in this article.[20]

Attitudes behind sex specific job advertisements

In order to find out about the attitudes behind the kind of formulation used in Figure 8, several personnel directors responsible for advertisements for an insurance salesman (*Vertriebsleiter*) using similar wording were contacted by telephone. Two personnel directors refused to answer questions concerning the advertisements. Others were surprisingly open in admitting that these advertisements were not expected to draw applications from women, and that they thought it highly unlikely that they would consider hiring a woman. Justification for this stance ranged from the fact that women were not likely to have the necessary qualifications even if they did apply, to the idea that women would not feel comfortable in such a male-dominated environment. The personnel directors even indicated that they would refrain from offering women such a position even if they were adequately qualified, to 'avoid placing them in such an uncomfortable setting'.

If the masculine is not what it used to be, what is it today?

During my search for advertisements that would constitute the data for this review of present-day German job-advertisements I came across an advertisement by the German Automobile Industry that had been placed in a youth magazine. It was searching for the 'geniuses/engineers of the future' by asking '*Wo sind die Genies der Zukunft?*', the word '*Ingenieur*' spanning the entire page at the top, and featuring generic masculines along with some neutral references (*Menschen* 'human beings', *Nachwuchs* 'junior staff') throughout.[21]

A German genius is grammatically neutral (*das Genie*), and the word is orthographically contained in *der Ingenieur*. A telephone inquiry to the writer of the advertisement revealed that *Ingenieur* was explicitly intended as a generic masculine and chosen to avoid the awkwardness of *Double Formulations*. The decision for the generic masculine was taken in a gender-mixed project planning group after long and heated discussions, but the final decision was unanimous. The general campaign was motivated by a recent decrease in engineering students and was directed towards high school graduates, attempting to convince them of the advantages of taking up engineering studies. The campaign was not specifically aimed at girls, but girls were meant to be included. This was given as the reason for positioning a young girl at the center of the picture used in the advertisement.

An informal survey of some female university students who were mostly majoring in social sciences indicated that they did not feel excluded from the group of addressees by the use of generic/masculine forms. This is paralleled in observations I have made about the language use of my students concerning gender-specific titles used in assignments. In several cases I have found that the female lecturer will be mentioned as *Dozentin* ('lecturer-fem') on the cover page of a written assignment or at the top of a hand-out, whereas the female student will be mentioned as a generic *Referent* ('presenter') on the hand-out or *Verfasser* ('author') on the written assignment.[22] Likewise, the use of the *Binnen –I* (e.g. *StudentInnen*) is also uncommon among people in their early twenties. When questioned, most of these students, both male and female, are not aware of their word-choices, or they consider linguistic equality a nuisance, boring, or unnecessary. They do not think that obvious linguistic representation or non-representation of women affects them personally in any way.[23]

Analysis of the job advertisements seems to show that the masculine is indeed no longer what it used to be. Generic uses of nouns without any means of signaling the inclusion of women in the group of addressees are infrequent, and at least in terms of job advertisements we can say that a generic masculine is not a wide-spread phenomenon in German at this point. Regarding the low number of subversively or openly discriminatory advertisements, we may even be able to claim that, in job advertisements, the generic masculine is nearly 'dead'. Listening to people speaking in the halls of universities and on the streets, however, the picture is markedly different. In academic and non-academic settings, equal linguistic treatment is a fragile, if not failing patient (see also

Dittmann, forthcoming on feminine references in academic texts). Even all-female groups overwhelmingly and consistently refer to themselves with masculine/generic forms in spoken interaction. Conscious attempts to use feminine forms in spoken interaction either go entirely unnoticed or cause raised eyebrows, but rarely draw similar word-choices from others.[24]

Thus it seems that the masculine has indeed changed, at least on the surface of public discourse (i.e. newspaper job advertisements), verifying Pusch's (1998a) claim that the masculine is 'not what it used to be'. A large majority of job advertisements now abide by the legal regulations that oblige employers to indicate that all jobs must be available to women and men alike. Whether this has had any effect on the numbers of female employment in general, and on women in leading positions in particular, is a question that would require further investigation in another kind of study.

While Pusch admits that German is still far from being a language that treats women and men equally,[25] she insists that feminine forms are fast gaining ground. This optimism is not reflected in reality, however. The real-life problem is that German strongly resists an easy-to-use equal linguistic treatment of women and men. An argument (perhaps facetious) for using the feminine form generically because it visually includes the masculine form, is a strategy that has met with as strong a resistance as any of the others mentioned above.

Equal linguistic representation still requires great effort on the part of German speakers, and it is apparent that these speakers lack sufficient motivation to make this effort. As long as the majority of women do not themselves use gender-inclusive language, and do not demand to be addressed in this manner in all contexts, not just in the opening lines of politicians' speeches or job advertisements, there is a very poor chance that linguistic equality will be achieved in the near future. In fact, in ordinary spoken discourse the masculine generic is certainly 'alive and kicking', if not fast (re)gaining lost ground. Perhaps this indicates a new stage of development in the process of language change – the evolution of a truly generic form?

Notes

1 Nicola Daly assisted with the editing of this paper.

2 Statistical analysis of the frequency with which the different strategies were employed was not possible at this point and does not enter into the description. Such an analysis would, however, also have been extremely difficult as the strategies most frequently do not appear in such clear-cut examples as presented below, but are used in a complementary (or muddled) manner. The illustrative examples that follow were all chosen for their representative status. I would like to thank Gudrun Nelle for her assistance in the preliminary analysis of the wording in thousands of job advertisements.

3 Objections usually present 'proof' of the kind where a text that has a rather complicated structure anyway is enriched or revised with double mentionings, leading to over-extended sentences that resist comprehension. The examples given often are from legal texts or government regulations: '*Der Minister oder die Ministerin* für Bildung, Wissenschaft, Jugend und Kultur kann für den Bereich der Landesaufgaben nach Anhörung des Senats *einen ständigen Vertreter oder eine ständige Vertreterin des Kanzlers oder der Kanzlerin* bestellen; *der Vertreter oder die Vertreterin* nimmt die Aufgaben *des Kanzlers oder der Kanzlerin* wahr, wenn *der Kanzler oder die Kanzlerin* verhindert ist oder die Vertretung angeordnet hat.' (Revised version of Schleswig-Holstein Hochschulgesetz (University Legislation), quoted from Ulrich 1991: 107, my emphasis). Translation: 'After hearings in the senate the minister-*masc* or the minister-*fem* for education, science, youth and culture can appoint a substitute-*masc* or a substitute-*fem* for the chancellor-*masc* or the chancellor-*fem*; the substitute-*masc* or the substitute-*fem* takes over the duties of the chancellor-*masc* or the chancellor-*fem* when the chancellor-*masc* or the chancellor-*fem* is prevented from coming or has ordered the substitution.'

4 'Dies sind meines Erachtens alles keine überzeugenden Lösungen, schon deshalb nicht, weil die Kürzel nicht sprechbar sind und so geschriebene und gesprochene Sprache nicht wechselseitig übertragbar bleiben.' (Ulrich 1991: 108). My own experience contradicts Ulrich's claim. I find that I indeed do make a phonetic distinction between reference to all-female groups with -*innen* as a feminine ending and a mixed group with -*Innen*, and frequently have heard other speakers do likewise. The distinction consists of the insertion of a minimal pause before the capitalized *I* in the case of the mixed group. The *Binnen-I* ('internal I' – see text) could thus be considered the rare instance of a phonetically-distinguished morpheme in German – to my knowledge, there exist no others at this point.

5 The text from footnote 3 above, which contains a number of articles, but only relatively few adjectives, would then be slightly shorter, but not necessarily more

easy to read, and would appear as follows: 'Der/die Minister/in für Bildung, Wissenschaft, Jugend und Kultur kann für den Bereich der Landesaufgaben nach Anhörung des Senats eine/n ständige/n Vertreter/in des/der Kanzlers/in bestellen; der/die Vertreter/in nimmt die Aufgaben des/der Kanzlers/in wahr, wenn der/die Kanzler/in verhindert ist oder die Vertretung angeordnet hat.' For a (humorous?) illustration of the illegible results that the mentioning of all kinds of endings may produce, see also Leisi's (1992) title.

6   These objections, of course, run parallel to the discussion amongst feminists and advocates of de-gendered language use regarding whether an explicit mentioning of women through derivational forms is indeed desirable, simply to make women seen and heard in language, or whether the use of derivational forms as such is discriminatory since the feminine forms are usually based on the masculine word stem. This discussion has led to a long list of more or less playful or provocative suggestions for reforming language use. These include, among others, a strategy by which (derived) feminine forms would be made visible wherever possible as 'ärztinlicher Rat' (instead of *ärztlicher Rat*), or a depatriarchalized (*entpatrifiziert*) version of German (Behlert 1998). All of these conscious attempts at premeditated language reform, however, are usually faced with the question of acceptability in public.

7   Interestingly, *Kaufleute* is the traditional plural form of *der Kaufmann* instead of *die Kaufmänner/*'salesmen'. Nevertheless, women employees in banking or business environments were long denied the right to be called -*kauffrau* in the singular form.

8   Bürgerliches Gesetzbuch, §§ 611a, 611b, in particular § 611b concerning the wording of advertisements: 'Der Arbeitgeber darf einen Arbeitsplatz weder öffentlich noch innerhalb des Betriebes nur für Männer oder nur für Frauen ausschreiben, es sei denn, daß ein Fall des § 611a Abs. 1 Satz 2 [daß ein bestimmtes Geschlecht unverzichtbare Voraussetzung für diese Tätigkeit ist] vorliegt.'

9   *Augsburger Allgemeine, Badische Neueste Nachrichten, Frankfurter Rundschau, Hannoversche Allgemeine Zeitung, Mainpost Würzburg.*

10   The approximate numbers result from the fact that advertisements may include plural reference to the position, indicating that several positions of this kind are open, or an advertisement may list several different kinds of positions; in these cases the advertisements were still counted as only one advertisement.

11   This appears to be a rather recent phenomenon that took place in the last dozen years; compare Brockhoff (1987), where she claims that equal linguistic treatment of women and men in job advertisements is still not happening, and Schoenthal (1998b).

12   Translation: 'We are open towards your successful future, because we can attain our goals only with successful colleagues. All over Europe Vermop is a name

that stands for innovation and competence in the realm of professional office cleaning. The continuous expansion of our leading position on the market demands high standards in the quality of our cleaning equipment and client orientation. Rising productivity and continuing growth require the strengthening of our team. We are looking for management trainees. Your profile: [. . .] Our offer: [. . .] Have we awakened your interest? Then we are looking forward to your application.'

13   See Ludwig (1989) on the history of the *Binnen-I*.

14   These advertisements with a *Binnen-I* are even more noteworthy because of the areas for which they appear, a company for safety-techniques in construction, and a plaster company.

15   For example, '*Die Universität wirkt bei der Wahrnehmung ihrer Aufgaben darauf hin, daß Frauen und Männer die ihrer Qualifikation entsprechenden gleichen Entwicklungsmöglichkeiten haben und daß für Frauen bestehende Nachteile beseitigt werden. Die Bewerbung von Frauen ist der Universität daher besonders willkommen. Schwerbehinderte Bewerberinnen oder Bewerber werden bei gleicher Eignung bei der Einstellung bevorzugt.*' (Universität Köln, Botanisches Institut, Die Zeit, Feb. 11, 1999). Translation: 'The university is aiming to offer women and men professional and developmental opportunities that are in accordance with their qualifications, and to eliminate disadvantages for women. Applications by women are therefore specifically welcomed by the University. Disabled applicants-fem. and applicants-masc. will be given preference where other factors are equal.'

16   Incidentally, the suffix/lexeme -*beauftragte* is one of the very few words in German that seem to have a truly generic potential and can take both masculine and feminine articles: *die/der Beauftragte* ('representative'), similarly *die/der Angestellte* ('employee').

17   The fact that *Sekretärin* is a derivative from the masculine form *Sekretär*, a perfectly acceptable position for men until approximately the invention of the typewriter, could be obscured by the fact that *Sekretär* also has a second meaning in German ('desk') which, if not more frequently used in that meaning, seems to be more prominent in Germans' minds than the 'male assistant for writing matters'.

18   This is an instance where grammatical gender seems to influence world-perception and thus severely interferes with equal rights for women and men. German *die Fee* ('fairy') seems to preselect a semantic component +FEMALE that inhibits a transfer of the saying *eine gute Fee* about a male person. In addition, I cannot recall an instance of a male fairy in any of my (originally German) childhood fairy tales. Male personae from the realm of non-humans usually are members of the class of *Elfen* or *Trolle* or *Zauberer* ('elfs', 'trolls', or 'sorcerers').

19   Another example that would have illustrated this strategy, but for which permission to reprint was denied, included the following 'generic nouns': 'suchen wir . . .

einen Elektroniker Instandhaltung. . . . Ansprechpartner bei . . . Ihr Profil: Techniker/Meister Elektronik'. Translation: 'we are searching for an electrician in maintenance . . . first contact for . . . your profile: technician/master craftsman . . .' (advertisement by WOODBRIDGE FOAM DEUTSCHLAND GmbH, *Frankfurter Rundschau* June 5, 1999).

20   The full text of the advertisement is quoted verbatim here: 'Für unser E-Center in Aichach suchen wir Marktleiter-Stellvertreter in Vollzeit, Kassierer/innen in Voll- oder Teilzeit sowie Verkäuferinnen in Voll- oder Teilzeit. Ihre Bewerbung richten Sie bitte mit den vollständigen Unterlagen an das E-Center, Münchener Straße 32, 86551 Aichach, Telefon 08251/52916, Frau Rauscher.' (Augsburger Allgemeine Zeitung, June 5, 1999). Translation: 'For our store in Aichach we are searching for the assistant store manager (full-time), cashiers (full- or part-time) and sales women (full- or part-time). Please send your complete application to . . .'

21   See also objections against using 'female forms' instead of 'generic' forms from some female professors. Viet (1991) considers such singling out of women dangerous. She claims that present-day usage of generic forms will be changed to the worse if feminine forms are introduced and used. As a female professor for mathematics she certainly wants to be 'included' when the talk is about the professors of the university: 'Ich jedenfalls möchte auch in Zukunft – für alle deutlich – *mitgemeint* sein, wenn von den Professoren einer Universität die Rede ist' (Viet 1991: 421, my emphasis).

22   This may be due to the fact, however, that Augsburg University is located in Bavaria, a traditional and strongly conservative region in German. I have been told that students in cities in other federal states are very much aware of the need to use gender inclusive language (H. Kotthoff, personal communication), as I myself remember from my student days.

23   This changes in other contexts, however. In journalism, editorials nowadays frequently address female and male readers alike, as in '*Liebe Leserinnen und Leser!*' ('Dear readers-fem and readers-masc'), but reports and articles in newspapers – with the exception of the left-wing paper *taz* – are far from consistent. It seems that the reporters' personal stance on the issue determines the use in an article, and generic references are far from out of vogue.

24   My request to a friend about whether it would be possible for her to use feminine forms to refer to our all-female group drew her response 'If you need it. . .'.

25   'Aber wir sind von einer gerechten und bequemen Sprache für beide Geschlechter noch weit entfernt' (Pusch 1998: 27).

References

Behlert, Matthias 1998. *Die Häsin und die Igelin: 15 Grimmsche Märchen, überarbeitet und in entpatrifiziertes (gerechtes) Deutsch übertragen.* Unpublished manuscript.

Brinkmann to Broxten, Eva 1990. Der allgemeine Mensch ist immer männlich. Frauen wehren sich gegen ihr Dasein als Außenseiterinnen in der Sprache. *Der Sprachdienst* 34,141-148.

Braun, Friederike 1996. Das große I und seine Schwester – eine kritische Bewertung. *Der Deutschunterricht* 48, 54-62.

Brockhoff, Evamaria 1987. Wie fragt Mann nach Frauen? *Die ZEIT* 2.1.1987.

Bundesministerium für Familie, Senioren, Frauen und Jugend (ed) 1996. Gleichberechtigung von Frauen und Männern. Wirklichkeit und Einstellung in der Bevölkerung 1992, 1994, 1996. *Schriftenreihe des Ministeriums, Bände* 117, 1, 2, 3.

Burkhardt, Armin 1984/85. Frauenlinguistik. *Muttersprache,* 95, 309-310.

Bussmann, Hadumod. 1995. *Das* Genus, *die* Grammatik und – *der* Mensch: Geschlechterdifferenz in der Sprachwissenschaft. In Hadumod Bussmann & Elisabeth Bronfen (eds) *Genus – zur Geschlechterdifferenz in den Kulturwissenschaften.* Stuttgart: Kröner, 114-160.

Dittmann. J. (forthcoming) Personenbezeichnungen und opake Geschlechtsreferenz. Am Beispiel von Wissenschaftstexten. In Ortrud Gutjahr & Claudia Schmidt (eds), *Kultur und Geschlecht. Gedenkschrift für Gisela Schoenthal.* Hg. Würzburg: Königshausen & Neumann.

Gewehr, Wolf 1995. Zur Genusmarkierung im Deutschen. In Götz Hindelang Eckard & Rolf Werner Zillig (eds), *Der Gebrauch der Sprache.* Münster, 121-134.

Gleichstellungsstelle für Frauen der Landeshauptstadt München (ed) 1995. *Mädchen-Frauenbild in Stellenanzeigen.*

Grabrucker, Marianne 1993. *Vater Staat hat keine Muttersprache.* Frankfurt a.M: Fischer.

Guentherodt, Ingrid, Marlis Hellinger, Luise F. Pusch, & Senta Trömel-Plötz 1980. Richtlinien zur Vermeidung sexistischen Sprachgebrauchs. *Linguistische Berichte* 69, 15-21.

Jakobson, Roman 1960. Closing statement: linguistics and poetics. In Thomas Sebeok (ed), *Style in Language.* Cambridge: MIT Press, 350-377.

Johnson, Sally & Ulrike Meinhof (eds) 1997. *Language and Masculinity.* London: Blackwell.

Kargl, Maria, Karin Wetschanow & Ruth Wodak 1997. *Kreatives Formulieren: Anleitungen zu geschlechterneutralem Sprachgebrauch.* Wien: Institut für Sprachwissenschaft der Universität Wien.

Leisi, Ernst 1992. Frauenbenennung als linguistisches Problem: 'Der/die Stellvertreter/ In des/der Vorsteher/S/'. *Neue Züricher Zeitung* 23, 9.

Leiss, Elisabeth 1994. Genus und Sexus. Kritische Anmerkungen zur Sexualisierung von Grammatik. *Linguistische Berichte* 152, 281-300.

Linke, Angelika 1993. Sprache und Geschlecht. Ein Einblick in den Forschungsbereich. *Praxis Deutsch* 122, 2-8.

Lorenz, Dagmar 1991. Wider die sprachliche Apartheid der Geschlechter. *Muttersprache* 101, 272-277.

Ludwig, Otto 1989. Die Karriere eines Großbuchstabens – Zur Rolle des großen 'I' in Personenbezeichnungen. *Deutschunterricht* 6, 80-87.

Lutjeharms, Maedline 1987. 'Liebe Leser' oder 'Liebe Leserinnen und Leser': Zum Verhältnis von Genus und Sexus im Deutschen. *Germanistische Mitteilungen* 26, 33-41.

Pusch, Luise 1984. *Das Deutsche als Männersprache*. Frankfurt: Suhrkamp.

Pusch, Luise 1989. *Alle Menschen werden Schwestern*. Frankfurt: Suhrkamp.

Pusch, Luise 1998a. 25 Jahre feministische Sprachpolitik: 'Liebe Wählerinnen und Wähler'. *Psychologie Heute Compact* 26-29.

Pusch, Luise 1998b. *Die Frau ist nicht der Rede Wert*. Frankfurt: Suhrkamp.

Scheele, Brigitte & Eva Gauler 1993. Wählen Wissenschaftler ihre Probleme anders aus als Wissenschaftler/nnen? Das Genus-Sexus-Problem als paradigmatischer Fall der linguistischen Relativitätshypothese. *Sprache & Kognition* 12, 59-72.

Schirmacher, Käthe 1988 (1906). Der Sexualismus in der Sprache. *Frauen und Schule* 2, 8-10.

Schmidt, Antje 1990. Frau vermißt – die unmerkliche Diskriminierung. *Sprachpflege und Sprachkultur* 3, 75-77.

Schoenthal, Gisela 1998a. Wirkungen der feministischen Sprachkritik in der Öffentlichkeit. In Gerhard Stickel (ed), *Sprache – Sprachwissenschaft – Öffentlichkeit*. Berlin/New York, 225-242.

Schoenthal, Gisela 1998b. Von Burschinnen und Azubinnen. Feministische Sprachkritik in den westlichen Bundesländern. In Gisela Schoenthal (ed), *Feministische Linguistik – Linguistische Geschlechterforschung*. Zürich, New York: Hildesheim, 9-32.

Schoenthal, Gisela (ed) 1998. *Feministische Linguistik – Linguistische Geschlechter-forschung*. Hildesheim, Zürich, New York.

Stickel, Gerhard 1983. 'Frau Müller ist Diplom-Bibliothekar' – Zur sprachlichen Form von Diplomgraden. *Mitteilungen des Instituts für Deutsche Sprache Mannheim* 9, 31-41.

Strunk, Klaus 1994. Grammatisches und natürliches Geschlecht in sprachwissen-schaftlicher Sicht. In Venanz Schubert (ed), *Frau und Mann. Geschlechter-differenzierung in Natur und Menschenwelt*. St. Ottilien, 141-164.

Studer, Liliane 1989. Eine Studentin ist kein Student. Auch nicht ein weiblicher. *Terminologie et Traduction* 2, 47-56.

Ulrich, Miorita 1988. 'Neutrale' Männer – 'markierte' Frauen. Feminismus und Sprachwissenschaft. *Sprachwissenschaft* 13, 383-399.
Ulrich, Winfried 1991. Movierte Feminina und motivierte Feminina – männliche und weibliche Personenbezeichnungen in der deutschen Sprache und ihre Akzeptanz in der gegenwärtigen Sprachgemeinschaft. In Winfried Ulrich (ed), *Mädchen und Junge – Mann und Frau: Geschlechtsspezifik in Verhalten und Erziehung.* Frankfurt, 103-112.
Viet, Ursula 1991. Professor/in/en/innen? Gegen die Verwendung von weiblichen Endungen. Universitas 5, 419-422.
Wegener, Hildburg, Hanne Köhler, Cordelia Kopsch 1990. *Frauen Fordern eine Gerechte Sprache.* Gütersloh: Gütersloher Verlag.

The 'Xena' paradigm: women's narratives of gender in the workplace

Su Olsson

Massey University

Introduction

Organisational myths and stories have become an increasing focus of interest in organisation and management studies (Boje 1991; Gabriel 1998). At the level of myth making, archetypal stories of the corporation and of 'the senior manager as heroic and transformative leader' are promoted by current management gurus (Clark & Salaman 1998a: 137). These myths seek to construct organisational unity, inspiration, values and role models to function as vehicles of communication change and management (Kaye 1995; 1996).

Both myths and stories 'can foster widespread understanding of the cultural and political realities of an organization's life' (Kaye & Jacobson 1999: www reference). And both involve the creation of occupational selves or identities from the manager as hero to the 'right types and wrong types' of professional or worker (Marshall & Wetherell 1989; Kaye 1996; Clark & Salaman 1998a).

This paper examines women's narratives of gender in the workplace within the larger context of the dominant organisational myths, with their associated images of 'heroic masculinism' (Sinclair 1994: 188), that provide the official role models for organisational identities. I argue that women's narratives of gender form a vibrant subcultural strand of stories that women tell other women, which parallel the managerial archetype represented in the heroic quest of Ulysses, while they provide parodic versions of the trials, giants, sirens and monsters that threaten the life of their career identities. The themes of these stories range from

Xena Warrior Princess to the Cookie Monster tale to make up a distinctive female paradigm that challenges stereotyped attitudes to women while at the same time forming a resilient depiction of women's organisational experience and identities.

The organisational context: stories within stories

At whatever level organisational stories occur, they are 'stories within a story', constructed and reliant on the 'other' story. Cash (1997) points out that all forms of narrative from drama to cartoons 'need the "other" or "hidden" story set up in the minds of the listener to have their effect' (1997: 160). Cash argues that story or narrative is a form of learning, which is intent on resolving paradox or conflicts:

> The hidden story unveils the surprises, twists, revelations and 'epiphanies' implicit in a different way of looking at the story or 'facts', thereby surfacing the assumptions on which the 'surface' story rests. (1997: 160)

On the one hand, the dominant 'rational' discourse or organisational story can attempt to subjugate alternative stories in a monological account (Potter & Wetherell 1987). On the other hand, stories within this dominant story, while reliant on the dominant story for their effect, can also provide critical insights into the dominant or underlying 'hidden' story, which may work to resolve the conflicts or the contradictions between different ways of looking at the 'facts'. In order to examine a particular group of stories such as women's narratives of gender, it is first necessary to look briefly at the way dominant myths function to provide the official organisational story and role models.

Organisational myths and heroic masculinism

One form of dominant organisational myths is the corporate saga of the specific organisation. This saga forms part of a company's official rhetoric, reflecting corporate ideals and values. Salzer-Morling (1998) describes the entrepreneurial rise of the Ikea furniture corporation from one man in a village in Sweden to an international company. While not always as dramatic as the Ikean success story, creation sagas, rags-to-riches stories, David and Goliath triumphs, and Herculean myths are all ways in which corporations attempt to unite workers and infuse them

with the spirit and values of the particular enterprise.
In turn, with some help from management gurus (Clark & Salaman 1998a) the leaders of corporate culture often assume the position of archetypal heroes, for example, Ulysses and his epic quest, Theseus killing the Minotaur, Zeus, and even the American Superman myth (Sinclair 1994, Kaye 1996). In a study of eleven Australian executive managers, Sinclair (1994) describes the values embodied in the manager as heroic and transformative leader as 'heroic masculinism' and likens the images of corporate success to Ulysses epic journey. While the corporate use of such images seeks to provide inspiration for aspiring heroes and lesser mortals, the models also operate as forms of managerial manipulation and control which attempt to dismiss the learning possibilities of alternate stories and identities within the corporate culture (Kaye 1995). In this sense, there are 'right stories' and 'wrong stories' and the rewards of corporate life are promised to those who construct themselves as the 'right' identities.

Two unquestioned factors within these dominant organisational models impact on women and make gender a central issue within their career identities. The first is the 'myth of meritocracy' (Maier 1997: www reference) which suggests that all workers have equal opportunities to succeed if they are talented and work hard enough, and that the merit principle provides fair and objective criteria of organisational advancement. The second, related factor is the 'tendency to take the masculinist paradigm for granted' (Maier 1997: www reference). In other words, the organisational playing field is far from equal or level, since organisational members are expected to conform to selected masculine criteria.

The embedded paradox of women's career identities

Both women and men may feel either ease or dis-ease in constructing their occupational selves within the dominant masculinist culture. However, whether or not women incorporate masculinist styles and values, they remain, in contrast to men, gendered identities (Olsson 1996) and they 'typically experience differential evaluations when they engage in identical behaviours' (Maier 1997).

Thus within the dominant organisational discourse, women's construction of career identities involves an embedded paradox. On the one hand, Maier (1997: www reference) points out that 'hegemonic masculinity assures that 'man' becomes the generic but hidden referent.' He quotes Dale Spender's well known reinforcement of this point, 'Women can only aspire to being as good as a man; there is no point in being 'as good as a woman" (1984: 201). On the other hand, women know well how to tell the appropriate stories and construct the 'right' identities in order to operate successfully within the dominant discourse. Yet even the women who take up the subject positions of heroic masculinism often experience differential evaluations to their male counterparts. In Cash's (1997) view, the resolution of such paradoxes may require a change in attitude to the dominant myth (in this case heroic masculinism) or a change in story type.

I argue that the stories of gender that women tell other women in the workplace challenge the assumptions of the dominant discourse while they create a change in story type. These stories within a story, which are often unheard, dismissed, or untold in the workplace, make up an untapped and vibrant subculture of organisational storytelling. In these stories women's 'heroic' qualities and competencies are a given, and humour is often used to deconstruct the masculinist assumptions of the 'hidden' story and to 'slay the monsters' of women's corporate experience'. This subcultural vein of narratives involves the sharing of experiences of gender that are transformed through the interactive process of storytelling to provide inspiration, role models, cautionary tales and parodic challenges to the dominant corporate myths of equity and meritocracy. As a parallel but distinctive strand of storytelling, I term these narratives the cultural 'battlefields' of Xena, warrior princess and her followers.

The Study

This study of workplace narratives employed a qualitative approach. Written stories were collected over a period of three years from students enrolled in a course in the College of Business at Massey University, New Zealand. At the very outset of the course class members were asked to write a short vignette or story, based on their personal organisational experience of a situation or an incident that illustrated a gender issue for them.

The class members were all mature, distance students, many of whom had first degrees. Others were in the process of gaining degrees or diplomas to add to their career achievements. They were predominantly women, although some men also took the paper to try to increase their understanding of gender issues in the workplace (the men's stories are not discussed here). Many of the women held senior positions in organisations and all were concerned with the career journey as shown by their investment in seeking further qualifications.

Participants were asked to indicate whether or not they were willing to share their stories with other class members in order to foster a co-operative learning environment. On two successive years some of the vignettes were put together in booklets and sent out to the group. Most of the participants were happy to share their experiences; some of these people wanted their stories to be reproduced under their own names, while others wanted their name and the name of their organisation to be changed or omitted. In this paper complete confidentiality has been ensured by changing the names of all writers and their organisations.

A total of 96 shared stories were collected (87 by women, 9 by men). These stories were given a simple numerical code (S 1, S 2, S 3, . . .). They were analysed and then grouped on the basis of recurrent thematic concerns. These themes were then looked at within the context of organisational myths and storytelling.

The Ulysses paradigm

In line with Sinclair's (1994) study of Australian male executive culture, I draw upon the myth of Ulysses to represent the heroic managerial archetype which forms the 'hidden story' for women's 'stories within a story'. Ulysses (Odysseus) is 'a mythical king of Ithaca . . . one of the leading chieftains of the Greeks in Homer's *Iliad,* and the hero of his *Odyssey,* represented by Homer as wise, eloquent and full of artifices' (Brewer 1974: 1113). Ulysses sets out on an epic ten-year quest, leaving his faithful wife Penelope at home. In his journey he faces many life-threatening disasters, he battles with giants and monsters, and he withstands the temptations of those who would seduce him from his quest, for instance, the Lotus Eaters and the Sirens.

The modern day norms of the heroic quest are described by Maier (1997: www reference):

The cultural system that predominates in most organisations is marked by an emphasis on objectivity, competition and getting down to business. Being hard-nosed and adversarial is taken for granted. Managers are expected to be single-mindedly devoted to the pursuit of organisational goals and objectives, to be competitive, logical, rational, decisive, ambitious, efficient, task- and results-oriented, assertive and confident in their use of power.

Maier argues these form universalistic standards, which recognise the chain of command and deem external factors such as family commitments to be irrelevant. The heroic journey, together with these norms form the hidden story or paradigm for the discussion of the women's narratives in this study.

The Xena paradigm

In a distinctive parallel to the Ulysses archetype, I liken the career journeys described by women in this study to the 'battlefields' of Xena, warrior princess and her followers. Xena is, of course, an invention of the modern entertainment industry, and not a figure of classical mythology. At the same time, the cult-following that the Xena character has acquired in parts of America and elsewhere, suggest that she triggers subconscious archetypes of women as leaders (albeit previously hidden or invisible within the dominant discourse).

While there are some women who 'walk the walk, and talk the talk' of heroic masculinism, the 'Xena' women in the following narratives acknowledge both their womanhood and the issues of gender in their careers, and many of them also privilege 'the discourse of femininity' (Olsson 1996: 25). In the transformative, and often humorous, act of telling their stories, Xena women may speak of incidents of victimisation and discrimination, but they do not present as victims. These women are confident and good at what they do, and are appreciated for their contributions by many of their male and female colleagues. They are well able to fulfill leadership roles and succeed as women in their progression towards executive or managerial positions.

Like Ulysses, the Xena warrior princess has embarked on a long journey, although (with one exception) in these stories, they have not left a 'Penelope' at home to deal with family and provide an audience to

Xena's achievements. Many Xenas combine family and career, many mention supportive partners in their personal life who sometimes feature as business partners also. In parodic inversions of the Ulysses story, the trials Xena women face and subvert in their stories are not to do with proving their abilities through feats of corporate strength, although many mention the hours, training, effort, and achievements of their careers. *The trials Xena women describe are rather to do with the **attitudes** they encounter from some people at times in their career journeys.*

In the following account, these attitudes are discussed under four inter-related headings: sexuality, invisibility, emotion and stereotyped expectations.

Sexuality

In the Ulysses myth, women are depicted either as temptress or as faithful supporter in a classical rendering of the whore/madonna dichotomy. Comparable attitudes affect women who set out on the modern day career quest, rather than form the supporters of male careers. Xena women see qualifications as one means of negating such attitudes, while furthering their career paths and choices. Some stories relate difficult attitudes from bosses and from male colleagues to their seeking these qualifications (S 13, S 25). However, the completion of a qualification does not always ensure acceptance. After June graduated with a commercial pilot license, she wrote to a number of small charter organisations enquiring about work:

> Some organisations wrote back, others did not. Some replies were encouraging, others were not. One man wrote, 'Find a compatible single man with an air transport license – the rest is easy.' (S 71)

Few examples were as blatant as this one, but the theme of a single woman's need to 'find a man' did recur (S 66).

If the single woman faces sexist attitudes, some employers find a woman's shift to the married state equally problematic. Notions still linger that marriage will mean a lesser commitment to the job, or even worse, babies (S 19). Many of these attitudes are parodied in Penny's story:

> I watched my employer get nervous about the prospect of my

marriage – it meant that I would no longer be able to attend evening meetings because I would be cooking for my husband. Breakfast meetings would also be difficult as I would be cleaning up furiously after my husband, helping him in the morning to get to his job. I would be so distracted with the intention of pleasing my man my mind would not be on my work. One manager said all the good relationships I had built up with 'the guys wouldn't be the same now, as a single woman is always more fun to deal with. And what's more I was going to get myself pregnant at the drop of a hat leaving them in the lurch with having to fill my position while I had a good time at home.' (S 23)

Actual motherhood (the madonna state) brought comparable attitudes. Stella was assured she could take maternity leave, but her boss suggested she would feel differently about coming back when she had that little baby in her arms, 'It was only natural. He had seen it all before!' (S 8). Harder to combat was the change in attitudes some women encountered to their competencies and abilities (S 5), and Cathy stated that with motherhood she became 'not simply female but another gender altogether' (S 2).

Underlying many of the stories of motherhood is the recurrent attitude from others that family commitments are 'women's work' (S 7, S 16, S 76, S 83). Ulysses should have had such problems! Ironically, in terms of opportunities and promotions, family commitments were sometimes used to favour men as the apparent 'breadwinner' (S 31, S 7).

Several stories relate to women's sexuality within the workplace. These included stories of sexual harassment, sexism and ageism (S 10, S 20, S 28, S 55, S 58,). Marie tells of blatant sexual harassment when she was starting out on her career, but points with self-parodic humour to her own ambivalence about the situation:

I was somehow elevated from Office Junior to Sexually Desirable Woman. I am still astounded and constantly peeved by how entrenched this *desire to be desired* is in me and, quite often I observe, in other women. (S 28)

One woman manager complained to her General Manager about an incident after a business dinner with the regional manager from another area. Her own manager was indignant on her behalf, but a managerial colleague told her that she had to expect that sort of thing. In Xena fashion she replied, 'Why, did he squeeze your hand too?' (S 27).

An interesting group of stories concern the dress codes required of women in a range of positions. Predictably perhaps, the 'uniform' required for some waitressing positions comes under fire from women working to support themselves through study:

> We were a culinary delight, tantalising, decorative pieces of meat, who were meant to be looked at but not touched. We were made to wear this skimpy little black skirt and this shirt that was verging on the obscene. (S 53)

Different variants of this 'dress code' are linked to the view of some organisations that 'women don't wear trousers'. This often unspoken code occurs in a range of occupations from secretaries, to bankers, to scientists. One woman scientist, for example, writes about the problems of having to row out across an oxidation pond in a skirt every day to check her samples (S 46).

Invisibility

A recurrent theme of women's career journeys is a lack of recognition for or acknowledgement of their contributions to the organisation. I have labeled this theme the invisible Xena. One strand of this theme is the attitude from clients, and more rarely from staff, that women are not able to advise clients even though they have formal qualifications in areas such as management, accountancy, computer technology, finance, property studies, and so on (S 33, S 40, S 43, S 44, S 64). Sometimes professional women are taken to be the 'office girl' (S 56).

Often employees and/or colleagues contribute to forms of invisibility for aspiring Xenas to combat. These stories include tales of males being paid more for doing the same job (S 32), restructuring processes in which the reduction in middle management is accompanied by a preference for males over the previously senior women for the new team leader or management positions (S 22), and stories in which women do all the research, or come up with new ideas, but have their work taken over and presented by male colleagues (S 15). One form of rendering Xena invisible is by giving women the responsibilities of management but denying them the title of manager (S 26, S 63). 'It's only a name' one General Manager said. 'Too many people in this organisation concern themselves with titles – it's a power play' (S 26).

The modern day Xena, however, is not prepared to accept either invisibility or career blocks and inequities. More and more aspiring Xenas now resist the temptation to become Lotus Eaters by staying with organisations that fail to reward or acknowledge their contributions. This flexibility is demonstrated in a number of stories that describe why and how women move on to more appreciative and supportive organisational cultures and greater achievements (S 19, S 22, S 24, S 29, S 46, S 69).

Emotion

Maier (1997) points out that two major themes of masculinist management are 'No Sissy Stuff : The Stigma of Anything Vaguely Feminine' and 'Give 'Em Hell: The Aura of Aggression, Violence and Daring' (1997: 4). In other words, only 'masculine' emotions are permitted on the heroic quest. Certainly, women are aware of the injunction against displays of so-called feminine emotions in the workplace as distinct from the 'Give 'Em Hell' behaviours. As a woman manager said in a previous study, 'You can scream and yell and you can slam a door and kick a desk. But apart from that you wouldn't show any other sort of emotion' (Olsson 1996: 22).

The ultimate 'no, no' for women in the workforce is the 'cry baby' scenario. Karen's story from her time as a prison officer in a male institution provides a delightfully comic illustration of the 'No Sissy Stuff' code in operation. One day after working an extra shift to help out a fellow (male) officer, Karen is called into the Chief's office and blamed for something that does not concern her. Karen explains that when she is really, really angry, she cries. The story continues:

The Chief stops what he is saying and I begin to answer his accusations, but he does not hear me. He has a funny look on his face and I can almost see the words, 'Fuck, what do I do now' run across his forehead. Staff have done a number of things in his office in the ten years he has occupied it, but *never* before have they cried. Generally they hold it together while in the office, then go out and abuse an inmate or go home and kick the cat, but never have they cried. (S 36).

The meeting is terminated and the Chief avoids Karen for the next few days. Then Karen is asked to report again to his office:

> After a few seconds of silence during which he shuffles his feet and coughs nervously, he makes reference to the previous conversation we have had and makes the statement, 'You need to know you can't do that if you want to do well in the prison service. I'm unsure exactly what it is I can't do, although I assume it to be that I can't challenge what the Chief says, so I ask. His response was to leave me speechless and to this day provokes a smile: 'You can't cry when you don't get your own way.' (S 36)

Stereotyped expectations of women

While the previous stories involve stereotyped attitudes to women, this last group of stories exposes stereotyped expectations of women as nurturers. The title of one woman programme leader's narrative, 'Born to serve' sums up the 'monsters of stereotype' that Xenas combat. Examples include the assumptions that women, including senior women, will always take the minutes (S 21, S 79), make tea, not policy (S 67), 'mind the wife' of an important visitor (S 72), and prepare the food for a meeting with sponsors (S 24).

A final story in this group typifies the way in which issues of gender are transformed through humour in the narratives women tell other women. Parody effects a slaying of the monster that is initiated by the title, 'The Cookie Monster Tale':

> There has been one major event, which I have classified as the 'Cookie Monster' incident. During an early afternoon meeting a new cookie recipe was the topic of discussion. The chocolate chip recipe was received via the Internet and the reviews had been fantastic. My boss instantly gave me a copy and asked if I could 'whip some up'. I declined, citing the inadequacies of our stove. At home that evening, my husband offered to cook a batch to prove cooking wasn't a female chore. To my horror the next day the whole department was summoned to taste Debbie's cookies. Debbie works a

couple of offices down the corridor. My boss was beaming, he raved about the taste, his success in finding a great cook and Debbie's proven skills. Despite my stubbornness, I felt strangely inadequate. (S 42)

Concluding remarks

Organisational stories are governed by and reliant on the dominant myths of the organisational culture. Yet alternate stories within the dominant or 'hidden story' can provide different ways of looking at the 'facts' that make up the cultural and political realities of organisational life..

As the narratives in this paper illustrate, women have no difficulties with competency criteria of careers or with organisational goals and objectives. They display qualities which range from decisive to confident in their use of power. The Ulysses archetype is paralleled by the Xena archetype.

At the same time, the Xena stories provide different ways of looking at the assumptions of the dominant discourse such as the 'myth of meritocracy', gender equity, and the level playing field. The overwhelming challenge of women's narratives of gender, however, is to the attitudes and stereotyped expectations women encounter in their career quests. Cultures and managers who persist in remaining locked within masculinist attitudes and assumptions, risk losing Xena women's abilities when the women move on to find more supportive and satisfying colleagues and organisations.

Finally, I suggest that in order to achieve changes in cultural consciousness of organisations, women's often 'unspoken' narratives of gender in the workplace need to be heard, repeated, and given the same status as other workplace stories. These transformational, and often humorous acts of storytelling make up a distinctively female paradigm which may bring about differences in organisational outlooks that would benefit both women and men in the workplace. More importantly, this subcultural vein of Xena stories provides a vibrant assertion of women's abilities and experiences; these narratives give women a place to stand and a place to recognise themselves, so that they no longer feel isolated in their resistance to genderised attitudes.

References

Boje, D.M. 1991. Consulting and change in the storytelling organization, *Journal of Organizational Change Management* 4, 7-17.

Brewer 1974. *Brewer's Dictionary of Phrase and Fable*, Centenary Edition. London: Cassell.

Cash, Michael 1997. Stories within a story: parables from 'The New Zealand Experiment'. *The Learning Organisation* 4, 4, 159-167.

Clark, T. & G. Salaman 1998a. Creating the 'right' impression: towards a dramaturgy of management consultancy, *Services Industries Journal* 18, 1, 18-38.

Clark, T. & G. Salaman 1998b. Telling tales: management guru's narratives and constructions of managerial identity, *Journal of Management Studies* 35, 2, 137-161.

Gabriel, Y. 1998. Stories and sense making. In D. Grant, T. Keenoy & C. Oswick (eds), *Discourse and Organization*. London: Sage, 84-103.

Handy, C. 1995. *Gods of Management*. London: Arrow.

Kaye, B. & B. Jacobson 1999. True tales and tall: the power of organizational storytelling, *Training and Development* 53, 3, 45-50. http: //www,massey.ac.nz/ ~wwwlib/

Kaye, Michael 1995. Organisational myths and storytelling as communication management: a conceptual framework for learning an organisation's culture, *Journal of Australian and New Zealand Academy of Management* 1, 2, 1-13.

Kaye, Michael 1996. *Myth Makers and Story-tellers*. Sydney: Business and Professional Publishing Pty Ltd.

Maier, Mark 1997. Gender equity, organizational transformation and challenger, *Journal of Business Ethics* 16, 9, 943-962. http: //www,massey.ac.nz/~wwwlib/

Marshall, J. 1996. Women leaders: Making career and life choices. In Olsson, S. & N. Stirton (eds), *Women and Leadership: Power and Practice, International Conference Proceedings, 1996*. Palmerston North: Massey University, 33-48.

Marshall, H. & M. Wetherell 1989. Talking about career and gender identities: a discourse analysis perspective. In S. Skevington & D. Baker (eds), *The Social Identity of Women*. London: Sage, 106-129.

Olsson, S. 1996. Gendered identities?: a discourse analysis approach to women managers' self- representations, *Working Paper Series 96/5*. Palmerston North: Massey University.

Olsson, S. 1996. A takeover? Competencies, gender and the evolving discourse of management. In S. Olsson & N. Stirton (eds), *Women and Leadership: Power and Practice: International Conference Proceedings 1996*. Palmerston North: Massey University, 359-378.

Potter J. & M. Wetherell 1987. *Discourse and Social Psychology: Beyond Attitudes and Behaviour*. London: Sage.

Salzer-Morling, M. 1998. As god created the earth: a saga that makes sense? In Grant et al. (eds), *Discourse and Organisation*. London: Sage, 104-118.

Sinclair, Amanda 1994. The Australian executive culture: Heroes and women. In P. Carrol (ed), *Feminine Forces: Redefining the Workplace: Women and Leadership 1994 National Conference Proceedings*. Perth, W.A.: Edith Cowan University, 180-193.

Wilson, F. 1995. *Organizational Behaviour and Gender*. New York: McGraw Hill.

Gender trouble in the workplace: 'language and gender' meets 'feminist organisational communication'

Deborah Jones

Victoria University of Wellington

Introduction

In this paper I treat 'language and gender' and 'feminist organisational communication' as if they are two friends of mine. I want to introduce the 'feminist organisational communication' literature to a 'language and gender' readership. I feel that they have a lot to offer each other. My purpose here is to contribute to the interdisciplinary development of 'language and gender' studies, by pointing to sources in organisational studies which can add contextual richness to linguistic analysis of workplace communication. I also believe that linguists have much to offer the field of organisational communication generally, not only in the domain of gender. Over the last decade discourse analysis has become increasingly central to organisational studies. However, few organisational scholars have specialised expertise in theorising and analysing language. Like all interdisciplinary scholars, they risk over-simplifying or misunderstanding the key principles of an unfamiliar discipline. Linguists do have the specialised expertise to critique and contribute to language-based forms of organisational analysis. Reciprocally, organisational scholars have much to offer in the way of framing workplace communication, both theoretically and in organisational practice.

In introducing 'feminist organisational communication', I need first to name and describe a rather varied and complicated set of relatives. In doing this, I have kept in mind what I think the 'language and gender' reader might want or need to know from outside her disciplinary field.

I have aimed to gradually weave together the different relationships involved in building up a description of 'feminist organisational communication', while trying to avoid the impression that the boundaries of any of these disciplines or sub-disciplines are cast in stone. In fact it is their permeability that makes the intersections of gender/communication/organisation so interesting.

The intersection of 'language and gender' and 'feminist organisational communication' is a fertile site for the integration of linguistic and organisational analysis. This is no coincidence. Feminist studies of language have long paralleled the broader development of women's studies in their drive towards disciplinary comparison and synthesis around the theme of gender difference (Cameron 1995). Secondly, in their orientation towards political change, feminist linguists have addressed what language does in key arenas of women's lives, and these include the workplace. Finally, outside linguistics, feminists have been drawn to the interpretive or linguistic turn in social sciences (Canning 1994). It offers a 'denaturalizing critique' that enables change by challenging the idea that identity is 'natural' and therefore essentially stable (Butler 1990: 110). I will focus in this paper on those aspects of 'feminist organisational communication' that can be drawn on to make what feminist theorist Judith Butler called 'gender trouble' – that is, to disrupt assumptions about gender differences (ibid.).

Possibilities of transformation: language and organisational change

I draw the phrase 'possibilities of transformation' from French philosopher Michel Foucault's work on language and change (Foucault 1972: 120). Foucault made discourse central to social change, conceptualising it as a complex interweaving of language, practices, power, institutions and identities. He proposed that discourse analysis is the central critical activity which creates possibilities of transformation. Such an analysis allows us to explicitly challenge the taken-for-granted 'truths' about identity, power, and organisation. Equally importantly, he argued that we will just repeat the same old patterns without realising it unless we are able to carry out this kind of analysis (for a range of his work on discourse see Foucault 1977, 1983, 1984, 1988, 1991). From a feminist perspective, identity and power are key issues in considering organisational communication. Feminist philosophers like Judith Butler have appropriated Foucault's work because it offers ways out of what seems like the intractable problem of collapsing back into unchangeable stereotypes whenever we talk about gender differences (Butler 1990, 1993, 1995a, 1995b). For linguists and communication scholars, Foucault's approach offers challenges and possibilities in the ways we theorise discourse ('language', 'communication') and its relation to identity and power. I go on now to introduce the field of 'organisational communication', and will loop back later to show how it has been influenced by Foucault's work.

The literature which is demarcated as 'organisational communication' has developed from a rather complicated and rapidly developing family of sub-disciplines. Associated with these sub-disciplines are critical perspectives which have located themselves in their margins. For instance, both mainstream management writing (e.g. Hamel & Prahalad, 1994, Martin & Frost 1998, Peters & Waterman 1982) and critical management studies texts (Law 1994, Oswick & Grant 1996, Putnam, Phillips & Chapman 1996) share a growing preoccupation with the ways that language and organisational change are intermeshed. But their theoretical assumptions about language, and their political agendas, are very different. Mainstream management writers argue that language can be used by senior managers to meet their strategic goals. In this account, language is seen instrumentally as a tool of management. More traditionally, it is deployed as a kind of magic bullet to transmit operational data and strategic frameworks (Conrad 1994). More recently, the emphasis has turned to the rhetorics and narratives which are intended to generate organisational visions that will mobilise and align the aspirations of employees (Barry & Elmes 1997). In this respect mainstream management writings can be seen to appropriate postmodern and interpretive perspectives on language, but to leave out the critique of power and the more sophisticated account of what discourse is and does.

By contrast, much of the work in recent critical management studies takes a foucauldian approach to focus on how power relations and identities are created through organisational discourses (Knights & Morgan 1991, is a seminal text). In this model, 'discourse' is not the unproblematised instrument of a given speaker. For instance, 'management' is seen as a discourse in itself, one which creates the horizons within which the identities, strategies, and communicative practices of managers come to be taken for granted as thinkable and reasonable. The management literature can be criticised for its rather simplistic account of how language can be 'used' to create top-down, management-driven organisational change. On the other hand, the critical literature tends to focus on the critique of managerial discourse, and is, so far, not well-developed in theorising discourse in ways that change agents can draw on in seeking to create 'bottom-up' or participatory change.

As well as drawing from organisational and management literatures, 'organisational communication' is also grounded in the North American literature of communication studies. This field tends to draw on social psychology, and on sociology, rather than on linguistics for its theoretical base (Jablin et al 1987, Miller 1995, Putnam & Pacanowksy 1983). Again, within communication studies there is a strongly developing critical stream, which has a social constructionist base. Its topic is not just 'communication' as a component of organisational life, but a more thorough-going account of organisations and management practices which are seen as *consisting of* communicative activities (Deetz 1992; Deetz & Mumby 1990; Kovacic 1994; Mumby 1987; 1988; 1993a; 1993b). There is still little connection between the 'organisational communication' literature and the growing interest in discourse in organisational studies – both as a 'topic' and as a mode of analysis. There is also quite a lot of theoretical confusion about how 'discourse' is theorised in organisational analysis. In particular there is a lot of confusion around the relationship between what is 'done' and what is 'said' – the 'walk' and the 'talk' (Hardy & Palmer 1997) – and about whether there are organisational concepts or practices – such as strategy – that can be conceptualised as separable and distinct from discourse (Hardy & Palmer 1999). These are also issues that feminist communication scholars address.

Why make gender trouble?

Both feminist theorists and critical organisational scholars have been attracted to the idea that discourse constitutes identity. Making change means finding ways to disrupt these identities and the power relations that are inherent in them. I want to briefly review Judith Butler's key proposition: that the first priority of feminist theorists should be to find the 'best way to trouble the gender categories that support gender hierarchy.' (Butler 1990: x). For Butler, 'gender' is 'a set of repeated acts within a highly rigid regulatory frame that congeal over time to produce the appearance of substance, of a natural sort of being (ibid: 33).

This definition evokes for me the picture of a photographic plate that is exposed over time to a series of regular movements. Over time the repeated exposure to the same movement will produce an image that seems solid. The repeated practices that create the appearance of solidity are obscured. Butler argues here that gender (or any other aspect of identity) is *not* substantial, but is the effect of a series of practices. Once recognised, these practices can be interrupted to create change, to 'deregulate identity' (Butler 1990: 147). The strategy she advocates is to use a denaturalising critique draw attention to the cracks in the wallpaper of identity, to the 'gender troubles' that may appear as points of strain in the 'lines of coherence' (ibid: 24) which maintain the effects of gender. This kind of critical discourse analysis a la Foucault allows us not only to critique powerful institutional discourses, but to be reflexive *about our own* discursive positions, to look at their assumptions and their political implications (Weedon 1987: 22).

For instance: the literature on women's communication in the workplace paints pictures of a world in which the very existence of women as managers troubles boundaries. If she talks like a manager she is transgressing the boundaries of femininity: if she talks like a woman she no longer represents herself as a manager (see for instance Pearson, Turner & Todd-Mancillas 1991). As Susan Chase puts it, for the woman 'professional', 'identity as a woman cannot be taken for granted . . . , but is subject to standards for action and speech' (Chase 1988: 276). The literature of 'assertiveness' in the workplace is just one index of the anxiety experienced by women as they attempt to perform as managers in this twilight zone. Here we see that 'lines of coherence' are threatened when the subject is positioned in two or more contradictory discourses – say, 'being a manager' and 'being a mother'. The subjects may describe themselves as under strain, as attempting to suppress or control, the contradictions, or perhaps deliberately resisting the regulation of gender by transgressive behaviour. The tendency in the practitioner literature is to try to 'fix' this kind of problem, by repeating the proposition that men and women are different. This strategy has the effect of moving our attention away from looking at how gender differences are actually created in these organisational processes. It means taking differences for granted – reinforcing them, even – and going on from there, rather than contesting those differences.

Butler's argument for creating 'gender trouble' is a political one, an argument which advocates a strategy for feminist theory. There are also emerging practical problems in the kinds of research which use gender as a variable, and sets out to precisely establish linguistic or communication 'differences'. Fewer and fewer claims to universality are being made (Freed 1995: 8-9). These 'differences' now appear by no means as straight-forward as they once seemed to be: Staley & Shockley-Zalabak (1989), in a review of twenty years of research in the field of 'women's communication', characterize the research results as 'fragmented, mixed and controversial' (1989: 242, see also Wilkins & Anderson 1991). Their call for 'converging methodologies', however, does not address theoretical problems of identity and epistemology. The problem of 'sandbagging' – 'the tendency for increased empirical study to stifle the original gender effects' (Bird 1998: 3) – has proliferated in gender difference research across a range of disciplines. As contextual factors have been more and more carefully considered in follow-up work, early dramatic results are harder and harder to replicate. In her review of 'difference' research in psychology, feminist psychologist Lise Bird points out that, in this research tradition, 'much more weight is given to testing of small-scale hypotheses than to deeper conceptual analysis. This tends to leave the big questions raised by feminists out of the picture' (ibid). Researchers are trapped, 'sandbagged into a corner' (ibid: 6) by ever more elaborate attempts to demonstrate essentialised gender differences. The answer here is not ever-more 'sand-bagging' – refined variable definition, or more rigorous 'triangulation' (Staley & Shockley-Zalabak 1989) – but a re-think of the research questions. Issues of subjectivity and signification ('making meaning'), and an emphasis on communicative practices in specific situations (as against 'sociolinguistic universals' (Holmes 1993)), have emerged as key issues in the interdisciplinary 1990s project of 'gender and communication' (Cameron

1995; Crawford 1995; Freed 1995; Hall & Bucholtz 1995b; Mills 1995a; 1995b; Rakow 1992).

Placing the discussions on 'gender and communication' within this transformative frame, the most interesting questions become those which reverse the formula of the earlier question: 'do men and women talk differently?' (Coates 1986), to ask instead how 'talk' creates or constitutes categories of gender difference. The next step is to question how these processes can be disrupted to create 'gender trouble'. I am not suggesting that we should simply reject studies of how men and women might communicate differently, but rather I propose a change in emphasis, so that 'talking differently' could be seen as one of the practices whereby gender takes on 'the appearance of substance'. US communication scholar Lana Rakow raised this issue in a review of feminist communication research in the late 80s, proposing that: 'gender research should mean being engaged in questions about the role of communication in the construction and accomplishment of a gender system' (Rakow 1986: 12). In other words, we should examine the ways in which 'communication creates genders who create communication' (ibid: 23, see also Rakow 1992). In taking this approach, we need to consider its theoretical implications: for instance, if we say 'communication creates genders' are we splitting 'communication' from 'gender' (and identity generally)? Feminist post-structuralist writers such as Judith Butler would say rather that gender is *constituted in* 'discourse' – that discourse and identity are in fact inseparable.

Similar theoretical issues arise in the feminist literature which asks how women 'resist and subvert hegemonic notions of gender', as Hall & Bucholz put it in their 1995 review of (mainly US) gender and communication literature (Hall & Bucholtz 1995a: 13). These are similar to the ones that writers in management studies are struggling with. They concern the relationship between language and action, and the question of whether and how language can be 'used' instrumentally to create desired changes. However, while managers are seeking to control or generate certain kinds of organisational behaviour, feminists are asking about bottom-up change, about change as resistance. What makes it possible for women to 'resist'? Can women somehow stand outside language and use it as a 'tool' of resistance? For feminists too these are difficult theoretical questions which require careful thinking about how we see language and identity. They are central not just to academic analyses, but to how we imagine change takes place. I will leave these as open questions here. My main wish is to flag that they are of central concern to feminist scholars who are considering the relationships between language, gender, and change. I do not think the answers can be taken for granted in writing our research. I pick up this issue in relation to the discourse of 'managing diversity' at the end of this paper.

Feminist organisational communication

'Feminist organisational communication' is still a small and rather marginalised field in relation to traditional disciplines, although it exists in the intersections of the hot points of several emergingly important disciplinary fields. Dennis Mumby, a central and influential US scholar of critical organisational communication, claimed in a 1997 review of communication studies that 'organizational communication has almost completely ignored feminism' (Mumby 1997: 24). In a feminist review of the 'organisational communication' literature, US communication scholar Marlene Fine argues that little feminist research in 'organisational communication' has been published because both 'organisational communication' and feminist perspectives are still (she writes in 1993) marginal in management and organisational literature (Fine 1993). Writing in the same year, Connie Bullis talks about the 'silence with which organisational communication has greeted feminism' (Bullis 1993: 144).

The field of critical organisational communication has intersected with critical trends in organisational studies, especially in the 1990s, when post-structuralist and post-modern perspectives are generating links in the form of the 'linguistic turn'. These trends have been showing up in an intensified interest in cultural perspectives on organisations: metaphor analysis, story analysis, deconstructive techniques applied to organisational documents and practices (Barry & Elmes 1997; Boje & Dennehy 1994; Boje, Gephart, & Thatchenkery 1996; Calas & Smircich 1996; Czarniawska 1997; Deetz 1992; Grant, Keenoy & Oswick 1998; Hassard & Parker 1993; Law 1994; Mumby 1993b; Putnam & Pacan-owsky 1983). Foucault's influence has been especially strong in fields related to the analysis of human resource management (HRM), where the deconstruction of the discourses has generated new ways to think about identity, language, and the new forms of disciplinary power in organisations (Austrin 1994; Findlay & Newton 1998; Jermier, Knights & Nord 1994; Rose 1990; 1996; Townley 1994). In fact, it is I possible to re-frame much of what goes on in organisational studies as within the boundaries of an enlarging 'organisational communication', given the preocupation with various types of discourse analysis. The same convergence can be seen in the more specifically feminist literature.

In the last few years that the literatures of women's studies and organisational studies have begun to 'meet, intersect, and enrich each other' (Brown 1995: 197). The trend in feminist organisational studies towards 'gendering organisational analysis' (Mills & Tancred 1992) goes beyond simply 'adding gender' as a topic of organisational analysis, or documenting inequality and difference. 'Gendering organisational analysis' means paying attention to the 'patterns of gender difference and subordination' in organisational processes as well as discourses of organisational theory (Acker 1992: 249). The search for explanations of the 'apparently endless reorganization of gender and permutations of male power' (ibid: 248) has turned attention towards constructionist views of gender, and the meaning-making processes by which identity is produced. In this way the feminist theoretical concerns of gender and organisation run in parallel to those in 'gender and communication'. A wide range of influential feminist writers have drawn on forms of discourse analysis to consider specific topics in organisational life, such as the gendered division of work (Game & Pringle 1983); bureaucracy (Ferguson 1984); relationships between bosses and secretaries (Pringle 1988); and policy formation (Yeatman 1990).

The feminist 'organisational communication' literature has functioned primarily as a critique of mainstream 'organisational communication' (Bullis 1993; Buzzanell 1994; Fine 1991; 1993; Marshall 1993; Natalle, Papa & Graham 1994; Spitzack & Carter 1989). Its thrust has been to create an alternative feminist account of communication and of organisation in terms of gender and power, noting who has been included and excluded from the 'subject' of organisation communication, whose voices have been authorised as writers and as research subjects, and whose have been excluded. It is also seen as a way into analysing feminist organisational change issues in organisations from a new perspective: for instance, Gregg foregrounds the meaning-making processes by which women carry out union organising (Gregg 1992; 1993a; 1993b); Bingham re-thinks sexual harassment as discursive practice (Bingham 1994).

Emerging issues

I have taken a strong position in favour of making 'gender trouble', and I have marginalised writings which seek to make positive statements about gender difference. However, this does not mean that attempts to 'sandbag' points of difference do not continue to be prominent in the academic and popular literature about gender, communication and organisations. To give just a few recent examples: Stuhlmacher and Walters have carried out a recent 'meta-analysis' of 'gender differences in negotiation outcome' (1999); good old Mars and Venus are investigated 'in the meeting room' (Meyers 1999); 'genderflexing' is proposed as way for 'men and women' to 'speak each others' language at work' (Zielinksi 1998); and gender continues to be investigated as a variable in communication competencies in the workplace (Reinsch & Shelby 1997).

A common theme here is the pressing question of how to address issues of gender and communication in the workplace in a practical way. In the examples given above, the suggestion is made that individual changes in communicative styles or competencies can remedy, for individual speakers, the perceived disadvantages of gender differences in the workplace. I am sceptical about this, both as a political tactic and as an account of how language works. But I am concerned with organisational change, and much of the critical material which sets out to deconstruct gender does not offer practical ways to be in action to create organisational change. This gap needs to be addressed. In doing so I am picking up on the questions raised above in the discussion of 'gender trouble': What makes it possible for women to 'resist'? Can women somehow stand outside language and use it as a 'tool' of resistance?

In this final section I want to highlight two possibilities for directions in feminist organisational communication:
* the possibility of taking action about gender issues in organis-ations while taking a sceptical and experimental approach to the 'languages' we use;

- the possibility of 'using' communicative techniques to transform discourses of gender in organisations.

I will use the discourse of 'managing diversity' to illustrate the need for a sceptical approach to the languages that we use – what Denise Riley calls an' ironic spirit' (Riley 1988). This irony does not mean a kind of 'postmodern' lack of commitment, but rather an ability to engage politically with issues of gender, while accepting that we cannot simply step 'outside' the discourses that constitute our own points of view. It involves, for instance, recognising that various versions of western 'feminism' have been saturated with assumptions about culture and class. Effective change agents will draw strategically on the various available discourses to create change – while recognising that 'strategy' itself is an aspect of discourse. A crucial element in this strategic approach is the ability to evaluate when 'the language of resistance' has been lost, as one EEO practitioner expressed it. I am drawing here on my own study of the discourse of 'managing diversity' in New Zealand government organisations (Jones 1998; see also Jones, Pringle & Shepherd, forthcoming). The objective of the study was to observe and theorise how communication processes create frameworks for dealing with issues of difference and equality. In 1994 'managing diversity' was emerging as a new vocabulary for addressing issues of difference – gender, ethnicity, culture, sexuality – in organisations (Pringle & Sowcroft 1996; Sauers 1993; Thomas, D. & Ely 1996; Thomas, R. 1991). EEO practitioners were sceptical about this new language and very aware of its political implications: as one woman put it, 'there's a whole lot of politics around those terms'. While 'managing diversity' was being touted by some consultants as the latest thing, the replacement for EEO, a more inclusive way to address change in a business context, EEO practitioners saw 'managing diversity' as signalling a specific move *away* from identifying disadvantaged groups, and towards a depoliticised individualism where every individual is 'diverse' in different ways, and 'managing diversity' offers 'something for everyone' (EEO Trust 1992). Most EEO practitioners in the study fought the replacement of EEO by 'managing diversity' as a framework for dealing with organisational difference. Their concern was that while the language of 'managing diversity' might be more acceptable and less threatening in their business environment, the effect would be to incorporate bottom-up equality perspectives within a managerial framework in which all differences were represented as equal. This is a debate about language as strategy: as a change agent, how far can you enter the dominant discourses of gender without losing your impetus for change?

The study indicated that unless change agents had alternative discourse communities in which they could discuss their objectives in a feminist language, it was more and more difficult for them to move strategically between different discourses, as opposed to getting stuck in the managerial perspective. In this respect the study illustrates what communication scholars know: effective communicators are able to draw on a wide communicative repertoire appropriate to context. However, to create organisational change in terms of gender is a major and collective task. 'Using' a discourse effectively within its own framework of assumptions is not the same as learning how to 'interrupt' discourse; in Butlers' terms, to rework it so that the frameworks of gender change. Among other things, this task requires the ability to analyse the discourses of gender in a given situation in order to create 'gender trouble', to intervene in them, rather than just reinforce them. This means always remaining sceptical and experimental, for instance, about what the effects of a discourse such as that of 'managing diversity' will be. In terms of 'feminist organisational communication', it would be very useful to seek out examples of how practitioners have successfully carried out this kind of intervention. A related possibility is collaborative work carried out by researchers with practitioners in the context of experiment and action learning, relating critical discourse analysis to organisational action.

The use of communicative techniques to create organisational change is emerging in feminist organisational communication for two key reasons. First, there is a general impulse in management discourse towards what I see as communicative and collaborative practices for creating organisational change: reflective practice (Schon 1987); action learning (Daudelien 1996); appreciative inquiry (Hammond 1998) and the concept of the learning organisation (Senge 1990). These practices have been given new life by the emerging discourse of 'knowledge work', although it is important to be cautious in assuming that the old command-and-control models have been drastically re-configured. Nonetheless, the opening is there. Secondly, feminist interventions at the cusp of the

20th century take place in a discursive context quite different from that
of 10 or 20 years ago. While feminist discourses of Equal Employment
Opportunities, diversity and sexual harassment, for instance, may be
well-established in organisational life, so are their counter-discourses.
Resistance to feminist discourse is well-established. To create further
changes, new forms of discourse need to be used that will not push the
old familiar buttons, but will nonetheless address the issues. An
understanding of organisational communication is central to these new
feminist initiatives. In their recent 'modest manifesto for shattering the
glass ceiling', published in the influential *Harvard Business Review*,
Debra Meyerson and Joyce Fletcher advocate a 'small wins' strategy
that 'creates change through diagnosis, dialogue and experimentation'
(Meyerson and Fletcher, 2000: 128). Drawing on their research as well
as their experience as consultants in organisational change through
Boston's Centre for Gender in Organizations, they argue that gender
inequity has 'gone underground' in US organisations, taking the form
of problems with 'no name'. They advocate the collaborative creation
of 'new metaphors to capture the subtle, systemic forms of discrimination
that still linger' (ibid: 136), and they emphasise that these forms will
often be highly contextual in specific organisations. In similar work,
Nanci Zane (1998 1999) and Mary Hale (1999) advocate forms of
organisational discourse that will 'diagnose' issues of gender and
resistance to change through structured 'conversations' between women
and men (Hale 1999), and track change through generating and
monitoring 'new conversational patterns' (Zane 1998). (It is important
to remember that we are referring here to organisations where feminist
discourse is already accepted at some levels, and where discrimination
is 'subtle' rather than gross.)

    In these examples the job of 'feminist organisational commun-
ication' is to generate the communication models that will enable this
kind of conversation to occur in workplaces, the analyses to monitor
new conversations, and the strategic frameworks that will monitor their
effects. A further caution: I have already argued that unless change agents
have communities – inside or outside their organisations – in which
they can continue feminist 'conversations', it is difficult for them to
create strategic frameworks which can transform dominant organisational
discourses. They need to stand back, to be critical, to be reflective, and

to engage in this strategic work collaboratively with other women. If it is true that organisational communication is seen by senior managers as ever more important in 'aligning' individuals with organisational 'visions' and strategies, it is ever more important for feminists to be able to analyse and engage with organisational discourse in terms of our *own* visions and strategies.

References

Acker, Joan 1992. Gendering organizational theory. In A. Mills & P. Tancred (eds), *Gendering Organizational Analysis*. Newbury Park, CA: Sage, 248-260.

Austrin, Terry 1994. Positioning resistance and resisting position: human resource management and the politics of appraisal and grievance hearing. In J. Jermier, D. Knights & W. Nord (eds), *Resistance and Power in Organizations*. New York: Routledge, 199-218.

Barry, David & Michael Elmes 1997. Strategy retold: toward a narrative view of strategic discourse. *Academy of Management Review* 22, 2, 429-452.

Bingham, Charlotte (ed) 1994. *Conceptualising Sexual Harassment as Discursive Practice*. Westport, CONN: Praeger.

Bird, Lise 1998. Dances with feminism: sidestepping and sandbagging. In. E. Burman (ed), *Deconstructing Feminist Psychology*. London: Sage, 90-114.

Boje D. & R. Dennehy 1994. *Managing in the Postmodern World* (2ed). Dubuque, IA: Kendall Hunt.

Boje, David, Robert Gephart & Tojo Thatchenkery (eds) 1996. *Postmodern Management and Organization Theory*. Thousand Oaks, CA: Sage.

Brown, Rosemary 1995. Meeting and intersections: organizational theory encounters feminist theorising. *Women's Studies International Forum* 18, 2, 197-203.

Bullis, Connie 1993. At least it is a start. *Communication Yearbook* 16, 144-154.

Butler, Judith 1990. *Gender Trouble: Feminism and the Subversion of Identity*. London: Routledge.

Butler, Judith 1993. *Bodies that Matter: on the Discursive Limits of 'Sex'*. New York: Routledge.

Butler, Judith 1995a. Contingent foundations. In Seyla Benhabib, Judith Butler, Drucilla Cornell & Nancy Fraser, *Feminist Contentions: a Philosophical Exchange*. New York: Routledge, 35-58.

Butler, Judith 1995b. For a careful reading. In Seyla Benhabib, Judith Butler, Drucilla Cornell & Nancy Fraser, *Feminist Contentions: a Philosophical Exchange*. New York: Routledge, 127-143.

Buzzanell, Patrice 1994. Gaining a voice: feminist organizational communication theorizing. *Management Communication Quarterly* 7, 4, 339-383.

Calas, Maria & Linda Smircich (eds) 1996. *Postmodern management theory.* Aldershot: Ashgate/Dartmouth, 491-505.

Cameron, Deborah 1995. Rethinking language and gender studies: some issues for the 1990s. In Sara Mills (ed), *Language and Gender: Interdisciplinary Perspectives.* London: Longman, 31-44.

Canning, Katherine 1994. Winter. Feminist history after the linguistic turn: historicising discourse and experience. *Signs,* 368-404.

Chase, Susan 1988. Making sense of 'The woman who becomes a man'. In Alexandra Todd and Sue Fisher (eds), *Gender and Discourse: the Power of Talk.* Norwood, NJ: Ablex, 275-295.

Coates, Jennifer 1986. *Women, Men, and Language: a Sociolinguistic Account of Sex Differences in Language.* London: Longman.

Conrad, Charles 1994. *Strategic Organizational Communication: Toward the Twenty-first Century* (3ed). Fort Worth, TX: Harcourt Brace.

Crawford, Mary 1995. *Talking Difference: on Gender and Language.* London: Routledge.

Czarniawska, Barbara 1997. A four times told tale: combining narrative and scientific knowledge in organization studies. *Organization* 4, 1, 7-30.

Daudelien, Marilyn 1996. Learning from experience through reflection. *Organizational Dynamics* 24, 3, 36-48.

Deetz, Stan 1992. *Democracy in an Age of Corporate Colonization: Development in Communication and the Politics of Everyday Life.* Albany, N Y: State University of New York.

Deetz, Stan & Dennis Mumby 1990. Power, discourse, and the workplace: reclaiming the critical tradition. *Communication Yearbook* 13, 18-47.

EEO Trust 1992. *Making the Most of a Diverse Workforce: an Employer's Guide to EEO.* EEO Trust: Auckland.

Ferguson, Kathy 1984. *The Feminist Case against Bureaucracy.* Philadelphia, PA: Temple University Press.

Findlay, Patricia & Tim Newton 1998. Re-framing Foucault: the case of performance appraisal. In Alan McKinlay & Ken Starkey (eds), *Managing Foucault.* London: Sage, 211-229.

Fine, Marlene 1991. New voices in the workplace: research directions in multicultural communication. *Journal of Business Communication* 28, 3, 259-275.

Fine, Marlene 1993. New voices in organizational communication: a feminist comment-ary and critique. In S. Bowen & N. Wyatt (eds), *Transforming Visions: Feminist Critiques in Communication Studies.* Cresskill, NJ: Hampton Press, 125-166.

Foucault, Michel 1972. *The Archaeology of Knowledge.* London: Routledge.

Foucault, Michel 1977. Intellectuals and power: a conversation between Michel Foucault Michel and Gilles Deleuze. In Donald Bouchard & Sherry Simon (eds and trans.), *Language, Counter-Memory, Practice: Selected Essays and Interviews.* Ithaca, NY: Cornell University Press, 204-217.

Foucault, Michel 1983. Afterword: the subject and power. In H. Dreyfus & P. Rabinow, *Michel Foucault: Beyond Structuralism and Hermeneutics* (2ed). Chicago: The University of Chicago Press, 208-226.

Foucault, Michel 1984. What is an author? In P. Rabinow (ed), *Foucault: A Reader*. New York: Pantheon Books, 101-120.

Foucault, Michel 1988. Technologies of the self. In L. Martin, H. Gutman & P. Hutton (eds), *Technologies of the Self: a Seminar with Michael Foucault*. Amhurst, MASS: University of Massachusetts Press, 16-49.

Foucault, Michel. 1991. Questions of method. In Graham Burchell, Colin Gordon & Peter Miller (eds), *The Foucault Effect: Studies in Governmentality*. Harvester/ Wheatsheaf, 73-86.

Freed, Alice 1995. Language and gender. *Annual Review of Applied Linguistics* 15, 3-22.

Game, Ann & Rosemary Pringle 1983. *Gender at Work*. Sydney: Allen & Unwin.

Grant, David, Tom Keenoy & Cliff Oswick (eds) 1998. *Discourse and Organization*. London/Thousand Oaks, CA: Sage Publications.

Gregg, Nina 1992. Telling stories about reality: women's responses to a workplace organizing campaign. In L. Rakow (ed), *Women Making Meaning: New Feminist Directions in Communication*. New York: Routledge. 263-288.

Gregg, Nina 1993a. 'Trying to put first things first': negotiating gendered subjectivities in a workplace organizing campaign. In Sue Fisher & Kathy Davis (eds), *Negotiating at the Margins: The Gendered Discourses of Power and Resistance*. New Brunswick, NJ: Rutgers University Press, 172-204.

Gregg, Nina 1993b. Politics of identity/politics of location: women workers organizing in a postmodern world. *Women's Studies in Communication* 16, 1, 1-33.

Hale, Mary 1999. He says, she says: gender and worklife. *Public Administration Review* 595, 410-424.

Hall, Kira & Mary Bucholtz 1995a. Introduction: twenty years after language and women's place. In Kira Hall & Mary Bucholtz (eds), *Gender Articulated: Language and the Socially Constructed Self*. New York: Routledge, 1-22.

Hall, Kira & Mary Bucholtz (eds) 1995b. *Gender Articulated: Language and the Socially Constructed Self*. New York: Routledge.

Hamel, Gary & C. K. Prahalad 1994. *Competing for the Future*. Boston: Harvard Business School.

Hammond, Sue 1998. *The Thin Book of Appreciative Inquiry*. (2ed). Piano, TX.: Thin Book Pub Co.

Hardy Cynthia & Ian Palmer 1997. Re-Directions in Strategy Theory and Practice: Walking the Talk or Talking the Walk. Paper submitted for presentation in the refereed stream, Australian and New Zealand Academy of Management Conference, 3-6 December, 1997. Melbourne, Australia.

Hardy, Cynthia & Ian Palmer 1999. Discourse as a strategic resource. Paper presented at the Critical Management Studies Conference, Manchester, 14-16 July. http: // www.mngt.waikato.ac.nz/ejrot/cmsconference

Hassard, John & Martin Parker (eds) 1993. *Postmodernism and Organizations.* London: Sage.

Holmes, Janet 1993. Women's talk: the question of sociolinguistic universals. *Australian Journal of Communication* 20, 3, 125-149.

Jablin, Frederic, Linda Putnam, Karlene Roberts & Lyman Porter (eds) 1987. *Handbook of Organizational Communication.* Newbury Park, CA: Sage.

Jermier, John, David Knights & Walter Nord (eds) 1994. *Resistance and power in organizations.* London: Routledge.

Jones, Deborah 1998. Possibilities of transformation: Discourses of difference in organisational communication. Unpublished doctoral dissertation, University of Waikato, Hamilton.

Jones, Deborah, Judith Pringle & Deborah Shepherd Forthcoming. 'Managing diversity' meets Aotearoa/ New Zealand. *Personnel Review.*

Knights, David & Gareth Morgan 1991. Corporate strategy, organizations, and subjectivity: a critique. *Organization Studies* 12, 2, 251-273.

Kovacic, Branislav 1994. Introduction. In Branislav Kovacic (ed), *New Approaches to Organizational Communication.* New York: State University of New York Press, 1-37.

Law, John 1994. Organization, narrative and strategy. In J. Hassard & M. Parker (eds), *A New Theory of Organizations.* London: Routledge, 248-268.

Marshall, Judi 1993. Viewing organizational communication from a feminist perspective: a critique and some offerings. *Communication Yearbook* 16, 112-143.

Martin, Joanne & Peter Frost 1998. The organizational culture war games: a struggle for intellectual dominance. In S. Clegg, C. Hardy & W. Nord (eds), *Handbook of Organization Studies.* London: Sage, 599-621.

Meyers, Caryn 1999. Mars & Venus: in the meeting room. *Successful Meetings* 485, 46-50.

Meyerson, Debra & Joyce Fletcher 2000. A modest manifesto for shattering the glass ceiling. *Harvard Business Review,* Jan-Feb 2000, 127-136.

Miller, Katherine 1995. *Organizational Communication: Approaches and Processes.* Belmont, CA: Wadsworth.

Mills, Albert & Peta Tancred (eds) 1992. *Gendering Organizational Analysis.* Newbury Park, CA: Sage.

Mills, Sara (ed) 1995a. Conclusions. In Sara Mills (ed), *Language and Gender: Interdisciplinary Perspectives.* London: Longman, 257-259.

Mills, Sara (ed) 1995b. Introduction. In Sara Mills (ed) *Language and Gender: Interdisciplinary Perspectives.* London: Longman, 1-10.

Mumby, Dennis 1987. The political function of narrative in organizations. *Communication Monographs* 54, 113-233.

Mumby, Dennis 1988. *Communication and Power in Organizations: Discourse, Ideology, and Domination.* Norwood, NJ: Ablex.

Mumby, Dennis 1993a. Critical organizational communication studies: the next 10 years. *Communication Monographs* 60, 18-25.

Mumby, Dennis (ed) 1993b. *Narrative and Social Control: Critical Perspectives.* Newbury Park, CA: Sage.

Mumby, Dennis 1997. Modernism, postmodernism, and communication studies: a rereading of an ongoing debate. *Communication Theory* 7, 1, 1-28.

Natalle, Elizabeth, Michael Papa & Elizabeth Graham 1994. Feminist philosophy and the transformation of organisational communication. In Branislav Kovacic (ed), *New Approaches to Organizational Communication.* New York: State University of New York Press, 245-270.

Oswick, Cliff & David Grant (eds) 1996. *Organisation Development: Metaphorical Explorations.* London: Pitmans Publishing.

Pearson, Judy, Lynn Turner & William Todd-Mancillas 1991. *Gender & Communication* (2ed). Dubuque, IA: Wm Brown.

Peters, Tom & Robert Waterman 1982. *In Search of Excellence.* New York: Harpers and Row.

Pringle, Judith & Jennifer Scowcroft 1996. Managing diversity: meaning and practice in New Zealand organizations. *Asia Pacific Journal of Human Resources* 34, 2, 28-43.

Pringle, Rosemary 1988. *Secretaries Talk: Sexuality, Power & Work.* Sydney: Allen & Unwin.

Putnam, Linda, N. Philips & P. Chapman 1996. Metaphors of communication and organization. In S. Clegg, C. Hardy & W. Nord (eds) *Handbook of organization studies.* London: Sage, 375-408.

Putnam, Linda & Michael Pacanowsky (eds) 1983. *Communication and Organisations: An Interpretive Approach.* Newbury Park, CA: Sage.

Rakow, Lana. 1986. Rethinking gender research in communication. *Journal of Communication* 36, 4, 11-26.

Rakow, Lana 1992. The field reconsidered. In L. Rakow (ed), *Women Making Meaning: New Feminist Directions in Communication.* New York: Routledge.

Reinsch, N. Lamar Jr. & Annette N. Shelby 1997. What communication abilities do practitioners need? Evidence from MBA students. *Business Communication Quarterly* 604, 7-29.

Riley, Denise 1988. *Am I that Name?: Feminism and the Category of 'Women' in History.* MINN: University of Minnesota.

Rose, Nikolas 1990. *Governing the Soul: the Shaping of the Private Self.* London: Routledge.

Rose, Nikolas 1996. *Inventing Ourselves: Psychology, Power and Personhood.* Cambridge: Cambridge University Press.

Sauers, David 1993. Managing workforce diversity: a challenge for New Zealand business in the 1990s. *Asia Pacific Journal of Human Resources* 31, 5, 44-51.

Schon, Donald 1987. The art of managing: reflection-in-action within an organizational learning system. In P. Rabinow & W. Sullivan (eds), *Interpretive Social Science: A Second Look* (Rev. and updated). Berkeley, CA: University of California Press, 304-326.

Senge, Peter 1990. *The Fifth Discipline: the Art and Practice of the Learning Organisation.* New York: Doubleday.

Spitzack, Carole & Kathryn Carter 1989. Research on women's communication: the politics of theory and method. In Kathryn Carter & Carole Spitzack (eds), *Doing Research on Women's Communication: Perspectives on Theory and Method.* Norwood, NJ: Ablex, 11-39.

Staley, Constance & Pamela Shockley-Zalabak 1989. Triangulation in gender research: The need for converging methodologies. In Kathryn Carter & Carole Spitzack (eds), *Doing Research on Women's Communication.* Norwood, NJ: Ablex, 242-261.

Stuhlmacher, Alice F. & Amy E. Walters 1999. Gender differences in negotiation outcome: a meta-analysis. *Personnel Psychology* 523, 653-677.

Thomas, David & Robin Ely 1996. Making differences matter: a new paradigm for managing diversity. *Harvard Business Review,* Sept/Oct 1996, 79-90.

Thomas, R Roosevelt 1991. *Beyond Race and Gender: Unleashing the Power of your Total Workforce by Managing Diversity.* New York: AMACOM.

Townley, Barbara 1994. *Reframing Human Resource Management: Power, Ethics and the Subject at Work.* Thousand Oaks, CA: Sage.

Weedon, Chris 1987. *Feminist Practice & Poststructuralist Theory.* Oxford: Blackwell

Wilkins, Brenda & Peter Anderson 1991. Gender differences and similarities in management communication: a meta-analysis. *Management Communication Quarterly* 5, 91, 6-35.

Yeatman, Anna 1990. *Bureaucrats, Femocrats, Technocrats: Essays on the Contemporary Australian State.* Sydney: Allen & Unwin.

Zane, Nancie 1998. The discourses of diversity: the links between conversation and organizational change. *Diversity Factor* 71, 29-35.

Zane, Nancie 1999. Gender and leadership: the need for 'public talk' in building an organizational change agenda. *Diversity Factor* 73, 16-21.

Zielinski, Dave 1998. How 'genderflexing' might help to bridge the gender gap. *Presentations* 128, 44.

The cost of corporate culture: linguistic obstacles to gender equity in Australian business

Jennifer J. Peck

University of New England, Armidale

Introduction

This paper has two main aims: to describe some of the work that I have been engaged in with Australian business and industry, and to relate the findings that have emerged from this work to contemporary theories in gender and language.[1] The paper pays particular attention to Community of Practice theory, which offers possibilities for explanations of gender and linguistic performance that avoid reinforcing stereotypes of male and female performances (Weedon 1987; Weiner 1994).

A Community of Practice (CofP) is defined as 'an aggregate of people who come together around mutual engagement in an endeavor' (Eckert & McConnell-Ginet 1992: 464). An essential feature of a CofP is that group members are involved in an activity, and behaviours are relevant to that specific activity and thus to the construction of the community. The ways in which members perform may identify them as peripheral or core members of the community. Learning how to perform is a key feature of CofP theory, and appropriate production of in-group discourse or the expression in appropriate language of group values may identify previously peripheral members as having achieved core membership status.

A CofP framework is useful in demonstrating the ongoing process of learning: social actors are continually engaged in the process of learning how to perform in socially appropriate ways. Social identities of actors are not rigid constructs, but are subject to revision and re-definement. This is a valuable addition to social theory; it accommodates struggle, resistance and change. The discussion in this paper shows, however, that while CofP theory may allow for the redefinition of constructs such as gender, the practices of a community may effectively deny that possibility, by making gender, and discursive practices traditionally associated with 'men' and 'women', highly salient. While membership of a corporation may not be restricted on the basis of gender, group practices may work to exclude those who do not perform in accordance with traditional corporate (male) behaviours. This comment highlights one problem with adopting a CofP model to explicate corporate activity: while the communities under observation may be discrete and defined by mutual endeavour, their practices are routinely constructed on the basis of the legitimised social practices of wider constructs such as 'the corporation'; 'the legal profession'; 'the medical profession'. There may be local variation, but typically practices that have been legitimised in high prestige environments are made highly salient in the groups with which I have been involved. Competition for a turn and the sole-speaking floor are examples of linguistic practices that have been legitimised in this way. While this makes a CofP approach somewhat problematic for explicating corporate behaviours, one useful aspect of the theory is that it highlights this issue as a problem in many corporate environments.

CofP is particularly helpful in demonstrating the problems associated with moving from peripheral to core membership, and its differentiation between peripheral and marginal status is relevant here. I demonstrate that CofP provides useful insights into and explanations for the performances that I have observed, and that have been described to me, but that CofP alone fails to provide a complete theoretical account of the behaviours and problems encountered.

Bourdieu's (1990, 1991) work on the habitus and symbolic capital is also relevant to the discussion of linguistic performance and the exercise of linguistic power in corporate environments. Concepts from Bourdieu discussed later in this paper are the habitus and hexis, symbolic power and notions of capital. These terms will be explained and exemplified in relation to the research, but summary definitions are provided here. Bourdieu uses the term 'habitus' to refer to the learned predisposition to speak and act in ways that are congruent with one's social space. According to Bourdieu, to be positioned outside a social space with which one is congruent can lead to hesitancy in speaking, and even to the inability to speak. This is clearly appealing to a discussion of the problems women encounter when they 'invade' social space that has traditionally been designated male territory. The concept of symbolic power describes power that derives from the combination of different types of capital: economic, cultural and social. Again, this is a concept that is useful in explaining both male and female behaviour in corporate environments.

Bergvall's (1999) argument is particularly relevant to my discussion: linguistic performances cannot be explained solely in terms of the practices of the community with which an individual social subject is engaging at a particular time, in a particular context. Linguistic performance, and gendered linguistic performance, is part of what we 'do' (cf West & Zimmerman 1991) from birth or possibly before; it is achieved, and it is thrust upon us. (Bergvall here adapts Shakespeare's *Twelfth Night*.)

I first discuss the practical work in which I have been involved and the findings that have emerged. I then discuss this in relation to CofP theory, and then to some concepts drawn from Bourdieu. The paper concludes with a brief comment on the value of praxis-oriented linguistics for corporate environments.

Subjects and activities

Throughout 1999 I have been involved in praxis-oriented work: taking academic research into public domains, facilitating the engagement of participants in business and industry with research issues, and developing and applying strategies that directly relate to the needs of the community that I am addressing. My approach has been to carry out interviews, seminars and speeches with government agencies (such as Human Rights and Equal Opportunity Commission, Affirmative Action Agency), private corporations and business groups. These activities have taken place in Australia in Sydney, Brisbane and regional New South Wales. The dynamics that have developed are interesting. Initial interviews have resulted in invitations to present to large groups, and large group presentations have led to approaches from individuals who have wished to pursue personal issues further in a private setting.

I have carried out formal interviews with senior personnel from private and public organisations. Formal interviews have been conducted with nine private corporations, three professional groups and four government agencies and departments. Key personnel involved have been directors of human resources and diversity management. Some outcomes of these meetings have been invitations to address executive groups, to speak at formal lunches and dinners, and to address business conferences. I have addressed 12 groups in seminar and speech format.

Most of my observations are drawn from these corporate situations, though some have been recorded during tutorials at the University of New England, Armidale, NSW. Courses at this university provide a particularly fertile ground for this type of material, as the majority of students are mature-age students studying externally, many of whom have extensive experience of business work environments. The comments of students attending Residential Schools have sometimes been recorded and some are used here. The exchange between men, which is reproduced later in this paper, is taken from my transcription recorded while I was working within a large corporation in Brisbane.

I have maintained written records of the comments, stories and experiences described. The need for confidentiality in a highly sensitive arena has prohibited tape-recording, but I have frequently been able to revisit individuals or groups to discuss issues and transcribe significant details. In one-on-one meetings this has never been problematic.

Specific examples of exchanges recorded in this text are taken from the personal experiences that have been reported to me and transcribed by me. Generalisations are made from my recording of the debates and issues raised as being of significant concern, either as a business concern, (eg. the isolation of women and consequent high attrition), or of concern to many women, (eg. the criticism of them as being excessively feminine or masculine). In all cases individuals have given their permission for their comments to be transcribed and reproduced.

I began conducting the work solely based on issues relating to gender. The program has extended to include other issues of diversity and business practices. Diversity issues that I have focused on include the communication practices of some Asian cultures, some Aboriginal Australian communities and vision-impaired people. Features that are salient in one community appear as equally relevant in a different group. For instance, the communication practices of some indigenous Australian cultures intersect with those of vision-impaired people. And the practices of vision-impaired people intersect in interesting ways with findings from gender and language research. These complexities are discussed elsewhere (Peck 1999), but it is worth recognising at this point the need to incorporate diversity into discussions of linguistic practices (Bing & Bergvall 1996); to recognise that diversity results from membership of a number of overlapping social communities of practice that must be accounted for by theory (Eckert & McConnell-Ginet 1992; Bergvall 1999); and also that some practices that identify group membership may also be performed by members of other groups. This might occur because of cross-group membership, but sometimes the practice serves quite different needs in different communities. In this paper I shall concentrate on gender-related issues.

Talking of men and women

In the public arena I speak of male and female behaviours, or the behaviours or ways of acting of men and women. When I use such terms I repeatedly stress that I am talking about tendencies rather than absolutes, and that the claims or suggestions I make are generalisations about gendered performances. It is necessary to use such terminology in order to make research accessible to a wider audience. The responses I receive confirm that there are different learned behaviours and different expectations about how men and women should behave, especially in relation to language use. I have used this terminology in this paper because these are the issues that I am addressing and that are continually presented to me in the contexts in which I am working. I wish to formally acknowledge here that 'masculine' and 'feminine' are problematic concepts, from the assignment of biological sex at birth through the socialisation into gendered subjectivities and the general social requirement that the 'successful' achievement of gender is reproduced and displayed.

The dangers of stereotypes

I am sensitive to the warnings from within academia concerning the distribution within the public arena of generalisations and stereotypes about women's and men's linguistic behaviours (Holmes 1993; Cameron 1995). Sally McConnell-Ginet (2000) makes the valid point that we should avoid giving gender difference the cachet of science, which could serve to validate differences. She points out that one consequence of this could be that women who fail to conform to the stereotype will be judged as deviant. These are valid points and need to be constantly considered in any presentation of academic research to, for instance, business groups or corporations. This potential problem should, however, be weighed against the value of taking academic research into a wider forum. This can have very positive results. A major response of women in business to exposure to academic research on gender and language has been relief: they learn that they are not 'deviant', but that their linguistic behaviours are acknowledged as acceptable performances, sometimes indicative of a gendered socialised position. Recognising that their linguistic performances may represent their successful social achievement, some women report feeling that they have received permission to continue to produce performances with which they are comfortable. Others say that they have gained the confidence to challenge and subvert social norms that have been 'thrust upon them'.

Linguistic features

It is accepted in many business organisations that the practices of the dominant corporate culture are inhibiting to women and to other minority groups. Private and public organisations recognise that they are losing the business of these groups, but more important for some organisations is the high attrition rate, particularly of women. There is a direct financial business loss when women leave: businesses invest heavily in human resources and the high attrition rate of women involves high cost. Business is also failing to capitalise on the skills that women bring to the business environment. Not only could women use their 'soft' skills (Burton & Ryall 1995: 8) to obtain business, but also these attributes could relieve the competitive and isolationist culture that pervades the masculine ethic of the corporate world.

Management agrees that the situation regarding gender and communication is a serious one, with major consequences for women, for business success and for the culture in general. Executives involved in human resources or in diversity are keen to implement action which will improve communication and change traditional, male-oriented culture. This situation is documented in business management literature: 'The culture has a corrosive effect on women' (Schwartz 1992), and

while they may persist in business for a time, 'the culture is so awful
... that women do not want to stay' (Squirechuck 1994: 126).

Some of the specific linguistic features that I discuss with business
groups are minimal responses, overlapping speech, completion of
sentences, and different types of turn taking: women favour the shared
floor, men the individual floor (West & Zimmerman 1983; Edelsky 1981;
Fishman 1983; Coates 1989; 1994; 1996). I also discuss women's tendency
to heavily modalize statements with utterances such as *maybe, perhaps,*
and their tendency to incorporate inclusive language with modalization,
producing utterances like *It might be a good idea for us to try, We could
think about doing* . . . (Holmes 1995; Coates 1996; Peck 1998). I point out
that women are disadvantaged in business situations, especially in
meetings, because they are often not using the speech style that they are
familiar with, and that they are expected to use a competitive style but are
condemned as being aggressive and unpleasant when they do.

Women in business are also more inclined to display their emotions
than men are, and this can be seen as a sign of female weakness. Coates
(2000) shows that male attempts at self-disclosure regarding their
emotions and fear are silenced by the conventions of masculinity. I have
observed in business settings the frequent denial of worry or nervousness.
An example of this occurred when a group of men in mid-management
positions were discussing a tender. Asked by a male colleague about the
stress associated with this, one man replied 'Yeah, it's been really worr-
no, no not *worrying,* I'm not *worried,* it's a *challenge'.* Here we have an
example of the type of heroic masculinity that Coates observed in her
data. Men deny their 'weaknesses' and construct themselves as heroic
figures in a way that is unfamiliar to most women.

When I describe linguistic features that some research associates
with female speech, I receive strong affirmation from the women in my
research that these are the types of linguistic strategies that women use,
and that it is seen as a problem when they do. They also describe the
condemnation they directly receive, or learn of, when they use assertive
or competitive strategies. Women who are assertive often feel alienated
by both men and women in the organisation.

In my discussion with business and industry I propose that 'women's
style' should be incorporated into business culture. That collaboration
and support should be affirmed and used, rather than denigrated and

abandoned. And I suggest some practical strategies, particularly consciousness-raising and education and training processes that advance women's position. At some seminars I discuss intervention techniques of the type proposed by Holmes (1992), and the ideas are well received by women. Some strategies they particularly respond to are: refusing to give up the floor in meetings; discussing in advance with other women when you want to contribute to a meeting, and handing the floor to another woman whom you know has a valuable point to make on a topic. Women have also commented that it can be easier for another woman to point out that offensive or silencing strategies are being used by men, rather than the woman who is on the receiving end of these strategies.

I have found that simply *talking* about these issues affirms women's sense of self. There is often a sense of revelation in seminars and following speeches: women have often been struggling in secret with communication problems. There is a high level of self-disclosure in these groups, and it is generally triggered by the women's exposure to academic research. It does therefore seem to be a useful enterprise.

Clearly many women feel that they are in a difficult position in relation to group practices and they are often uncomfortable within the corporate social space. In the following section I analyse corporate practice in terms of CofP theory and Bourdieu's concepts of symbolic power and the habitus.

Communities of practice theory

The participants in this research belong to a corporation or organisation and are engaged in joint projects. Eckert & McConnell-Ginet define a CofP as:

> An aggregate of people who come together around mutual engagement in an endeavor. Ways of doing things, ways of talking, beliefs, values, power relations – in short, practices – emerge in the course of this mutual endeavor. As a social construct, a CofP is different from the traditional community, primarily because it is defined simultaneously by its membership and by the practice in which that membership engages (1992: 464).

According to this definition, the performances of both the women and men in the groups that I have been involved with fit within the CofP: as members, they are participants in the construction of the practice. The use of a CofP theory becomes problematic when considering to what extent most of the women are considered by the core group to be members of the community. This issue can be analysed in terms of three crucial dimensions identified by Wenger (1998: 76) and elaborated by Holmes & Meyerhoff (1999): mutual engagement, joint enterprise and shared repertoire.

Mutual engagement

'This typically involves regular interaction: it is the basis for the relationships that make the CofP possible' (Holmes & Meyerhoff 1999: 175). The individuals or groups that I have been involved with are typically engaged in shared projects and meet regularly both formally, to discuss progress and to distribute and assess work; and sometimes informally, occasionally for lunch but more often for drinks after work.

Women fit within this category according to their involvement at work and in projects, but women have repeatedly reported that despite their efforts, they are excluded from all but directly work-related activities. For example, a number of women said that they followed sport on TV, but despite their displays of knowledge and interest, would routinely be excluded from casual discussions that occurred between men.

More importantly, while 'ways of doing things, ways of talking, beliefs, values' do emerge as part of the mutual endeavour associated with a work project, conflicts are often described as existing between typically 'masculine' and typically 'feminine' ways of doing things, beliefs and values (see Gilligan 1982, 1983, 1986, Belenky, McVicker Clinchy, Goldberger & Mattuck Tarule 1986, Peck 2000 regarding morality and gender).

Joint enterprise

This refers to the notion that the enterprise is more than a goal: it is a negotiated venture that involves the mutual accountability of the members of the community (Wenger 1998: 80; Holmes & Meyerhoff 1999: 175). The groups that I have been involved with appear to have shared goals (though these are often designated by the wider organisation). The notion of negotiation is often more clearly apparent, both through the negotiation of the way as project or enterprise develops, and the ways in which tasks are negotiated and subsequently allocated.

In terms of this dimension, women appear to fit within the CofP. Interestingly, this category is in some ways particularly relevant to gender analysis. Men and women reported that tasks were negotiated and assigned on the basis of skills that seemed to the participants to have a gender bias. It was reported that women in teams tended to have more of a 'perfectionist' attitude than men. In production of proposals and tenders, for instance, women were reported to be extremely particular about correctness of style and format. In a similar vein, it was reported that women were concerned about the accuracy of a result, while men were more concerned to finalise the process. Some project managers said that these different approaches could be usefully deployed. This is an unsupported point, but was widely made, and is in line with the notion that the practice of a community involves negotiation, complex relationships, and shared accountability.

Shared repertoire

Shared repertoire develops over time as a result of the shared enterprise. The repertoire of the CofP includes a range of resources for negotiating meaning (Wenger 1998: 85). Ways of coming to decisions, ways of talking in meetings, shortcuts in telephone talk, as well as social interaction outside work-related activities were all features that were mentioned by participants. All of these features appear relevant to this category.

The category of 'shared repertoire' is similar in many ways to my comments above regarding the dimension of mutual engagement. While there is a partial fit, the linguistic routines used in work environments and ways of coming to work-oriented decisions vary for some women from some of the practices of the group. Women also said they tended to 'chat' more than men when concluding a telephone call, and they 'talked' more on e-mail than their male colleagues. The absence of shared repertoire has been described by many of the women in this research as a major problem. Further, women are often excluded from social activities (and state that they are frequently ignored when they attempt to participate).

In terms of two of these dimensions (mutual engagement and shared repertoire), women's membership of the CofP is problematic. Many women in business could be analysed as peripheral group members, and many are attempting to become core members, often through the use of some CofP devices such as linguistic routines. Women tell me that they practise linguistic routines to their husbands or male partners in advance of meetings in order to ensure that their performances conform to the established group behaviours. Significantly, for a CofP analysis, they are practicing before men, but not men who are members of their local community. There seems to be an assumption within the general public that 'men' belong to a global group. (Clearly this is problematic in relation to CofP theory: the men are not involved in a mutual endeavour.) This generalisation may be being promoted by work such as Gray's (1992) *Men are from Mars, Women are from Venus*, though many women in business have said that while they do not support his thesis, Gray's work has helped by illustrating to their male colleagues that there may be performative linguistic differences.

Many women do not achieve core membership status of the local group who are engaged in mutual activities within the organisation (for instance within a small project group). They remain marginal in Wenger's (1998) terms, failing to become even peripheral members of the community, often despite concerted efforts to do so. A number of linguistic features that are used by men in their work environment are described by women in my research as defining women as outsiders and as unacceptable to the dominant group. Many of these features correlate with those described by Wenger (1998: 130-31) as critical characteristics of a CofP. Features that fall into this category are:

Sharing stories and knowing laughter
Jargon and shortcuts to communication
Styles displaying membership
Shared discourse reflecting a certain perspective of the world.

A large proportion of the women that I have met during this project feel excluded by masculine story-telling, laughter, and the discursive practices which they feel alienates them from the group and demonstrates their categorisation as belonging to a different experiential world. These women disclosed their feelings of isolation in an alien environment. The process of marginalisation of these women had apparently been successful. It is important for this discussion to make the point that many women leave large corporations when they have been in senior management positions for about a year, and that isolation is recognised by organisations as being a crucial factor in the dropout rate of women.

However, some groups of women appear to constitute their own CofP: establishing themselves as members of an elite group with greater prestige than other women in the contextual setting. This was displayed in some seminar and large group settings. Methods of display of group membership were story telling and laughter, 'shortcuts' to commun-ication, and shared discourse that was associated both with work and knowledge of the other in-group members' personal experiences. These practices often demonstrated solidarity within the smaller, all-female group. My observations of this type of performance were of highly successful senior women, many of whom stated that they had succeeded in business under very difficult circumstances. The fact that gender is a highly salient factor in the construction of these local groups is confirmed by the topics of discussion frequently being associated with a gendered position. Laughter often accompanied discussions of clothes, and the need to wear high heels; children, and the difficulties associated with negotiating family and work; men in the workplace; and the struggles that the women endured.

Two points should be made in relation to these local, all-female groups. First, although these women held prestigious positions within the wider CofP, the local group exists only outside the practices and organisation of the group as a whole. None of the practices that I observed as constitutive features of these groups would transfer into the larger CofP. This is problematic because the notion of mutual endeavour would appear to be directly associated with the women's membership of the wider corporate community. Perhaps the endeavour of these communities is mutual support in the face of a potentially hostile environment.

Second, the construction of the core group isolates other women who have had different experiences, or who are currently less successful. Effectively, a further elite group is established, consisting of 'women who've succeeded against the odds', which may contribute to the margin-alisation of other women. (I do not include other men in this marginalisation process, since I have not observed the display of this elite group membership before men.)

Peripheral and marginal status

Wenger's distinction between 'peripheral' and 'marginal' members of a community is important. While I have said that the select women's group marginalises women, the main source of denial of women's status as peripheral (and thus potentially central) members is dominant (masculine) cultural practices. Women describe comments that are made to them in meetings, which effectively construct them as 'deviant'. They talk of the way they are ridiculed for using modalising strategies. One woman reports that a man repeatedly challenges her with the words 'Do you know or don't you?', which silences her and makes her dread meetings. Women and men agree that women tend to collaborate towards a resolution, and men treat this as a problem since confrontation is seen within this CofP as a marker of successful performance. As Coates (2000) says, men perpetually assert their masculinity. Women in business and in politics reported that 'one-up-manship' and competitiveness which includes verbal abuse are part of the routine of meetings and parliamentary sittings, and that their refusal to engage in these practices marks them as outsiders and failures according to the value system of the community.

Deviant women

Women regularly claim that they are accused of being either *too* masculine or *too* feminine. For instance, women who adopt male-type strategies are condemned on the basis of biology: one woman in middle management in a bank who identifies as reasonably assertive says that she's been introduced to visitors by her boss as follows: 'This is Sarah. She's permanently premenstrual'. A leading woman politician in Australia who has a relatively deep voice told me that on the floor of parliament she has received comments such as 'Do you take hormones to get that voice?'. Women in business frequently say to me that they're in a no-win situation: expected to be assertive but condemned as being castrating bitches when they are. Women who are 'too feminine' are deviant, women who are assertive are, to use Bergvall's term 'doubly deviant': 'not male nor yet fully female' (Bergvall 1999: 278).

Habitus and symbolic capital

Bourdieu's (1990, 1991) concepts of the habitus, hexis and symbolic power are relevant here. Bourdieu's discussions reveal his particular concern with linguistic performance and linguistic capital. Bourdieu associates the habitus with learning to speak within a particular position in social space. Part of what one learns is the value of speech; reinforcements or refutations provide a sense of the social value of linguistic usages and the relation between markets and usages (1991: 81). A sense of the value of one's own linguistic products is a fundamental dimension of the sense of knowing the place which one occupies in social space. Together with the value of one's own body they constitute the 'sense of one's own social worth' (1991: 81).

This is particularly relevant to the discussion of the linguistic behaviours of women, and the ways in which their 'aberrant' performances are condemned or refuted by those whose histories are more congruent with the social space that they occupy in the corporate world. If men in western societies, especially middle-class men, have been socialised into positions that are congruent with those of business ethics, while the histories of women from equivalent backgrounds have oriented them towards more nurturing social positions, then the histories of men are more congruent with their social space than the histories of women. As Thompson, discussing Bourdieu, says, 'when there is a lack of congruence . . . an individual may not know how to act and may literally be lost for words' (1991: 17). These theories are helpful in elucidating the comments made by and to the women in this program. As a result of their histories, the women appear to be located in a different social space from the men, and this is often unrecognised by the women that I have talked with. They may feel that they do not know how to act; they are either 'lost for words' or are silenced, but they usually have no explanation for this.

The histories of these men and women have led them to possess different quantities of linguistic capital in Bourdieu's terms (Thompson 1991: 17), and linguistic capital is related in specific ways to other forms of capital. Capital may be economic, cultural or social, and together they constitute symbolic capital (Bourdieu 1991: 230). These concepts are appealing to the explication of performance in the corporate world, since the different types of capital described by Bourdieu are all relevant to corporate performance. Economic success, the legal protection afforded to cultural or intellectual knowledge, and social capital that is legitimised through the systems of elitist social structures are all pertinent to successful corporate performance.

Further, as Bourdieu points out, 'there is no symbolic power without the symbolism of power' (1991: 75). It is an important feature of the corporate linguistic environment that linguistic power is made evident. This is achieved not only through male performances that assert power and provide demonstrations of the ownership of linguistic capital and thus symbolic power, but also through the denigration of female linguistic performances. Bourdieu (1991: 23, 51) also points out that symbolic capital requires the 'active complicity' (1991: 23) of those subjected to symbolic power. Women's complicity is arguably evidenced in their linguistic struggle and silence, and their abandoning of senior corporate positions.

Bourdieu includes the body (hexis), in his descriptions of symbolic capital, and he points to the fact that insignia (such as is worn by the military), and manners serve as reminders of institutionalised social positioning. I find it useful to extend this to include less obvious 'insignia', such as gender-differentiated corporate dress; the requirement that women in business wear cosmetics, and the occupation of bodily space which is also typically gender-differentiated, especially within conservative corporate environments. These features are strong reminders both of gender and of the positions traditionally assigned to gender. They serve to uphold and maintain the symbolic order, and effectively women are displaying, (and are regularly required to display), 'active complicity' in the system of symbolic power and subordination.

I have been told by women and men in business and industry, in both the private and public sectors, that as more women are perceived as being successful in business, men tend to increase their use of competitive linguistic strategies. Corporate culture, they say, is becoming more competitive and aggressive in areas where women are evident. Again, this could further explain the need to make gender relevant and visible: making femininity visible through the gender-differential use of the body, and gender-marked clothing and adornment may be facilitating the maintenance of the status quo.

Theoretical problems and explanations

The issues that I have approached in this paper are complex and far-reaching, and the attempt to locate my findings within a single theoretical system is clearly problematic. In some ways, CofP theory and Bourdieu's notions of capital and symbolic power are in conflict. CofP tends to look at a local group and show how group membership is enacted or resisted, and sometimes shows that membership of a local CofP can define opposition to wider social practices. CofP also serves to demonstrate the variety that constitutes 'society'. Bourdieu's notions of capital and symbolic power tend to address issues related to wider, institutionalised power structures and show how subordinates help to maintain the structures of power which subordinate them.

It has been shown here that both theories have useful applications. Of particular interest from CofP theory is the way that local communities can marginalise women. In the groups observed in this paper, the small, local groups tend to support wider structures. Bourdieu's theories of the habitus, capital, and symbolic power help to show how women in corporate situations are often occupying social spaces that are incompatible or incongruent with what they have learned. If the 'corporate male' is in a social space that is compatible with the habitus, he is likely to be more at ease than the female in a corporate world. Symbolic capital helps to explain the requirement that gender be displayed, and the ways that women's linguistic performances are condemned or ridiculed: through these mechanisms symbolic power can be retained and controlled.

Conclusion

Women and men are socialised (in various ways, and to varying degrees), into gendered subjectivities. And in business they are required to display their successful achievement of gender: in effect, both men and women have gender 'thrust upon them'. However, the result of displays of gender that represent socially successful achievement of gender in the wider community is received differently in the world of business, industry and politics. Displays of masculinity are likely to lead to success and acceptance within the CofP. Displays of femininity can result in derision and marginalisation. In many ways it is in the interests of the dominant group, who control symbolic capital, to ensure that gender is continually made relevant. However, in a business world where women are increasingly present (though often peripheral or marginal), and in societies where women are increasingly the economic decision-makers, it is a business need as well as a social responsibility to accommodate women and to eliminate prejudice towards displays of diversity. This may involve the acceptance of behaviours which evidence diversity, and the removal of the requirement that difference (such as gender), be constantly displayed.

The responses that I have received from people in business and industry confirm that it is useful to take academic research into public domains, and to present it in accessible ways. Women who feel that their linguistic performances are problematic say that they have benefited from the programs in which I have been involved. These women have typically been constructed as either 'too' weak or 'too' aggressive. The work provides forums that allow women (and men) to speak out in an environment in which their views and experiences will be accepted and validated. These forums reduce the isolation of those who feel marginalised by the practices of the dominant culture.

The sessions also provide contexts in which there is a possibility for the reconstruction of the practices of the community. Subversive joint action can be negotiated which may both validate collaborative linguistic practices and allow for the recognition of the usefulness of competitive strategies. At a micro level, subtle changes to community practices have the possibility to enact macro change. Affirmed by group effort and support, the women I have talked to say they intend to challenge existing practices.

The work also provides a possible starting point for management education programs, instigating change at all levels. Change to contemporary corporate culture is problematic, because of the vested interest of the majority group in maintaining existing practices. However, it is clear that change can be promoted as having a number of positive outcomes: it will be to the financial advantage of business and industry; will promote women and other minority groups, and has the potential to reduce stress levels of both women and men.

The theoretical discussion in this paper has shown that CofP theory can highlight ways in which CofP are constructed and enacted. An analysis in CofP terms demonstrates that women can be identified as part of local business communities of practice, and that women sometimes form exclusive communities of practice. An important feature of CofP is the distinction between marginal and peripheral membership. The paper has shown that women are often marginalised by the gendered performances that they produce, and that they are expected to produce. It is required that gender should be constantly displayed, and this display helps to support the status quo and works to ensure that symbolic capital remains in the control of the traditional owners.

While 'doing gender', and displaying the successful achievement of a gendered position is currently a highly salient feature of corporate culture, there are possibilities for challenge, subversion and change. Praxis-oriented work can promote these opportunities.

Notes

1   I wish to thank all those who have contributed to this paper through their participation in seminars, interviews and formal and informal discussions. I appreciate both the honesty of those who disclosed their experiences, and the warmth and support offered by audiences who heard them. Special thanks go to the public and private organizations who shared their problems; to the Director of HREOC, Sydney; the Director of the Affirmative Action Agency, Sydney, and the members of VIPHEO, Armidale.

References

Belenky, Mary Field, Blythe McVicker Clinchy, Nancy Rule Goldberger & Jill Mattuck Tarule 1986. *Women's Ways of Knowing: the Development of Self, Voice, and Mind*. New York: Basic Books.

Bergvall, Victoria L. 1999. Toward a comprehensive theory of language and gender, *Language in Society* 28, 273-93.

Bing, Janet M. & Victoria L. Bergvall 1996. The question of questions: beyond binary thinking. In Victoria L. Bergvall, Janet M. Bing & Alice F. Freed (eds), *Rethinking Language and Gender Research: Theory and Practice*. London: Longman, 1-30.

Bourdieu, Pierre 1990. *In Other Words: Essays Towards a Reflexive Sociology*. Trans. by Matthew Adamson. Cambridge: Polity Press with Basil Blackwell.

Bourdieu, Pierre 1991. *Language and Symbolic Power*. Trans. by Gino Raymond & Matthew Adamson. Cambridge: Polity Press with Basil Blackwell.

Burton, Clare & Carolyn Ryall 1995. *Enterprising Nation. Managing for Diversity.* Canberra: Australian Government Publishing Service.

Cameron, Deborah 1995. *Verbal Hygiene.* London: Routledge.

Coates, Jennifer 1989. Gossip revisited. Language in all-female groups. In Jennifer Coates & Deborah Cameron (eds), *Women in their Speech Communities.* London: Longman, 94-122.

Coates, Jennifer 1994. No gap, lots of overlap: turn-taking patterns in the talk of women friends. In David Graddol, Janet Maybin & Barry Stierer (eds), *Researching Language and Literacy in Social Context.* Clevedon: Multilingual Matters, 177-92.

Coates, Jennifer 1996. *Women Talk.* Oxford: Blackwell.

Coates, Jennifer 2000. *'So I thought bollocks to that': men, stories and masculinities.* See this volume.

Eckert, Penelope & McConnell-Ginet, Sally 1992. Think practically and look locally: language and gender as community-based practice, *Annual Review of Anthropology* 21, 461-90.

Edelsky, Carole 1981. Who's got the floor? *Language in Society* 10, 383-421.

Fishman, Pamela 1983. Interaction: the work women do. In Barrie Thorne, Cheris Kramarae & Nancy Henley (eds), *Language, Gender and Society.* Rowley, MA: Newbury House, 89-101.

Gilligan, Carol 1982. *In a Different Voice. Psychological Theory and Women's Development.* Cambridge, MA: Harvard University Press.

Gilligan, Carol 1983. Do the social sciences have an adequate theory of moral development? In Norma Haan, Robert N. Bellah, Paul Rabinow & William M. Sullivan (eds), *Social Science as Moral Inquiry.* New York: Columbia University Press, 33-51.

Gilligan, Carol 1986. Remapping the moral domain: new images of the self in relationship. In Thomas C. Heller, Morton Sosna & David E. Wellerby (eds), *Reconstructing Individualism.* Stanford: Stanford University Press, 237-52.

Gray, John 1992. *Men are from Mars, Women are from Venus: A Practical Guide for Improving Communication and Getting What You Want in your Relationships.* New York: Harper Collins.

Holmes, Janet 1992. Women's talk in public contexts. *Discourse and Society* 3, 2, 131-50.

Holmes, Janet 1993. Women's talk: the question of sociolinguistic universals, *Australian Journal of Communication* 20, 3, 125-49.

Holmes, Janet 1995. *Women, Men and Politeness.* London: Longman.

Holmes, Janet & Miriam Meyerhoff 1999. The community of practice: theories and methodologies in language and gender research, *Language in Society* 28, 173-83.

McConnell-Ginet, Sally 2000. *Panel Discussion: How Can Language and Gender Research Be Best Used in the Workplace?* See this volume.

Peck, Jennifer J. 1998. *The Performance of Gendered Subjectivities in Micro-Interactions.* Unpublished PhD thesis. University of Queensland.

Peck, Jennifer J. 2000. *Discursive Constructions of Expertise: The Salience of Gender and Sightedness.* To appear in *Discourse Studies.*

Peck, Jennifer J. 2000. Gender, language and morality: explaining differences in micro-linguistic performances. To appear in *Discourse and Society* 3.

Squirechuck, Rohan 1994. *Canberra Bulletin of Public Administration*, 126.

Schwartz, Felice 1992. Women as a business imperative. *Harvard Business Review*, March-April, 105-13.

Thompson, John B. 1991. Editor's Introduction. In Pierre Bourdieu, *Language and Symbolic Power*, 1-31.

Weedon, Chris 1987. *Feminist Practice and Post-Structuralist Theory.* Oxford: Blackwell.

Weiner, Gaby 1994. *Feminisms in Education. An Introduction.* Buckingham: Open University Press, 51-73.

Wenger, Etienne 1998. *Communities of Practice.* Cambridge & New York: Cambridge University Press.

West, Candace & Don H. Zimmerman 1983. Small insults: a study of interruptions in cross-sex conversations between unacquainted persons. In Barrie Thorne, Cheris Kramarae & Nancy Henley (eds), *Language, Gender and Society*. Rowley, MA: Newbury House, 103-18.

West, Candace & Don H. Zimmerman 1991. Doing gender. In Judith Lorber & Susan A. Farrell (eds), *The Social Construction of Gender*. Newbury Park: Sage, 13-37.

Forget Mars and Venus, let's get back to earth!: challenging gender stereotypes in the workplace

Maria Stubbe, Janet Holmes, Bernadette Vine and Meredith Marra

Victoria University of Wellington

Introduction

Gender differences in the use of language have been intensively studied by academics from a number of disciplines over the past three decades. The results of this growing body of research have also consistently attracted the interest of other groups in society. During the 1970s and 1980s, it was the work of feminist researchers such as Robin Lakoff and Dale Spender which was most visible outside academia. Their critical examination of the role of language in maintaining male social dominance was particularly influential amongst professionals and others involved in the educational equity and assertiveness training movements (c.f. Crawford 1995).

More recently, a number of books published during the 1990s as part of the burgeoning 'self-help' genre (e.g. Elgin 1993, Gray 1992, Rearden 1995, Tannen 1990, 1994b) have enjoyed great success with a much wider popular audience. These books take a rather different approach from earlier work which emphasised explanations centring on male dominance and power (e.g. Lakoff 1975, Zimmerman & West 1975, West 1984, Spender 1985). Drawing selectively on research which uses the notion of cultural difference as a metaphor for gender difference (e.g. Maltz & Borker 1982), as well as on a large stock of anecdotal examples, the popular books either directly or indirectly promote the theory that there are predictable 'natural' differences in patterns of verbal interaction between men and women which can be explained by cultural or even biological pre-programming. The assumptions on which they are based contrast with the consensus emerging from more recent research, which rejects the idea of dichotomising women and men into homogeneous groups, and instead proposes a dynamic social construc-tionist explanation of observed gender differences in communicative style (e.g. Bing and Bergvall 1996, Cameron 1996, Holmes 1997).[1]

The essentialist view of gender difference espoused in books like Gray's and Tannen's is reflected in many contemporary management texts and workplace communication training materials, which also tend to take a rather deterministic and over-generalised approach to language and gender issues (c.f. Cameron 1996). The 'gender as cultural difference' approach of these books and training materials clearly appeals to many people in the post-feminist nineties as an unthreatening and common-sense way to explain and deal with the gender differences and inequalities they observe around them on a daily basis. However, it is our contention that the 'equal but different' model has serious short-comings, particularly when applied to workplace settings.

Our argument is that deterministic explanations of gender differ-ences are problematic, first of all because there is good evidence that they conflict with the 'down to earth' reality of genuine workplace interaction, and secondly because they reinforce out-of-date and unhelpful stereotypes, with potentially serious implications for gender equity in the workplace. This second problem is nicely illustrated in a recent cartoon, which shows the following scene:

> Four men in business suits and two 'power-dressed' women are sitting round a table with papers in front of them. One of the men is saying, 'That was a fine report, Barbara. But since the sexes speak different languages, I probably didn't understand a word of it.'

This cartoon makes the important point that while it may be fashionable and entertaining to naturalise gender differences as writers like Gray do, there is a real danger that an uncritical acceptance of such views simply provides an excuse for justifying the status quo. Moreover, the 'Mars and Venus' approach also fails to account adequately either for the strongly institutionalised nature of status and power relationships in organisational contexts, or for the ways in which men and women in the workplace continually balance their various other social and professional roles with the expectations placed on them by their gender (see Bing and Bergvall 1996, Stubbe 1998a for further discussion of this point).

Our disagreement with the dualistic 'women do this, men do that' approach to gender difference in language use provided the starting point for the workshop we facilitated at the *Language and Gender Symposium*. The session began by examining the assumptions about gender and communication displayed in excerpts from three books aimed at a non-academic audience. Workshop participants looked at how these assumptions relate to common gender stereotypes, and how they might colour our perceptions of the communicative behaviour of individual women and men in the workplace. We then explored these issues in the context of recent developments in international research on language and gender, with a particular focus on the ways in which New Zealand women and men actually use language at work.

We looked in detail at aspects of management style, meeting talk and humour in examples of genuine workplace interaction taken from a corpus of local data gathered by Victoria University's Language in the Workplace project[2] to see in which ways this data challenges current stereotypes of gendered language. The extracts presented were representative of data from a large corpus of over 500 naturally-occurring workplace interactions collected as part of this project (see Holmes 1998, Holmes et al 1999a, 1999b). The project was designed to analyse the features of effective interpersonal communication in a variety of New Zealand workplaces. A methodology was therefore developed to record natural workplace interactions as unobtrusively as possible (see Stubbe 1998b, Stubbe and Ingle fc), with volunteers from each workplace tape-recording a range of their everyday work inter-actions over a period of two to three weeks. Some kept a recorder and microphone on their desks, others carried the equipment round with them. In addition, a series of regular meetings was video-recorded in a number of different workplaces.

Most of our data has been collected in white collar organisations, but we also have some data from factories and small businesses such as garden centres. We collected some excellent examples of natural workplace interaction ranging in time from 20 seconds to five hours. The complete dataset comprises a wide variety of different types of interaction, including small, relatively informal work-related discussions between two or three participants, more formal meetings of between four and thirteen participants, telephone calls and social talk.

The project team has analysed various aspects of these workplace interactions, including meeting and decision-making processes, problem-solving, directives, management style, humour, small talk, social versus business talk, miscommunication and problematic discourse, and workplace culture. These analyses have taken into account a range of social and contextual factors such as gender, ethnicity, power and status, and type of workplace. We are also committed to developing practical applications of the research, in particular communication evaluation and development programmes, and assessing how communication contributes (or not) to employment equity and to effective workplace relationships. Based on this work we are now in a position to critically examine what our data can tell us about gender differences in workplace communication in New Zealand.

This chapter provides a summary of the workshop content as described above, and briefly discusses the implications of the issues raised for gender equity in NZ workplaces.[3] We set out to explore two key issues. First of all, what is the relationship between common stereotypes or generalisations about gender difference in language use and the actual patterns that have been observed in the research, both internationally and in New Zealand workplaces? And secondly, where gendered styles do occur in workplace discourse, how should we interpret them? This last question has especially important implications for how the results of academic research get used in the 'real world' of the workplace.

Accessing the stereotypes

It is our experience that if we give a group of people a set of real-life scenarios or 'scripts' marked for gender, such as the examples based on the books by Gray, Tannen and Elgin we provided at the workshop (see Appendix A), and ask them to identify the aspects of male and female communication style illustrated in each case, they will readily come up with a list that looks something like the one in Table 1. This set of features also happens to provide a useful 'checklist' of the typical (and often stereotypical) comparisons of male and female interactional style which are the stock in trade of the various popular works.

Table 1: Widely cited features of 'feminine' and 'masculine' interactional style:

Masculine	Feminine
• direct	• indirect
• aggressive	• conciliatory
• competitive	• facilitative
• autonomous	• collaborative
• dominates talking time	• talks less than men
• interrupts aggressively	• has difficulty getting a turn
• task-oriented	• person-oriented
• referentially oriented	• affectively oriented[4]

(Holmes 2000a)

What this exercise demonstrates is that all of us, to a greater or lesser extent, have a similar set of expectations about how women and men as a group do (or should) behave linguistically. Most of us also have fairly definite opinions about which style is preferable or 'better' in different contexts. Thus it is common for women to be acknowledged as having superior interpersonal skills, and as being more likely to use 'proper' and polite speech. They are expected to be the peacemakers and 'social secretaries' in both family and workplace settings, and are generally acknowledged as having strengths in working collaboratively. However, these 'feminine' characteristics are strongly associated with the domestic sphere, and in the world of work, many people still 'think male' when asked to characterise what constitutes effective communication. In the workplace setting, it is the more competitive and task-oriented features from the 'masculine' end of the continuum which are usually perceived as being the most valuable and important. 'Feminine' styles of communication tend to be undervalued in the workplace, and are often denigrated as being too indirect and unassertive. The effect of these negative stereotypes is that women often feel they face a 'Catch 22' situation at work, whereby they are subject to criticism for being 'unfeminine' if they adopt a stereotypically 'masculine' style of communication, yet are seen as unassertive and weak if they retain a more 'feminine' interactive style (Lakoff 1990).

Challenging the stereotypes

In a context where women are often still seen as having a 'deficient' style of interaction and men are accused of using a more assertive style as a way of maintaining their dominance in the workplace, it is easy to understand why the 'different but equal' approach of the popular books appeals so strongly to many people, and especially to women. However, it can also be argued that books like Gray's and Tannen's are persuasive precisely because they tap into largely unquestioned and taken-for-granted stereotypes and cultural constructs about gender based on people's past experiences and social conditioning.

In support of this argument, Deborah Cameron (1997: 48) describes a 'thought experiment' used by Penelope Eckert in her teaching, in which students are presented with a typical gender-linked scenario, like Tannen's classic 'asking for directions' example, but with the genders reversed (Tannen 1990). Tannen uses this as an illustration of male reluctance to place themselves 'one down', but, as Cameron points out, invariably 'people will have no difficulty coming up with a different but equally plausible explanation' of the suggested gender difference if they are told that it is women who dislike asking for directions. She concludes:

> What this suggests is that the behaviour of men and women, whatever its substance may be in any specific instance, is invariably read through a more general discourse on gender difference itself. That discourse is subsequently invoked to *explain* the pattern of gender differentiation in people's behaviour.' (Cameron 1997: 48)

Another way to test the accuracy of our perceptions is to investigate what happens in situations where we *don't* know what gender someone is. How accurate are our predictions if we have to rely solely on linguistic cues? Of course, normally when we participate in or observe interactions, this issue does not arise – in most cases we can tell immediately whether a given participant is a man or a woman, and our perceptions are therefore automatically filtered through a gendered lens. However, gender may be masked in certain contexts, for example in written or electronic communication. If the 'Mars and Venus' model of gender difference is correct, then it should be easy to accurately determine the gender of participants from their interactional style. On the other hand, if it is speaker gender itself that is helping to construct our interpretations of what is happening in a given situation, rather than objective linguistic clues, then we would expect it to become much more difficult to assign gender confidently or accurately in situations where we are working 'blind'.

In the workshop, we tested this hypothesis on a set of brief excerpts from transcripts of actual workplace recordings. The workshop participants worked in small groups to deduce as much information as they could about the setting and the speakers in each excerpt, using only the linguistic clues available in the transcript (see Appendix B). This proved to be quite a difficult exercise, and there was considerable variation in the conclusions reached by each group. A number of people also commented that they felt uncomfortable trying to make judgements about social characteristics like gender and status on the basis of a brief transcript alone. This exercise provided a graphic illustration of how context-embedded our interpretations of interactions are in practice, as well as demonstrating how difficult it is to reliably link discourse features with social variables such as gender in specific interactions.

This is not to imply that gender is in any way irrelevant or unimportant in interpersonal interaction, whether in the workplace or in other settings. Clearly it is: gender is a highly visible and salient aspect of social organisation. We devote a great deal of time and energy to maintaining this most basic of social categorisations, and it is inevitable that this will be reflected in our use of language. But to what extent do the gendered stereotypes and 'cultural scripts' with which we are familiar actually reflect the reality of everyday interaction, as revealed by objective research?

The international research evidence

Extensive scholarly research over the past thirty years (e.g. Aries 1996, Coates 1996, 1998, Crawford 1995, Holmes 1995, Romaine 1999, Talbot 1998, Tannen 1993, 1994a, Wodak 1997) has quite clearly established that the interactional styles used by females and males do vary systematically along the lines of the masculine and feminine features summarised in Table 1. However, it is also clear from the research that neither gender uses one set of strategies exclusively, and there are few, if any, specific language features which have a direct and exclusive link to gender (c.f. Ochs 1992: 340). Although the findings are complex and sometimes contradictory and difficult to interpret, much of this research was well-conceived and carefully executed. As Cameron (1996) points out, the results have proved remarkably robust, and they continue to provide a useful and relevant starting point for analysing the communicative style of men and women at work.

However, the approach of researchers who write for a popular audience, such as Gray (1992) and Tannen (1990), has been heavily criticised by academics for the way they dichotomise male and female style and in the process '. . . emphasise differences, minimize similarities and largely ignore unequal power or status' (Bing and Bergvall 1996: 4). As Freed (1992) argues, such books work to reinforce gender stereotypes rather than challenge them, and mask the fact that female and male language and behaviour actually takes place along an overlapping continuum rather than in two distinct categories. The fundamental weakness of the popular books, as opposed to the original scholarly research on which they are based, is the inevitable over-generalisation and simplification involved in presenting such material for wide public consumption. Writers of popular tracts generally ignore the careful qualifications which surrounded the original research, as well as the many sources of diversity and variation (such as age, class, ethnicity, sexual orientation, and so on), which researchers indicate need to be taken into account in comparing women's and men's styles of interaction. Moreover, they take little or no account of the stylistic variation which arises from contextual factors, including the social and discourse context of an interaction, and the participants' goals (Holmes 2000a).

To summarise, the most recent academic research clearly concludes that gender differences are not absolute or exclusive, but instead form a continuum – with men and women simply more likely to cluster towards one or other end of that continuum. Moreover, gender is far from the only factor in determining how an interaction will proceed: many other aspects of the context and the social identity of the speakers must also be taken into account. The various generalisations summarised in Table 1 above represent well-established distributional patterns and gendered norms of interaction, but they cannot account for which parts of their linguistic repertoires each individual will choose to draw on in a given situation. This is exactly what our analysis of the New Zealand data shows.

The New Zealand evidence

If we turn now to some examples taken from real data in New Zealand workplaces, we will see that both women and men commonly engage in a wide range of verbal behaviours, and use elements of both 'masculine' and 'feminine' styles to achieve their goals. These examples are representative of more detailed research undertaken by members of the Language in the Workplace Project team which has established that the most effective communicators, whatever their gender, ethnicity or status, choose their strategies to suit the situation – there is no single formula for a successful interaction. Rather, the key factor is flexibility in selecting and switching styles as appropriate, which means using the most effective style to suit the topic or purpose of the discussion, the setting, and the people involved. There is no evidence in our data to support the idea that men and women stick to a narrowly prescribed range of sex-specific strategies. This finding is in line with the results of a study of group discussions among female and male managers in the United States which identified individuals using a 'wide-verbal-repertoire speech style', combining different proportions of masculine and feminine speech characteristics, as being the most highly rated communicators and managers by other members of the group (Case 1995: 150).

The brief excerpts discussed below are representative of many other examples from a range of New Zealand workplaces where both men and women can be seen to use a range of discourse features associated with both masculine and feminine styles of interaction. The discussion here focuses on just two aspects of discourse: (i) different strategies for giving directives and advice; and (ii) the use of contestive and collaborative humour during different kinds of meetings.

Giving directives

It has often been suggested that women typically use less direct means of getting people to do things. West (1990), for instance, found that female physicians used more mitigated directives to their patients than did male physicians, and she suggested that these hedged directives were more likely to result in the patients' compliance with the doctor's advice than the male physicians' use of direct imperatives. However, as the examples below illustrate, although the women recorded in Wellington workplaces certainly used indirect strategies such as hedges and requests in a variety of contexts to get others to do things, they used very direct forms equally often to give instructions. Such forms have stereotypically been associated with males rather than females, partly because they are appropriately used from a more powerful to a less powerful person (West 1990), and partly because they are associated more with an explicit orientation to the immediate task, and take less account of affective goals. Conversely, males were observed to make substantial use of indirect forms, as well as the direct forms associated with a masculine style. The context and relationship between the people involved seems to be the crucial factor here, rather than simply the gender of the speaker.

Ginette, a female factory team leader, for example, is direct and assertive in running team briefing meetings, using many explicit imperative forms, in a style somewhat reminiscent of a teacher's (Stubbe 2000). Example 1 is taken from an early morning team meeting, where Ginette is giving her team their instructions for the day's activities (directives are highlighted in bold):

Example 1

Ginette: if they don't match there's something wrong **STOP THE LINE** if the lay card says you've got five numbers . . . . **that's what you put in there not four** just cause it's got a zero on there doesn't mean it doesn't count it does count **so make sure you check then properly**

However she uses much less direct strategies when dealing on a one-to-one basis with individuals, as illustrated in Example 2, where she is talking to a male factory floor worker who has had difficulty under-standing what to do, and needs encouragement:

Example 2

Ginette: no the way you did it this morning is good **that's what**
we're supposed to do (9) **see how important important**
the checks a- are you know if you do them //properly

Sam: /well I yeah\\ well I yeah I I'm I'm usually pretty good on on
that sort of thing now so-

Ginette: yeah=/

Sam: /=if you go by the book you can't go wrong

Ginette: that's right + **just remember that when you're doing the**
check list you put down what YOU find not what it
should be + so you're checking against what it should be
if it don't match then there's something wrong

The next example, from a large evaluation meeting in a government
organisation, illustrates a man using relatively indirect forms for
conveying directives. Len is a male manager, and his role here is to
facilitate a wide-ranging discussion. (Directives are in bold).

Example 3

Len: how do we- can we capture some of these things that we
want to um

Brian: do you want me to write them down

Len: **can you #**
I mean I just think where we've we've identified //
some\thing we //want\ to carry that through 'cause later
on we may want to come back to it ... ...

Celia: one that I'm am surprised at is [institution] engineering

Len: **hang on can we can we stay in the- do this block first**

Celia: oh okay you want to //do service\ first

Len: /all right\\
um + do service first otherwise we'll we'll we'll dart a bit
I just want to try and deal with the a- do the scores make
sense with people's perceptions or if there's a difference
big difference in the scores that we've got some comment
that covers that big difference we've done that one

Our data demonstrates that both men and women have a wide range of directive strategies available to them, and draw on these as most appropriate to a particular setting. While quantitative studies of larger amounts of data like West's have indicated that there are patterns of gender difference in relation to the use of directives in particular contexts, this clearly does not allow us to make predictions based on gender for individual interactions.

Humour in meetings

Both popular and academic stereotypes frequently portray women as humourless participants in workplace interaction. However, our recent analysis of humorous contributions in 22 meetings recorded in a variety of New Zealand workplaces suggests there is reason to be sceptical about the accuracy of such stereotypes. Female participants typically contribute at least their share of humour to meetings; women's meetings often produced more humour than male-only meetings; and when in the role of chair, there is evidence that women encourage rather than stifle humour (Holmes, Marra and Burns fc).

Humour serves a number of complex functions in the workplace, all of which contribute to social cohesion (Holmes 2000b). It creates and maintains solidarity or collegiality (supportive humour), but it may also hedge or attenuate face threatening acts such as directives or criticism (controlling humour). Extrapolating from the masculine and feminine characteristics in Table 1 might lead us to predict that women would be more likely to engage in collaborative and supportive humour, while men would be more likely to produce controlling and contestive humour. Once again, however, our data suggests that such generalisations need to be qualified: attention to the precise context is a consistently relevant consideration.

The following excerpts provide examples of controlling humour from a male and a female. In example 4, Rob (Blair) arrives late at the 9am meeting being chaired by Sandy (a male manager). Sandy greets Rob with a sarcastic remark, which other members of the group pick up on. The tone is light, but Rob would have been left in no doubt that he was the butt of some (good-natured) criticism:

Example 4

Sandy: however it's a service we've provided for our customers
        good afternoon Mister Blair
Rob: I forgot it was on
All: [laugh]
Rob: I was sitting at my sitting at my desk
All: [laugh]
Peg: oh yeah
All: [laugh]
Seth: so you had a good //weekend then\
Rob: /and then I\\ finally opened my email and it's got oh meeting
All: [laugh]
Sandy: and you weren't sitting there at nine o'clock (when-)
Rob: can we strike this one from the record
All: [laugh]
Ange: I'll leave it out of the minutes

In Example 5, the group have got carried away on a topic that is not related to the job in hand and have broken into smaller groups. Penelope, the chairperson, attempts to control the conversation:

Example 5

Penelope: settle down
Group: [laughs]

Penelope uses a direct imperative here. Since this is obviously too strong in the context of a group of senior managers, she uses a humorous motherly tone of voice as a softening strategy. She acts like a mother or a teacher with a group of children, instead of the chairperson controlling a senior management meeting. The group takes the point that they have moved too far off track and the humour precludes anyone taking offence – to do so would appear unreasonable (Marra 1998).

Example 6 illustrates collaborative humour, this time involving both men and women, and again there is an overt gender dimension to the humour. It comes from the weekly reporting meeting of a mixed gender project team. Sandy is in the chair.

Example 6
Clara: the picture overstates the number of men in the call centre
Rob: oh okay
Clara: ///( )\
Sandy: /there's one\\ gigolo and one pimp and the rest of them are
Clara: [laughs]: call girls:
Sandy: call girls
Peg: [laughs]
Marlene: and you'll need some more //chunky gold jewelry\
Peg: /there's always a complete [name of organisation] service\
           though isn't it when you think about it [laughs] //[laughs]\
Clara: /and maybe a moustache\\
Marlene: yeah and a shirt that unbuttons (to the waist)
Clara: a shiny shiny shirt
Rob: what's ange then //the top moll or something\
Marlene: /( )\\
Clara: stuck on
Sandy: the madam
Peg: [laughs]: yeah she's the madam: [laughs]
Sandy: madam ange
           [general laughter]
Both women and men participate in this jointly constructed collaborative
sequence, each supportively building on and extending the ideas
introduced by the previous speaker. Clearly generalisations about the
way women and men use humour must be treated with caution;
contextualisation is crucial.

Interpreting difference

The existence of a large number of examples in our database like those
just described effectively debunks the idea that there are specific
discourse features or styles which can be reliably associated with males
and females, whether across the board, or in any given interaction. It is
not gender per se which is important in accounting for the forms people
select to get things done at work, but rather a whole range of more
subtle social and contextual factors which operate in interaction with
gender. Of course, in our New Zealand data, as in earlier research, there
are still distributional patterns along gender lines that we can identify

by means of quantitative analysis of larger amounts of data (c.f. Holmes, Marra and Burns fc), as well as differences in how different discourse strategies or 'styles' are perceived when used by men and by women. But our point here is that these generalisations must be applied with caution when it comes to individual interactions, where gender is just one variable to be taken into account. This kind of qualitative evidence provides strong support for the argument that we need to look for a more robust alternative to essentialist explanations of gender differences.

Our analyses of the New Zealand workplace data leads us to agree with international researchers who favour a social constructionist approach to interpreting patterns of gender difference in linguistic (and other social) behaviour. Rather than focusing on simplistic generalisations, we need to 'look locally, think practically' (Eckert and McConnell-Ginet 1992) when analysing the relationship between gender and language use. Doing this reveals how people orient to and manipulate well-established discourse norms and sociolinguistic stereotypes when talking to others, and how they balance their identities as women or men with other facets of their identities, like their professional role and status, ethnic group membership, or personal characteristics such as their wish to be considered friendly or well-informed (Stubbe 1998a; Holmes, Stubbe and Vine 1999a).

We will look at one example in detail to illustrate how such an analysis might work in practice. Example 7 is an excerpt from the final phase of a meeting between Jan, a Pakeha manager, and Heke, one of her senior staff, who is Maori.[5] The meeting has focused on a number of misunderstandings and differing work expectations, and Jan starts to wrap it up with a direct instruction aimed at resolving the last of these problems: *oh well just check out to see what happened 'cause there was clearly some miscommunication somewhere.* Despite Jan's attempt at softening her directive by providing a neutral reason for it, Heke seems to interpret this as an indirect criticism, which he counters by offering at some length to put more pressure on his team to improve their performance:

Example 7a
(Hedging devices are in boldface).
Heke: oh I think they're just taking a holiday from the stress really
Jan: yeah
Heke: but I'm keeping the pressure on [**laughs**] + **actually** I- I
         wanted to- get your advice about that_I want to do **a bit of a**
         wee sort of ra ra speech at the beginning of **like** of planning
         day tomorrow we ARE stretched people ARE starting to feel
         the pressure + but it's it's just the kind of thing **you know**
         it's- if if we want to be in the business you're gonna have to
         live with it **you know that kind of thing** but I want to say
         that in such a I'm starting to **really** become quite the
         manager now [**laughs**] um um + and I don't- er I **just** I do
         want to say that I want to say **you know** look um **you know**
         if we- if we're gonna be good policy advisers and we're
         wanting to be recognised alongside all the other central ones
         then unfortunately this is the nature of it and you're gonna
         have to work nights and compromise your [**laughs**]:
         weekends: **and things like that** and + um-

By suggesting this tactic, and using discourse strategies like hedging
and seeking advice, Heke positions himself as a hardworking subordinate
who is trying sincerely to meet Jan's needs and respects her greater
experience. At the same time he claims solidarity with her as a capable
new manager who is prepared to be tough with his own team when
necessary: *I'm starting to really become quite the manager now.* He
uses a large number of hedging devices in a short period of time,
sometimes heavily clustered eg.: *a bit of a wee sort of ra ra speech*,
which signal the tentative nature of his suggestions, while at the same
time claiming common ground with Jan by means of addressee-oriented
devices such as *you know that kind of thing*, both strategies which are
usually associated with women. However, Heke also uses this little
speech to draw explicit attention to his position at the top of the pecking
order in his own section, a strategy which serves to reinforce his
orientation to competitive male gender norms. Jan eventually breaks
into Heke's monologue to suggest a less full-on approach:

Example 7b

Jan: **although I mean I can appreciate the that sort of message but on the other other hand** um + don't **sort of** + **sort of** say that as something that sh- that should be the norm //**like** that's

Heke: /mm\\

Jan: really **you know** when things //are **really**

Heke: /from time to time\\

Jan: from time to time that it's not a good way of them expecting to organise their work all the time

Heke: ae yeah

Jan: that they need **you know** it's **the old** work smarter **sort of stuff**

Heke: yeah

Jan: and we need to- to **sort of** be aware of we being a (friend-) family friendly workplace

Jan offers no verbal feedback during Heke's long turn, and her comments here also make it quite clear that as his manager she does not agree with his intended approach and does not wish to be associated with it. But at the same time she demonstrates a typically 'feminine' consideration for the face needs of her interlocutor, and takes great care not to sound critical, and thus undermine Heke's attempted reconstruction of himself as an effective manager. Her rejoinder *don't say that as something that should be the norm* is also very heavily mitigated, and in the remainder of this excerpt, her speech is peppered with hedges like *sort of, like, sort of stuff* and the addressee-oriented device *you know.* She adopts a conciliatory tone, which is reinforced by using a higher pitch, and by repetition which signals her acceptance of Heke's proffered phrase *from time to time,* both features which are also associated with the feminine end of the style continuum.

Heke does not say much here, but responds positively by providing regular and explicitly supportive minimal feedback (eg. *mm, yeah, ae, from time to time*). Like hedging, a high frequency of verbal feedback is not considered to be a typical feature of a masculine style. However, although on one level Heke's positive responses could simply indicate his acceptance of Jan's advice, using such explicitly supportive feedback also assumes a certain level of solidarity between them, and therefore functions as a strategy to put him back on a more equal footing with Jan.

Jan's reference to the need for the organisation to provide a *family friendly workplace* also situates her in a gendered social space, as this is a concept which has mainly been promoted by women's groups in New Zealand. At the same time, it can be read as an appeal to the Maori value system, which accords the *whanau,* or family, high priority. It also positions her as a considerate and reasonable manager, who, while she does not expect her staff to work too hard, still wants to see good results: *it's the old work smarter sort of stuff.*

In this short excerpt then, we can see Jan using a variety of discourse strategies which clearly identify her as a woman in the workplace, while at the same time enacting her professional identity as a competent manager engaged in 'doing' both power and collegiality, and her role as a Pakeha in a Maori organisation who is sensitive to Maori cultural norms. Heke similarly uses a range of strategies to position himself more favourably with regard to the issue at hand. Interestingly, many of the discourse forms he uses (eg. hedges, addressee-oriented devices, supportive feedback) come from the 'feminine' end of the style continuum. However, when combined with his proposal to *keep the pressure on,* their effect is to show his awareness of the workplace hierarchy, and help him negotiate his way out of what he seems to perceive as being placed in a 'one-down' position.

Conclusion

Do men and women really live on different 'planets', or belong to different cultures which speak different languages? As we have seen, these metaphors have wide appeal and seem plausible because they offer a straightforward explanation for gender differences in behaviour that we all 'know' exist. If they were accurate, life would undoubtedly be much easier for discourse analysts with an interest in language and gender, but as this paper has shown, the reality is rather more complex and difficult to interpret. The research evidence and data excerpts presented here demonstrate quite clearly that the cultural difference theory, as promoted by a number of popular books, does not provide an adequate model of the interaction between language and gender in the workplace.

First of all, 'women' and 'men' do not constitute separate and homogeneous groups – there are as many differences between individual women and men as there are inter-group differences in language use. Rather, there appears to be a continuum of linguistic features which are more or less strongly associated with masculine and feminine values at either pole. These poles reflect social norms and expectations about gender which are reproduced to some extent in distributional patterns of usage, but there is no one-to-one correspondence between gender and the use of a given linguistic or discourse feature. Secondly, gender is only one of a number of relevant social variables and contextual factors affecting an interaction. Therefore, as we have seen, the same linguistic forms or discourse strategies may be quite differently motivated at different points in an interaction, or when used by different individuals and/or in different contexts, and it is overly simplistic to make a direct link with only one social variable such as gender. Thirdly, the cultural difference model does not account adequately for the relationship between gender and power. This is a major problem for researchers interested in workplace communication, as any analysis which focuses on gender in this context is also inevitably concerned with the ways in which power and solidarity are enacted through discourse.

There have been arguments amongst academics about how to explain gender differences in language use for many years, but the increasingly popular view that there are 'natural' differences in patterns of verbal interaction between men and women needs to be challenged, not simply because it is out of line with current theoretical views, but more importantly because widespread acceptance of this theory will have a negative impact on the achievement of gender equity in the workplace. In the first instance, the popular books reify inaccurate gender stereotypes and encourage overgeneralisation of those differences that do exist. For instance, the erroneous perception that indirect discourse strategies are unassertive and tentative, if coupled with the notion that these are characteristic of women, can act as a powerful barrier to women's success. Such negative stereotypes are disempowering, not least because the argument that there are 'natural' gender differences in communicative style offers a way of avoiding or explaining away the real issues of unequal status and power, and inequitable access to resources which underpin the glass ceiling. A widespread acceptance of this theory is therefore likely to act as a strong disincentive to change. The end result may be to reinforce rather than to challenge gender stereotypes, and thus help to perpetuate inequality.

Secondly, the dualistic 'women do this, men do that' model encourages a prescriptive approach to training and development, rather than encouraging people to become more aware of and reflective about their communication practices, and develop a repertoire of flexible strategies they might use to achieve the outcomes they want in different situations. Moreover, no two workplaces are the same – each has its own organisational culture and practices, and this makes a 'one size fits all' approach even less constructive. As the examples demonstrate, the most effective communicators in fact use a wide-verbal-repertoire style, integrating features into their discourse which are typically associated with both masculine and feminine speech styles in the research literature. It is also difficult to escape the implications of the fact that men have dominated most workplaces until relatively recently, occupying nearly all the influential and powerful positions. Hence, 'styles of interaction more common among men have become the workplace norm' (Kendall and Tannen 1997: 85). In this context, a dualistic approach can lead to an unhelpful emphasis on valuing masculine styles (regardless of who produces them), which means the world of work loses some of the benefits, such as high quality exploratory talk and good social relations, which are generated by cooperative, facilitative styles of discourse.

A social constructionist or performative model of language and gender has the potential to provide a much sounder basis both for understanding what goes on in workplace interactions and for developing constructive strategies for promoting gender equity. Unlike essentialist models which frame a particular aspect of identity like gender as 'given' and linked to a predetermined set of (linguistic) behaviours, this approach instead problematises gender, and examines it as a social construction, with discourse strategies playing a crucial role in the process. Within a social constructionist framework, language is viewed as 'a set of strategies for negotiating the social landscape' (Crawford 1995: 17), and as the site of the cultural production of social identity (Weedon 1987).

Such a framework fits much better with the complex reality of workplace interaction, and makes it possible to evaluate how gender-related differences in language use interact with other factors to contribute to inequitable outcomes for women. By looking closely at individual interactions and placing these in the context of the large body of language and gender research which has accumulated over the last three decades, it is possible to demonstrate clearly the dynamic and interactive relationship that exists between language, gender and professional identity in workplace interactions. Individual speakers do draw on and manipulate established norms of male and female discourse, but the linguistic resources they use are generally not exclusive to either group. Rather, they consist of features which cluster to create a continuum of styles which are available to construct a range of social meanings, including those relating to gender. Gender remains an important factor in how people communicate at work and how they perceive others, but it is important to be wary of approaches which over-simplify and stereotype gender differences. If we wish to promote the cause of women in the workplace, we should instead focus our efforts on identifying and challenging unhelpful stereotypes while continuing to explore how gendered language is constructed in practice.

Appendix A

Several popular books suggest that women and men have very different communication styles.

Scenario 1

Do you think a man or a woman would be more likely to produce each of the directives below? Why?
1. I wonder if you could help me move this table
2. Would you put this in that drawer for me?
3. I can't put all of this away
4. This kitchen is a mess; it really stinks. I can't fit anything else into the rubbish bag. I need it tied. Could you do it?
5. Would you bring the groceries in from the car?
6. Please pick up Ben from scouts
7. Empty the rubbish
8. You'll be going by the store. Lauren needs a bottle of milk. I just can't go out again. I am so tired. Today was a bad day. You could get it couldn't you?
9. Julie needs a ride home and I can't pick her up. Do you have

time? Do you think you could pick her up?
10. I need my shirt ironed
(Adapted from Gray 1992: 257)

Scenario 2

What aspects of male and female communication styles are highlighted in this scenario?

Amy was a manager with a problem: she had just read a final report written by Donald, and she felt it was woefully inadequate. She faced the unsavoury task of telling him to do it over. When she met with Donald, she made sure to soften the blow by beginning with praise, telling him everything about his report that was good. Then she went on to explain what was lacking and what needed to be done to make it acceptable. She was pleased with the diplomatic way she had managed to deliver the bad news. Thanks to her thoughtfulness in starting with praise, Donald was able to listen to the criticism and seemed to understand what was needed. But when the revised report appeared on her desk, Amy was shocked. Donald had made only minor, superficial changes, and none of the necessary ones. The next meeting with him did not go well. He was incensed that she was now telling him his report was not acceptable and accused her of having misled him. 'You told me before it was fine', he protested. Amy thought she had been diplomatic. Her praise was intended to soften the negative message. Donald thought she had been dishonest. He saw her suggested changes as optional.
(Adapted from Tannen 1994b: 21-22)

Scenario 3

What aspects of male and female communication styles are highlighted in this scenario?
Context: Mary made a complicated presentation based on months of work to a senior male group at work. It was well received but after congratulating her, the boss added a comment saying how much her attractive appearance and pretty face had brightened everyone's day. After the meeting another male colleague congratulated her on her 'strategy' of wearing a tight black sweater. She was furious. At home she described exactly what had happened to her husband, Frank.

Frank: Hey that's terrific. I **told** you I was sure the presentation
would fly, remember? Congratulations! Now what happens
next?

Mary: What happens **next**?

Frank: Right! Do they start the project now or are there more
meetings first or what?

Mary: You're incredible! You didn't understand a word I said did
you? My boss and his buddies knock themselves out to make
me look like some airhead that has to rely on batting her
eyelashes because she hasn't got a brain and all YOU can do
is congratulate me! **You're as bad as they are!**

Frank: Now wait a minute, let me check this out. I come home from
one of the worst days I've had in months and before I can
even eat my dinner you're telling me in excruciating detail
about your latest triumph. And I listen, right? And then when
I tell you how terrific I think it is you bite my head off.

Mary: All right. I'm sorry I brought it up. Just forget it and eat your
dinner.

Frank: You eat dinner. You've ruined mine!

(Adapted from Elgin 1993: 19-20)

Appendix B

Exercise:
Consider the following speech extracts from the Language in the
Workplace Project data.

1   Describe a possible social context for each extract: Who is
speaking to whom? Where? Why? How do you know?

2   What can you say about the relationship between the
participants? What is their relative status?

3   What linguistic clues did you use?

4   Thought experiment: Can you 'swap' genders and still make
sense of what is going on?

(A)

K: so no it was good I didn't have to worry about meals I didn't
have to worry about bills or kids or um work or anything just me

H: just holiday for you
K: yeah + [tut] it was UNREAL [laughs]
H: now listen are you going to be wanting to take time off during the
    school holidays

(B)

T: can I just have a quick word
G: yeah sure have a seat
T: [sitting down] great weather eh
G: mm
T: yeah been a good week did you get away skiing at the weekend
G: yeah we did + now how can I help you
T: I was just wondering if I could take Friday off and make it a long
    weekend
G: mm I don't see any problem with that – you will have finished
    that report by then won't you

(C)

V: she muttered something about not letting Len come and poke his
    finger round in it [laughs]
N: yeah yeah we'll build that into it [laughs] the Len factor
V: [laughs] I like that the Len factor [laughs]
N: [laughs] take account of the Len factor [laughs]
V: add [laughs] f- add five days [laughs] [laughs] um
N: [laughs]

(D)

W: he's found some [technical word]
D: some what?
W: [laughs]: yeah I I just like funny words: [laughs]

(E)

C: one that I'm surprised at is [institution] engineering
L: hang on can we can we stay in the- do this block first
C: oh okay you want to //do service\ first
L: /all right\\ do service first otherwise we'll
C: okay=/
L: /=we'll we'll dart a bit

Transcription conventions

All names are pseudonyms.
XX   Unidentified speaker
YES   Capitals indicate emphatic stress
[laughs] Paralinguistic features in square brackets
[drawls]
+   Pause of up to one second
. . .//. . . . . .\. . . Simultaneous speech
. . ./. . . . . .\\. . .
(hello)   Transcriber's best guess at an unclear utterance
?   Rising or question intonation
-         Incomplete or cut-off utterance
=   Utterance continues on speaker's next line
. . . . . . Section of transcript omitted
(. . .) Indecipherable speech

Notes

1   Rather than viewing a particular aspect of identity like gender as 'given,' and linked to a predetermined set of (linguistic) behaviours, this approach emphasises the ways in which we actively 'perform' or construct aspects of our social identity in interaction with others.

2   This project is funded by the NZ Foundation for Research, Science and Technology. We thank the many volunteers who allowed themselves to be recorded, and the research assistants who transcribed the data.

3   The views expressed here are our own, and do not necessarily coincide with the opinions of those present at the workshop.

4   Referential orientation means a primary focus on the information content of an utterance, while affective orientation entails focussing more on the socio-emotional content.

5   The analysis of this example is a modified version of one which first appeared in Stubbe and Holmes (2000).

References

Aries, Elizabeth 1996. *Men and Women in Interaction*. Oxford: Oxford University Press.

Bing, Janet M. & Victoria L. Bergvall 1996. The question of questions: beyond binary thinking. In Victoria L.Bergvall, Janet M. Bing & Alice F. Freed (eds), *Rethinking Language and Gender Research: Theory and Practice*. New York: Longman, 1-30.

Cameron, Deborah 1996. The language-gender interface: challenging co-optation. In Victoria L. Bergvall, Janet M. Bing & Alice F. Freed (eds), *Rethinking Language and Gender Research: Theory and Practice*. New York: Longman, 31-53.

Cameron, Deborah 1997. Performing gender identity. In Sally Johnson & Ulrike Hanna Meinhof (eds), *Language and Masculinity*. Oxford: Blackwell, 47-64.

Case, Susan Schick 1995. Gender, language and the professions: recognition of wide-verbal-repertoire speech. *Studies in the Linguistic Sciences* 25, 2, 149-192.

Coates, Jennifer 1988. Gossip revisited: language in all-female groups. In Jennifer Coates & Deborah Cameron (eds), *Women in their Speech Communities*. London: Longman, 94-121.

Coates, Jennifer 1996. *Women Talk*. Oxford: Blackwell.

Coates, Jennifer (ed) 1998. *Language and Gender: a Reader*. Oxford: Blackwell.

Crawford, Mary 1995. *Talking Difference: on Gender and Language*. London and Thousand Oaks: Sage.

Eckert, Penelope & Sally McConnell-Ginet 1992. Communities of practice: where language, gender and power all live. In Kira Hall, Mary Bucholtz & Birch Moonwomon (eds), *Locating Power: Proceedings of the Second Berkeley Women and Language Conference*. Berkeley April 1992. Berkeley, University of California: Berkeley Women and Language Group, 89-99.

Elgin, Suzette H. (1993) *Genderspeak, Men, Wonen and the Gentle Art of Self Defense*. New York: Wiley.

Freed, Alice 1992. We understand perfectly: a critique of Tannen's view of cross-sex communication. In Kira Hall, Mary Bucholtz & Birch Moonwomon (eds), *Locating Power: Proceedings of the Second Berkeley Women and Language Conference*. Berkeley Women and Language Group, Berkeley: CA, 144-52

Gray, John 1992. *Men are from Mars, Women are from Venus*. New York: Harper Collins.

Hay, Jennifer 1995. *Gender and Humour: Beyond a Joke*. Unpublished Master's thesis, Victoria University of Wellington, Wellington, New Zealand.

Holmes, Janet 1995. *Women, Men and Politeness*. London: Longman.

Holmes, Janet 1997. Women, language and identity. *Journal of Sociolinguistics,*1, 2, 195-223.

Holmes, Janet 1998. Victoria University's Language in the Workplace Project: goals, scope and methodology. In Janet Holmes & Scott Allan (eds), *Proceedings of the Sixth New Zealand Language and Society Conference. Te Reo* 42, 179-81

Holmes, Janet 2000a. Women at work: analysing women's talk in New Zealand workplaces. *Australian Review of Applied Linguistics* 22, 2, 1-17.

Holmes, Janet 2000b. Politeness, power and provocation: how humour functions in the workplace. *Discourse Studies* 2, 2 (in press).

Holmes, Janet, Meredith Marra & Louise Burns forthcoming. *Women's Humour in the Workplace: a Quantitative Analysis*.

Holmes, Janet, Maria Stubbe & Bernadette Vine 1999a. Constructing professional identity: 'doing power' in policy units. In Srikant Sarangi & Celia Roberts (eds), *Talk, Work and Institutional Order. Discourse in Medical, Mediation and Management Settings*. Berlin and New York: Mouton de Gruyter.

Holmes, Janet, Maria Stubbe & Bernadette Vine 1999b. Analysing New Zealand English in the workplace, *New Zealand English Journal* 13, 8-12.

Kendall, Shari & Deborah Tannen 1997. Gender and language in the workplace. In Ruth Wodak (ed), *Gender and Discourse*. London: Sage, 81-105.

Lakoff, Robin 1975. *Language and Woman's Place*. New York: Harper and Row.

Lakoff, Robin 1990. *Talking Power: the Politics of Power in our Lives*. New York: Basic Books.

Maltz, Daniel N. & Ruth A. Borker 1982. A cultural approach to male-female miscommunication. In John J. Gumperz (ed), *Language and Social Identity*. Cambridge: Cambridge University Press.

Marra, Meredith 1998. 'My job's a joke!': humour in the workplace. In Janet Holmes & Scott Allan (eds), *Proceedings of the Sixth New Zealand Language and Society Conference. Te Reo* 42.

Ochs, Elinor 1992. Indexing gender. In Alessandro Duranti & Charles Goodwin (eds), *Rethinking Context: Language as an Interactive Phenomenon*. Cambridge: Cambridge University Press, 335-358.

Rearden, Kathleen Kelley 1995. *They Don't Get it Do They*. Boston: Little Brown.

Romaine, Suzanne 1999. *Communicating Gender*. Mahwah, New Jersey: Lawrence Erlbaum.

Spender, Dale 1985 (2ed). *Man-Made Language*. Boston: Routledge.

Stubbe, Maria 1998a. Striking a balance: language, gender and professional identity. To appear in *Proceedings of the Fifth Berkeley Women and Language Conference April 24-26 1998*. Berkeley Women and Language Group: University of California.

Stubbe, Maria 1998b. Researching language in the workplace: a participatory model. *Proceedings of the Australian Linguistics Society Conference* Brisbane University of Queensland July 1998. http: //www.cltr.uq.edu.au/als98.

Stubbe, Maria 2000. 'Just do it . . . !': Discourse Strategies for 'Getting the Message Across' in a Factory Production Team. *Proceedings of the Australian Linguistics Society Conference* University of Western Australia September 1999. http: // www.arts.uwa.edu.au/LingWWW/als99/

Stubbe, Maria & Megan Ingle (forthcoming). Collecting natural interaction data in a factory: some methodological challenges paper presented at Murdoch Symposium on Talk-in-Interaction, Murdoch University, Perth, September 1999.

Stubbe, Maria & Janet Holmes 2000. Talking Maori or Pakeha in English: signalling identity in discourse. In Allan Bell & Koenraad Kuiper (eds), *New Zealand English*. Oxford: Blackwell. Wellington: Victoria University Press, 249-278.

Talbot, Mary M. 1998. *Language and Gender: an Introduction*. Oxford: Polity Press.

Tannen, Deborah 1990. *You Just Don't Understand: Women and Men in Conversation*. New York: William Morrow.

Tannen, Deborah (ed) 1993. *Gender and Conversational Interaction*. Oxford: Oxford University Press.

Tannen, Deborah 1994a. *Gender and Discourse*. London: Oxford University Press.

Tannen, Deborah 1994b. *Talking from 9 to 5*. London: Virago Press.

Weedon, Chris 1987. *Feminist Practice and Poststructuralist Theory*. Oxford: Blackwell.

West, Candace 1984. When the doctor is a lady. Power, status and gender in physician-patient dialogues. *Symbolic Interaction* 7, 1, 87-106.

West, Candace 1990. Not just 'doctors' orders': directive-response sequences in patients' visits to women and men physicians. *Discourse and Society* 1, 1, 85-112.

Wodak, Ruth 1997 (ed). *Gender and Discourse*. London: Sage, 81-105.

Zimmerman, Don & Candace West 1975. Sex roles, interruptions and silences in conversation. In Barrie Thorne & Nancy Henley (eds), *Language and Sex: Differences and Dominance*. Rowley, Mass: Newbury House.

Breaking through the 'glass ceiling': can linguistic awareness help?

Sally McConnell-Ginet

Cornell University

Introduction

Linguistic awareness involves paying explicit attention to who says what, how and when they say it, and, critically, to what sort of effect. Linguistic awareness is enhanced by the kind of scholarly work on the gender dimensions of discursive practices represented in this collection of papers. Such work can, I will argue, help dismantle male advantage in professional achievements. But, I will also argue, linguistic awareness is only part of the picture. Not only does any individual woman need strategies for effective action, there must also be collective action to effect the systemic social changes that are needed if those strategies are to work reliably.

In August 1998, Rita Rossi Colwell became Director of the National Science Foundation (NSF), an independent agency of the United States Government that provides support for research and education in science, mathematics, engineering, and technology. Immediately prior to becoming NSF Director, Dr. Colwell was President of the University of Maryland Biotechnology Institute and Professor of Microbiology at the University of Maryland, positions she had held since 1991 and 1972 respectively.

As the first woman to head the NSF, Dr. Colwell has frequently been interviewed on her views of women's participation in science and, more generally, in research and education. She has remarked on noticing at meetings that women's comments and proposals, her own included, often get attributed to men who have picked them up for repetition. Although the women then do not get 'credit' for their ideas, she goes on, worrying about who gets credit diverts us from getting things accomplished. Since Dr. Colwell did indeed eventually get tapped for leadership positions, it is obvious that somewhere along the line she finally did get some 'credit.'

Stories like Rita Colwell's have been heard from virtually every American woman who has recently achieved prominence in a professional or high-powered business position. These women have somehow managed to become successful in spite of finding themselves sometimes unfairly ignored. The 'sometimes' is important here: no one whose contributions are always ignored becomes a leader in her line of work. So it is possible for a woman eventually to make herself heard and acknowledged, even if she may often have trouble doing so. But for every woman who has made it in the face of such barriers, there is almost certainly another women who has lost out to a man who is objectively no better on the job than she is (and sometimes not as good). There is another woman who has accepted the implicit devaluation of her capabilities that such ignoring conveys, and who has consequently stopped making the requisite effort, and trimmed back her aspirations. (Uta Lenk's discussion of job advertisements, in this volume, points to other discursive practices that could limit aspirations before women even get into the workplace.) And there are women who never allowed themselves any such aspirations and thus never got the credentials needed for professional achievement. They decided in girlhood to focus their energy and talent in domains where females predominate: at home taking care of other family members and in various kinds of jobs that provide support to high-achieving professionals and executives.

In this paper, I explore some of the linguistic texture of the social practices and institutions that support the 'glass ceiling' that limits women's aspirations and achievement. The glass ceiling is, of course, the invisible barrier that seems to keep even some exceptionally capable women from ascending to the top in the many professions dominated by men. Its companion, the glass elevator, is the invisible leverage that propels even relatively mediocre men upward in female-dominated occupations. Both are created and sustained by gender practices of various kinds, including many that involve language. What are some of these practices and where do they fit in the more general picture of language and the gender order?

A practice-theory approach to language and gender

In joint work, some already published and some in progress, Penelope Eckert and I have been developing a practice-theory framework for thinking about the interaction of language and gender. (See Eckert & McConnell-Ginet 1992a, 1992b, 1995, 1999, forthcoming.) I will explain what this entails by first contrasting it with some of the approaches many of us first brought to this area, and which continue to be useful for certain purposes. Early research on language and gender took social structure, in particular the gender order, as given and then tried to correlate language with pre-existing gender categories and relations. This is not surprising. Commonsensically, there are 'women' and 'men', categories that sort people generally into two non-overlapping classes. There is a gender order that is patriarchal, in the sense of being characterised by male advantage, the concentration of social prestige and power in male hands. Approaching language and gender research in this way, the obvious way forward is to explore correlations that might exist between the socially given distinctions and language. Language itself is also typically viewed as given, a system to take off the shelf, use, and then re-shelve. So, using this approach, what we try to match to society are elements of a linguistic system. Typically these elements are linguistic expressions, where these might be structured from sound units, morphosyntactic units, or semantic units. The linguistic forms are tagged, then, as associated with women or with men, with the socially subordinate or the privileged

It can be quite useful to think of gender in structural terms. Virtually all societies not only provide for a binary categorisation of people into sex classes. They also have a gender order, an array of social institutions and structures that link to the sex-class categories. Sociologist Robert W. Connell (1987) has introduced a useful tripartite classification of the gender order: in addition to allocation of power and prestige, already mentioned, Connell identifies the division of labor, and the regulation of cathexis. *Cathexis* is originally a Freudian term that deals with the direction of libidinal energies, especially sexual. It can also somewhat more expansively cover the whole range of likes and dislikes, including but not confined to erotic desire and gender-based derogation of others. As Connell also points out, however, these different aspects of the gender order are interrelated, and, what is most important for our purposes, they are created and sustained by social practices of various kinds.

As linguists are well aware, it can also be very useful to view a language as a static structure with a grammar. That grammar includes phonology and phonetics, systematic sound patterns. It includes morphology, principles of word formation and inflection. It includes syntax, categorisations of words and principles for combining them into larger phrases and sentences. It includes a lexicon of words and other meaningful units that specifies for each unit its grammatical characteristics, its sound structure (and how it is written), and its basic meaning (which may be 'underspecified,' i.e. not completely fixed). Lexical semantics and syntactic structure feed into combinatorial semantics, principles for assigning meanings to complex structures on the basis of the meanings of their constituent parts. Japanese, English, and Finnish speakers have access to quite different grammars. But it is social conventions of linguistic practice that are the real basis of our saying that, for example, Japanese have access to or 'use' a grammar in which pronouns are gendered in all persons, whereas English speakers access a grammar in which pronouns are gendered only in the third-person singular, and Finnish speakers access a grammar in which pronouns are not gendered at all. In other words, what counts as the grammar (or grammars) accessed by a particular population – what language or languages they speak – depends on ongoing and always potentially shifting social practices in communities.

If we confine attention to language and gender as static systems, it is difficult to understand either interactions between them or possible changes in each system. A focus on the structural systems of gender and of language obscures the role of human agency and actions, including purposive uses of language, in creating and sustaining the gender order and in effecting gender and other social change. Staying at the structural level also obscures the role of agency and action, including that focused on gender distinctions and relations, in linguistic change of various kinds. Agency is completely external to both social and linguistic structures. What bridges the gap between structure and agency is social practice. Social (including linguistic) practice is constituted by the interplay between social (including linguistic) structure and our own actions. Social practice includes both the way we do things as individuals and the way in which such individual actions fit into the larger scheme of things. Ultimately social practice encompasses the effect of individual agency on social structure and the constraints social structure puts on individual agency.

So in a practice-theoretic approach to language and gender, the focus is on the place of language in the social practices that construct a gender order and the place of gender in the social practices that construct particular linguistic systems as those used by a population. In this paper I focus on some of the ways in which language figures in the social practices that create and sustain male advantage in power and prestige. When our interest is social practice, it is immediately apparent that decontextualised linguistic forms will give us only limited information. We have to consider not only who is speaking and with whom, where the interactants are and when the interaction is taking place, but also which utterances are attended to, and which ideas are taken up. In other words, we have to look at how others interpret and respond to what is said. Whether a particular person's talk and other actions affect many or few, it is the unfolding over time of a structured totality of situated acts that creates meaning in and for society. The meaning of gender unfolds continually, gradually modified by large and small acts. And that meaning is produced in social interaction, which involves actions and reactions in ongoing exchange. *Discursive practice* is a useful label for the generation of social meaning in practice, and *gender discourse* for discursive practice as it pertains to gender. We should keep in mind, however, that discursive practice in this sense goes far beyond what people say or understand others to say.

Early studies of language and gender distinguished sharply between two topics. One was the study of how men and women speak, what were sometimes called 'genderlects' or 'gendered styles.' The other was the study of how women and men are spoken of, a topic that includes, for example, 'sexist' language. (See, for example, the introductions to Thorne & Henley 1975, McConnell-Ginet, Borker & Furman 1980, Thorne, Kramarae & Henley 1983.) On a discursive practice approach, however, we can see that the two topics are intimately connected: the effects intended and produced by any utterance depend not only on the linguistic form proffered, but also on the place of that utterance in gender discourse, which draws on past history, as well as involving who utters it to whom, and the reactions it evokes (or fails to evoke, as in the case of the woman whose meeting comments seem to be ignored or mis-attributed). Discursive practice draws especially heavily on the kinds of face-to-face exchanges people have with one another in the course of their ongoing mutual engagement in various activities. For example, work colleagues constitute an ongoing group that develops a shared history of linguistic practices, including interpretations and evaluations of what different individuals bring to the group's exchanges. Drawing on work by Jean Lave and Etienne Wenger, Penny Eckert and I have emphasised the importance of understanding linguistic practices in light of their place in such groups, what Lave & Wenger call 'communities of practice.' (In addition to the Eckert & McConnell-Ginet references provided above, see Lave & Wenger 1991 and Wenger 1998.) Each individual's relation to discursive practice generally and gender discourse in particular depends on the various local communities of practice to which they belong and their forms of membership in those communities, relations of those communities to one another and to various institutions, and so on.

Engagement, content, and personas

In constructing language and gender, people collaboratively construct (1) discursive engagement, (2) discursive content, and (3) personas. In constructing engagement, people make social moves involving speech actions and activities, they manage interactions, and they connect themselves and others to ongoing discourse. Making suggestions or offering evaluations, getting and keeping the floor, building on what you or others have said earlier, acknowledging and developing others' contributions, asking questions of clarification or issuing challenges: such practices construct discursive engagement. Not surprisingly, much work on language and gender has focused on the terms of engagement. Being able to engage effectively is essential to achieving virtually any of the aims one might have. The woman who keeps talking even after a man (or perhaps another woman) has tried to interrupt her is shifting, however slightly, the gendered terms of discursive engagement.

In constructing discursive content, people label and categorise, and they invoke and convey all kinds of background assumptions. How we categorise not only ourselves but all of experience is critical to discursive practice. In the US, there is talk of the 'mommy track' in certain professions but there is as yet no parallel 'daddy track.' We talk about 'working mothers' but not 'working fathers,' of 'career women' as a special group but not 'career men'. News stories about successful women highlight their families (or comment on the absence of a spouse and children). Behind such construction of gender content there lies, of course, a host of implicit gender assumptions that might well be rejected if made explicit. Increased linguistic awareness can bring the gender content of discursive practice into sharper focus, thus helping to change that content. And of course content that is not directly 'about' gender may nonetheless be critical to gender discourse. Evelyn Fox Keller (1992), for example, has argued that scientific discourses have been gendered in interesting and important ways. A 'masculine' discourse of control and destruction dominated physics during the first two-thirds of the century; a more 'feminine' discourse of collaborative engagement and life-creating forces came into biology during the last decades. Does the increasing importance of the life sciences really make women more welcome participants in scientific enterprises? Perhaps, though the story is undoubtedly quite a complicated one. Still, it is clear that discursive content is of critical importance in all kinds of workplaces. Exactly what kind of content is constructed depends in part on how engagement is constructed, and both of these also depend on how participants' personas are constructed

In constructing personas, people use language choice and variation to negotiate the linguistic market, and they make social meaning visible through their stylistic choices. My presenting myself as a linguistics professor and getting others to ratify that presentation, to take me seriously in that persona, involves my speaking in certain ways and not in others, and involves others responding to what I say appropriately. At the same time, the collaborative construction of me as a woman relies on a different array of practices. A colleague may start our meeting by commenting, perhaps quite approvingly, on my clothes or some other aspect of my physical appearance. There may be appreciative little jokes about how meetings have been 'toned up' since women joined the working group, and perhaps also a little reminiscing about the 'dirty talk' that earlier characterised workplace meetings. I may assume a somewhat diffident and 'modest' style in advancing my ideas in order to forestall harsh judgments of me as an overly ambitious or self-aggrandising and thus unfeminine woman. Perhaps I will smile frequently and use intonational patterns that suggest I am seeking others' input rather than trying to impose my ideas on them. Or maybe I will rely mostly on nonverbal actions to construct myself as feminine: certain kinds of clothing, postures, jewellery. Occasionally gender identities may be completely irrelevant, but this is still less common than might be supposed. In most contexts, including most workplace contexts, gender attributions are not only made but have a fairly significant effect on perceptions of what people are contributing and evaluations of their work. Constructing gendered personas has implications, of course, for constructing discursive engagement and content and vice versa.

As I noted at the outset, linguistic awareness can be of some help in breaking through the glass ceiling and eventually, I hope, in removing the ceiling and the escalator altogether. I should make clear, however, that there is no quick purely linguistic fix for gender inequities to be found. In her very interesting *Talking from 9 to 5: how women's and men's conversational styles affect who gets heard, who gets credit, and what gets done at work*, Deborah Tannen (1994) has argued that the glass ceiling is a 'wall of words,' suggesting that conversational styles are at the root of women's failure to achieve authority and rewards commensurate to their skills and efforts. She is certainly right that language use enters centrally into our construction of gender and occupational status, but not, I think, in the implied suggestion that knowledge of different styles is the real key to women's breaking through the glass ceiling. That implication is often interpreted as meaning that women need to remedy deficiencies in their communicative styles in order to advance on the job, an interpretation that Tannen tries at points to forestall, but which is now well institutionalised in a variety of programs aimed at teaching women to 'improve' their communication skills. Tannen herself argues that it is not that women's styles are deficient, but that men do not understand or appreciate them. But she does not adequately acknowledge that many of the differences she discusses are part and parcel of the social practices that maintain men's advantage over women in the workplace: they are not minor cosmetic differences in individual style but connect to socially substantive matters of values and interests that sustain sexual inequality. There are at least two issues.

Firstly, the problem that Tannen does acknowledge, i.e. the double-bind to which linguist Robin Tolmach Lakoff (1975) first drew attention: women are faced with the dilemma that open verbal displays of their competence or authority can undermine their social attractiveness, especially their perceived heterosexual desirability. And secondly, there is the related problem that tacit and often quite unrecognised assumptions about gender can lead to women being undervalued no matter how they speak. Nonetheless, I agree with Tannen that attention to what we and others say, how it is said, and how others respond can be helpful in developing general strategies to get women the kind of recognition and rewards that their talents and work should but do not consistently bring. It is important, however, not to see the glass ceiling as 'merely' a wall of words, readily broken through by training individuals in linguistic difference and tolerance. And our focus should not be on helping token individuals break through, but on collective action to remove the ceiling for women generally and also for men who are disadvantaged by race, ethnicity, class or some other characteristic that ought to be, but is not, irrelevant to their chances for achievement.

Gender schemas

The best discussion I know of the difficulties women have faced and continue to face in professional life is Virginia Valian's excellent (1998) book, *Why So Slow? The Advancement of Women*. Although Valian's data on how women fare in academia and related high-status jobs come pretty much exclusively from US studies, I suspect that similar data could be found for New Zealand, Australia, the UK, and most of western Europe. The particular details will vary in different countries, in different institutions, in different workplaces. And the details are important. But there do seem to be some recurrent general patterns that we can usefully discuss.

Valian argues that the distorting lenses of gender schemas – by which she means our expectations of people on the basis of the sex to which we have assigned them – are not just distorting but actively operate to women's disadvantage in public arenas where competence and achievement are at stake. She cites a host of empirical studies that show that both women and men tend to expect men to function more effectively in high power jobs. In explaining achievements, both women and men tend to credit men with skill and hard work and see women as having had good luck, an easy task, or having exerted phenomenal effort. Men's successes tend more to confirm expectations, to bring to mind their other successes; women's tend to run counter to expectations and also tend not to redound to their credit. In explaining failures, both women and men tend to see women's failures as evidence of their lack of ability whereas men's failures are more likely to be explained in ways that do not bear on future accomplishments: the task was very hard, he had some bad luck, he didn't try as hard as he should have. Men tend to be compared to other men, no matter what the task, whereas women tend to be compared to other women only when doing 'feminine' tasks. In tasks seen as masculine, women who fail are seen as doing so BECAUSE they are female. In tasks seen as feminine, men often are seen as *succeeding* BECAUSE they are male. Valian cites a host of empirical studies that show this pattern, a pattern of which most of us are unaware because gender content is so often implicit. Noting one's own and others' explanations of successes and failures is an important first step to changing these gender-biased patterns.

More generally, Valian argues that gender schemas influence evaluations to women's detriment, in turn making it difficult for women to accumulate advantage at the same rate as men, and she goes on to suggest several ways to nullify the negative professional consequences of gender schemas and to equalise men's and women's ability to accumulate advantage (1998: 303). She does note that gender schemas can be detrimental to women's self-confidence and their capacity not only to present their achievements in the best possible light but actually to achieve at the level of which they are capable, i.e. that individual women may often benefit from taking steps to change their own attitudes and behaviour. But, in sharp contrast to Tannen, and also to the cottage industry that has sprung up to train women in asserting and displaying themselves, Valian is quite clear that there is a systemic problem.

> No woman should think that if she just does everything 'right' she will succeed. No woman should think that any modifications she may make in her everyday demeanor will guarantee success. Observers' views of women as a class constitute an entire structure that no individual woman can change. It is that structure that needs changing (1998: 322-23).

Of course this does not mean that individual women's efforts are irrelevant. Structural change necessarily involves individual-level changes, and women can indeed engage in 'self-improvement' programs that do help them in their lives, both personal and professional. But the critical point emerging from Valian's research is that it is not women or their differences from men that are the major problem. The sex differences that matter most and that almost certainly make a major contribution to the hypothesised sex differences in personalities and interests and the disturbing documented sex differences in workplace achievement still found are differences in how people are judged and evaluated, the 'advantages' they receive, depending on the sex to which they have been assigned (certainly these results fit with what Su Olsson, this volume, reports on women's workplace narratives: women find their biggest problem to be how others, especially but not only men, treat them). Both women and men expect different things of women and of men, and these expectations lead them to respond to and evaluate women and men quite differently, often in professional contexts undervaluing women's talents and work and overvaluing men's. This happens in various ways even from people who are sincerely committed to promoting gender equity.

Valian uses the example of meeting dynamics to which Rita Colwell alluded to illustrate how very small differences in advantage or disadvantage can add up to major differences in position over the long term, just as tiny differences in savings or debt can be dramatically multiplied by the compounding of interest. Speaking and having your contributions recognised are part of constructing engagement, of positioning yourself and being positioned by others in ongoing discourse. As Valian notes, not only are some comments not taken up, participants in the group also tend to register who is credited and who is not and form expectations for future creditable performance on this basis. The person whose contributions are ignored or not credited this time may find even less receptivity in the audience the next time around. Her prestige has suffered, albeit slightly, whereas the male colleague who got credited for her suggestion has enjoyed a slight increase in prestige. Part of constructing men as more capable and knowledgeable than women in affairs of consequence is treating their comments as more worthy of attention, more credit-worthy. Their getting the floor may be easier in some contexts but, even more critically, they seem to find it easier to get their suggestions and ideas taken up by others – and, importantly, taken up as *their* ideas. Sometimes of course there may be belated recognition that many of the most influential ideas that have affected the practices of some particular community have actually originated with some woman rather than with the men who initially got the credit for them. But such delayed recognition does not always come, and women and men interested in seeing women achieve on an equal basis with men need to devise ways for getting credit to women who deserve it. This does not mean that women themselves need to be preoccupied with whether they get credit. As Colwell notes, such preoccupation can actually impede making credit-worthy contributions. What it does mean is that everyone concerned about equity issues needs to be alert to the need for appropriate crediting. If Mary's idea is picked up by John and then later called John's idea, either John or another of Mary's colleagues, Linda perhaps, can point out that the idea really came first from Mary. Simply alerting those responsible for personnel evaluations to the well-documented tendency to differentially attend to women's and men's contributions can help effect a shift to more equitable patterns of giving credit.

Male advantage in constructing engagement does not begin in business or research meetings. It is already well attested in research on elementary and secondary schools and has sometimes been observed in university classrooms as well. Even cartoonists have noted the phenomenon. Gary Trudeau in his Doonesbury cartoon strip has a sequence in which Alex, a very bright computer-wise young girl, is shown in the classroom trying to get the teacher to notice her raised hand as boy after boy is called on and praised for stumbling and confused comments. 'Maybe I should lose weight,' Alex speculates. Alex's counterparts are in many classrooms, even ones in which teachers consciously believe in gender equity. Punch had a cartoon some time ago showing a professor addressing the class after a young woman has just spoken: 'That's an interesting point, Miss Jones; perhaps we can get a man to make it now.'

In scholarship, the equivalent is citation practice; men do not cite women in the same proportion that other women do, though both sexes tend to under-cite women. A particularly notorious scientific case is that of Rosalind Franklin, whose data were essentially stolen by Francis

Crick and James Watson and used with quite minimal credit in their Nobel-winning work on the structure of DNA. A number of analysts have observed that Franklin might well have been first to light on the helical structure had her best X-ray picture not been shown to Watson and Crick without her permission and that they certainly could not have made their breakthrough without access to her data. Watson's (1968) book on the race to understand DNA spoke condescendingly of 'Rosy' and commented quite patronisingly on her painstaking work and even about her personal appearance and her 'nervous' interactional style. In the second edition (1980), published after Franklin's tragically early death from cancer, Watson apologised for having underestimated her and her work, noting that he had not earlier appreciated the obstacles faced by women in science. Of course, the apology came too late for Franklin. A happier ending is the story of Barbara McClintock (see Keller 1983), the biologist denied a regular research job and somewhat dismissively regarded as a bit of a crank until others' work showed the tremendous importance of her ideas and led to her receiving a Nobel Prize towards the end of her long and productive life.

Professional advancement, Valian observes, depends on being able to parlay small gains into big ones.

If everyone understood explicitly what some people understand implicitly – that success comes from creating and consolidating small gains – no one would counsel women to ignore being ignored. The concept of the accumulation of advantage lets us see that the well-meaning advice often given to women – not to make a mountain out of a molehill – is mistaken. That advice fails to recognise that mountains *are* molehills, piled one on top of the other. Fairness requires appreciating the importance of each molehill of advantage and disadvantage and taking steps to ensure that molehills do not accrue to individuals on the basis of their group membership (1998: 4-5).

Colwell's advice, then, to focus on getting things accomplished and not to worry about getting 'credit' is problematic. It *is* important not to get diverted from one's main goals by minor setbacks: for some women, a focus on getting things accomplished plus a certain amount of good luck may eventually led to their accruing advantage and ultimately to their advancement. But so long as they remain a small group of 'exceptional' women, the glass ceiling will stay in place.

Angier (2000), a *New York Times* feature on the 'glass ceiling in the sky' that women in astronomy continue to encounter, reports on recent surveys of astronomy departments in the US. Dr. C. Megan Urry, an astronomer who has been very active in spearheading such studies, says that, despite perceptions to the contrary, women did not really share in the rapid expansion of the field during the 1990s. Their numbers rapidly decline as one goes up the academic ladder, in spite of the fact that there have been distinguished women astronomers for centuries. Is it overt discrimination? David Gelernter, a computer scientist at Yale, has argued that it is women's lack of abilities or interest that has impeded their advancement in the sciences.

> If women aren't being kept out of science by force, they must be choosing not to enter, presumably because they don't want to, presumably because (by and large) they don't like these fields or (on average) don't tend to excel in them, which is nearly the same thing. They're also less prone to the intense cut-throat aggressiveness that usually marks the successful research scientist or engineer.

As Dr. Urry points out, Gelertner's view completely misses the cumulative effects of small slights and disadvantages that mount up over time. There are much subtler kinds of things going on as a look at what is written about or said to women clearly demonstrates. The article cites some anecdotes that recently appeared in *Status*, a biannual report on women in astronomy published by the American Astronomical Society. One letter of recommendation for a female applicant for a postdoctoral position emphasises twice how tiny, sweet and charming the applicant is, and gives a specific example of how amusing and cute it is to watch the applicant in the laboratory wrestling with astronomical equipment larger than she.

A woman graduate student in astronomy reports having just passed her PhD oral exam. A well-intentioned senior male faculty member approached her with a handshake and remarked, 'I am very proud of your accomplishment, knowing how hard astronomy and physics is, especially for a woman . . .'

Another young woman astronomer tells of approaching two male colleagues in her field at a conference, one of whom was a senior astronomer whose work was very close to hers. They were talking about a scientific issue with which she was quite familiar and continued their conversation until the senior astronomer finally acknowledged her presence by saying, 'Ah, but we are boring this sweet young girl. What can I do for you, dear?' That such experiences persist into the new millennium suggests that molehills are still often piling up into mountains for women scientists, who face kinds of scepticism about their abilities and commitment that male scientists do not encounter.

Gender discourse and 'backstage semantics'

Gender discourse applies what psychologist Helen Haste (1993) calls the 'sexual metaphor' to gender attributes, activities, and even things. The sexual metaphor uses the female-male contrast to organise thinking about a host of other binary contrasts and, typically, to present those binary contrasts as polar opposites, as incompatible with one another. Rationality and instrumentality, for example, are constructed as masculine while emotionality and affectivity are constructed as feminine. (Let me note parenthetically that language and gender research reports have contributed to this aspect of gender discourse.) Women who venture into 'masculine' realms such as science can thereby jeopardise their perceived femininity. Some women use the strategy of ostentatiously constructing themselves as feminine on other dimensions to get around this obstacle: they use make-up, wear feminine clothes, practice many feminine virtues, and smile a lot as they continue to pursue success in traditionally masculine preserves. A recent obituary for a very successful Chicago lawyer spent some time on how kind she was to clients and colleagues, while at the same time noting that she had achieved a kind of prominence shared by few other women. Some women make it clear that being seen as 'feminine' simply does not concern them: this is most likely from women who are not, for whatever reasons, concerned to be seen as heterosexually attractive.

For a variety of reasons, this attitude is rare among adolescent or young adult women. Few women at that vulnerable life stage can afford not to worry about whether men will find them attractive or, more generally, will admire them. Many a teenaged girl in an American high school still keeps quite silent (or lies) about her achievements in the highly rational and thus highly masculine areas of science and mathematics. She does so for fear of seeming less than desirable to her male peers. In the 1950s wearing eyeglasses was seen as a sign of intellectual seriousness, and the slogan was 'boys don't make passes at girls who wear glasses'. The slogan itself is dated, but recent reports suggest that rationality is still gendered masculine, and nested within it are types of intellectual activity like science and mathematics that inherit masculine gender. A true story from the late 1990s can illustrate. A young woman whom male peers found quite attractive surprised them all by winning the high school's physics prize. She had not spoken out in class, and she had concealed her perfect test scores. Next thing she knew, comments that 'she must have slept with the physics teacher' or that 'her dad or brother or boyfriend must have helped her' were filtering back to her. She had been trying to keep her 'unfeminine' achievements invisible from her peers; when those achievements got broadcast, they also got either denied (and her success attributed to her 'feminine' attractions), or transferred to males. How did this young woman come to believe that some might see intellectual competence, especially in a science like physics, as inconsistent with attractiveness to men? Perhaps she heard someone say 'Linda is at the top of her physics class but quite good-looking', thus presenting Linda's combining excellence in the physics classroom with good looks as somehow surprising, especially remarkable. The same speaker might also have said 'Jim is at the top of his math class and quite good-looking', making it clear that for Jim the combination of good looks and outstanding performance in math is not especially remarkable. Speakers are often unaware that they have said *but* rather than *and*, and the choice may be only faintly registered by their hearers. Nonetheless words like *but* and *even* and other presuppositional triggers do have effects, albeit often very subtle ones. Of course, the process is far more complex than this: it is a whole discursive history that leads a young woman to try to construct herself as desirable by constructing herself as (somewhat) incompetent, at least in traditionally masculine areas. The response to the revelation of her competence will itself enter gender discourse: perhaps it will anger and galvanise her into abandoning her policy of hiding her talents, leading her to work hard and openly for success in the sciences. Or perhaps the response might simply confirm her of the wisdom of her self-deprecating policy and lead her to turn away from scientific endeavors altogether. This high school experience is closely linked to the kind of minor harassment so many women encounter on the job, eg. excessive and unwanted attention to their appearance ('you look so pretty today') unmatched by similar attention to male colleagues or inappropriate expressions of interest in their personal lives ('stay out late last night?'). Women astronomers who get so far as completing PhDs have undoubtedly been tripping over such molehills for many years.

Gender schemas are typically constructed very early. Parents, teachers, and other children busily convey messages to a child about differing expectations for females and for males. Sometimes the messages are pretty explicit. I remember hearing a little Scottish boy tell my two-year-old daughter, who was happily playing with her Matchbook miniature cars and trucks, that 'wee lassies shouldna' play wi' wee motors'. Sometimes different expectations are conveyed rather more subtly. Both my son and my daughter picked up on my use of *shit* as an occasional expletive when I was particularly annoyed by something. A neighbour reported to me that another neighbour, on hearing this word from my daughter's mouth, had gently remonstrated 'oh dear – such a pretty little mouth shouldn't say such an ugly word.' To my son, the correction was 'I don't like to hear that word'. Both children got the message that the word was somehow taboo, but it was suggested to the girl that speaking that way might jeopardise her 'prettiness' and to the boy only that he should be careful of the audience. At just about the same time my kids were getting this kind of feedback in response to their use of 'bad' language, the professors in a leading academic department in a major U.S. university were discussing whether to hire their first woman. The candidate was a very distinguished scholar in the field, and a number of the faculty were keen to have her as a colleague. What carried the day, however, was the sentiment of those who said that hiring a woman would mean 'cleaning up our language at lunch and meetings' and that collegiality would be seriously impaired. This was back in the late 1960s, and few if any would advance the 'freedom to talk dirty' argument when discussing an academic hire any more – at least not in a general departmental meeting from which it might be publicly reported. Nonetheless, the threat to camaraderie of introducing women into their numbers was still being taken quite seriously only a couple of years ago by the Viennese Philharmonic Orchestra, many of whose members insisted that their distinctive and much admired ensemble playing would be jeopardised if they were forced to admit women as peer colleagues.

Gender schemas that potentially distort judgments of women and men are still being actively constructed, though often without explicit recognition. A couple of years ago I happened to see a news clip about a program that used professional sports stars to help encourage kids to read. The clip showed a large American football player talking with a boy of about six or seven. The boy was actually engaged in reading a book, and the sports star looked over his shoulder. 'Oh,' he said, 'that book's about a girl. Why don't I help you find something more interesting?' The news commentator who introduced the clip did not comment at all on this gender message, but the kid certainly must have registered that his hero did not think girls or their activities of much interest. The athlete did not say explicitly that girls are relatively boring, but that message was certainly conveyed by what he did say. And not too long ago there were studies that showed males figuring much more prominently than females in school textbooks, and more often doing things while females observed or cheered them on. In these cases, a message is conveyed by a general *pattern* of what is and what is not said. That is, no one need say explicitly that females are or are supposed to be passive, and males are or are supposed to be active: this is a generalisation that emerges from the general pattern of talk about women and men, girls and boys, and it is a generalisation that figures in gender discourse, and thus plays a role in gender schemas even where it is not overtly acknowledged.

More often than not, gender schemas are conveyed covertly, their tenets often not explicitly recognised even by those who help to convey them. Even gender-liberal parents in the U.S. tend to give their children sex-specific names and dress them in sex-specific ways (after all, one of the first questions parents are asked about a newborn is 'is it a girl or a boy?'), to steer their girls more than their boys towards preparing for household responsibilities and for nurturing roles ('when'- not 'if'- 'you get married and have kids . . .'), to push their boys but not their girls to develop math and technology skills, and in a host of different ways to reinforce the message that sex is of paramount importance to personal identity and to the division of labour. Adults often speak of 'girls and boys' rather than 'kids', cast kids' opposite sex-friendships in romantic terms ('oh, Scott is Lisa's boyfriend!'), and suggest that Michael play with cousin John rather than with cousin Betsy, even though Betsy is nearer Michael's age and shares more of his interests. In late September of 1999, a *New York Times* article on home decor reported a mother objecting to her three-year-old son's preference for a 'Spice Girls' motif in his bedroom, trying to get him to go for football-adorned bedclothes instead. Adults have not given up pushing gender and sexual conformity, even though they may be less frequently overt about it.

Still there are many more communities of practice now than there used to be in which there is an explicit commitment to gender equity. Teachers in some U.S. schools encourage young boys to play with dolls and girls to build with blocks; they read children stories about men taking care of children and about women fighting fires or having exciting adventures on their own rather than waiting for princes to come to their rescue. This does not mean that gender discourse is completely neutral in these communities, but such practices have certainly had some effect. Not only are U.S. girls becoming quite involved in competitive sports, but high-powered career aspirations are far more common for them in the late 1990s than they were in the 1950s or 1960s. Discourses of gender egalitarianism, especially directed towards children and advanced by people recognised as leaders and authorities, can go some way to promoting egalitarianism.

In addition, there have been dramatic changes created by equal opportunity legislation and its implementation in the late 1960s and the 1970s. U.S. women now hold about 45% of managerial and executive jobs (compared to under 17% in 1970), they constitute about 42% of college faculty (29% in 1970), they are 46% of economists (11% in 1970), 44% of pharmacists (12% in 1970), 62% of psychologists (39% in 1970), 33% of vets (5% in 1970), 18% of architects (4% in 1970). They outnumber men among entrants at several of the top medical schools and account for 41% of medical degrees overall as well as 44% of law degrees; they are now the vast majority of graduates in pharmacy and veterinary science (both, it should be noted, relatively low paying fields). For every 100 men now graduating from college, 123 women get degrees. (Figures from the U.S. National Center for Education Statistics and from the Bureau of Labor Statistics, cited in Hacker 1999.) These are all changes that have not only strengthened women's credentials for professional and executive jobs but have also increased women's desire for such jobs.

And yet, only three of the 1000 largest U.S. corporations are headed by women. At my own university, there are still only a handful of women with named chairs or six-figure U.S. $ salaries, a much lower proportion than of men. Overall, U.S. women still earn approximately .75 for every dollar men earn. It is still assumed that issues like childcare and eldercare are 'women's issues' rather than general social issues. Men may 'help' with the children and the household chores, but women continue to assume the primary responsibility in most cases. One study reported that both women and men think their arrangements are 'equitable' even when women spend about twice as much time as men in taking care of family needs. Women only begin to feel overworked when their share rises to 70% or more whereas men feel overworked when they are doing 35 to 40% of the job.

Interviews with successful women often ask them how they manage to combine family and career (or else mention that the woman involved does not have a family). Interviews with successful men do not usually ask those questions. As a college senior, some time before it was illegal in the U.S. to ask about women's childcare arrangements or similar matters, I was interviewed for a Woodrow Wilson (WW) Fellowship, then given for people contemplating a career in college or university teaching. I do not know the proportion of women who applied – I think it was in the neighbourhood of 30% – but recipients included only 10% women. I was a nervous 20-year old, who had given rather little thought to how I might indeed combine a career and family, or even whether I wanted to. The interviewers said 'Well, you're an attractive young woman and you'll probably get married. How do you plan to manage a family and a career in college teaching?' (I should add the obvious: the interviewers did not ask that same question of my male classmates who were interviewed the same day.) 'Well,' I said, 'I'll probably marry someone who is also a professor [as indeed I did], and we'll be able to arrange our schedules so that we can take turns taking care of the children.' Little did I know how much more might be involved! For example, I ended up asking to switch my fellowship from Harvard to Ohio State because that was where my husband was working; neither of us even thought about his trying to find a job near Harvard while I worked on my PhD. It was not that we said to ourselves that we needed to stay where his job was, but rather that we never considered any other option. It was some years before it occurred to us that we had simply assumed that his job would determine where we lived. When my transfer request arrived, I suspect that someone at the WW Foundation office said something like, 'that's why these things shouldn't go to women'. For some time now, however, I have wished that when the interviewers asked me about how I would manage family responsibilities, I had thought to smile sweetly and say, 'How do you gentlemen manage?' Of course, I would then probably not have been awarded the fellowship, but it would have been satisfying. The point of this anecdote is that the Woodrow Wilson interviewers and I both helped construct a gender discourse in which women have primary responsibility for children and the personal needs of their husbands and other household members, whereas men have primary responsibilities in the public world of work.

Gender schemas are mainly conveyed through what I sometimes call 'backstage semantics.' That 'how do you plan to manage a family and a career?' could be seen as a reasonable question to direct to a female but not to a male indicates that it was, and often still is, simply taken for granted that women's primary responsibilities lie in the domestic domain rather than in the world of paid employment, and thus that their career commitment may be at issue. Men's focus on career even at the expense of family is similarly assumed. These messages need never be explicitly conveyed, but they are part of what helps us make sense of the explicit linguistic actions that we do encounter – not just individual actions but their overall patterning. In other words, meaning depends not just on particular utterances but on their being situated in a rich discursive history. Gender discourse results in powerful and influential gender schemas in part because so much of the content of gender schemas is constructed covertly.

I mention to a colleague, for instance, that a student who had been doing splendidly on the in-course work had fallen apart on the exam. The colleague responds 'Did you suggest that she practice by taking old exams?' My colleague is presupposing, taking for granted, that this student is female. If that is not the case, I might say something like 'Well, actually, this student is male, but I think your advice might be good for him'. Or I might just say 'No, I didn't but I will,' leaving intact the assumption of femaleness. If the student is indeed female, I am quite likely indeed to say simply 'No, I didn't but I will', a response that does not explicitly confront the presumption that females are more likely than males to fail in high pressure performance situations. Neither I nor my interlocutor may notice explicitly that we have just implicitly ratified that presumption, strengthening a gender schema that may have negative consequences for women. Such assumptions can lead, for example, to suggesting that one of the male members of the research team present a paper, while 'protecting' female members from that kind of pressure situation and thus from that chance for increasing their professional visibility. 'Chivalry' of this kind ultimately harms rather than helps women's chances for professional advancement.

Gender discourse is saturated with gender content that is seldom if ever made explicit. In constructing content, much work is done 'backstage' as the examples with 'but' and the unwarranted 'she' illustrate. One thing we can do is train ourselves and others to notice such backstage semantic moves, to bring them to our own and others' explicit attention and thus help reduce their potency. The 'change the sex' test is often useful for making glass ceiling supports visible. When discussing Mary and her work, do we say the same kinds of things we would say if Mary were Jim and vice versa? Do we mention Mary in the same kinds of situations where we would mention Jim and, if so, how do we talk about her as compared to him? How do we respond to her as opposed to him? Do we hesitate to offer her substantive criticism because we fear she 'can't take it'? Do we promote her brother because 'it means more to him'? Do we pay her less so that her husband won't feel he's failed?

It can be useful to let people know that women may do more to facilitate others' contributions to conversation than men, and that they may be far less comfortable than men in offering or facing direct challenges. Those responsible for evaluating women and men on the job can be alert to these possible differences and can try to take steps to ensure that they do not result in unfair advantage for men. But it may be even more important for evaluators to realise that it is *expectations* of profound differences of women in general from men in general that lead to biassed evaluations of individual women and men. This means it is very important to make sure that our own findings about how gender differences are constructed linguistically are properly contextualised and do not strengthen problematic aspects of currently dominant gender discourses. Just as the fact that the average height of men is greater than the average height of women does not tell us anything about the relative heights of a particular male and female, so findings that women orient themselves more collaboratively towards conversational interaction do not mean that a given woman does not or should not care about being credited for her discursive contributions. Similarly, we should not take it as given that a man does not or should not care about the communal good or is unwilling to take direct responsibility for meeting the personal needs of others with whom he shares a household. Of course we may well want not only to change gender discourse but also to change the discourse of achievement so that nurturing and support are given more recognition than they now are. An important first step, though, is to take and give credit where appropriate and more generally to work collectively on making visible the gender schemas supporting the glass ceiling so that we can begin to curtail their effects.

References

Angier, Natalie 2000. For women in astronomy, a glass ceiling in the sky. *New York Times*, February 15, 2000, F5.

Connell, Robert W. 1987. *Gender and Power: Society, the Person, and Sexual Politics.* Stanford, CA: Stanford University Press.

Eckert, Penelope & Sally McConnell-Ginet 1992a. Communities of practice: where language, gender, and power all live. In Kira Hall, Mary Bucholtz & Birch Moonwomon (eds), *Locating Power: Proceedings of the Second Berkeley Women and Language Conference* 1, 89-99.

Eckert, Penelope & Sally McConnell-Ginet 1992b. Think practically and look locally: language and gender as community-based practice. *Annual Review of Anthropology* 21, 461-90.

Eckert, Penelope & Sally McConnell-Ginet 1995. Constructing meaning, constructing selves: snapshots of language, gender and class from Belten High. In Kira Hall & Mary Bucholtz (eds), *Gender Articulated: Language and the Socially Constructed Self.* London: Routledge, 459-507.

Eckert, Penelope & Sally McConnell-Ginet 1999. New generalizations and explanations in language and gender research. *Language in Society* 28, 185-201.

Eckert, Penelope & Sally McConnell-Ginet forthcoming. *Language and Gender Practice*. Cambridge/New York: Cambridge University Press.

Hacker, Andrew 1999. The unmaking of men. *The New York Review of Books* XLVI, 16 October 21, 1999, 25-30.

Haste, Helen 1993. *The Sexual Metaphor*. New York and London: Harvester Wheatsheaf.

Keller, Evelyn Fox 1983. *A Feeling for the Organism: the Life and Work of Barbara McClintock*. New York: W.H. Freeman & Co.

Keller, Evelyn Fox 1992. *Secrets of Life, Secrets of Death: Essays on Language, Gender and Science*. New York/London: Routledge.

Lakoff, Robin Tolmach 1975. *Language and Woman's Place*. New York: Harper & Row.

Lave, Jean & Etienne Wenger 1991. *Situated Learning: Legitimate Peripheral Participation*. Cambridge: Cambridge University Press.

McConnell-Ginet, Sally, Ruth Borker & Nelly Furman (eds) 1980. *Women and Language in Literature and Society*. New York: Praeger. Reissued in 1986 by Greenwood Publishers.

Tannen, Deborah 1994. *Talking from 9 to 5*. New York: William Morrow & Co.

Thorne, Barrrie & Nancy Henley (eds) 1975. *Language and Sex: Difference and Dominance*. Rowley, MA: Newbury House.

Thorne, Barrie, Cheris Kramarae & Nancy Henley (eds) 1983. *Language, Gender and Society*. Rowley, MA: Newbury House.

Valian, Virginia 1998. *Why So Slow? The Advancement of Women*. Cambridge, MA: MIT Press.

Watson, James D. 1968. *The Double Helix: A Personal Account of the Discovery of the Structure of DNA*. New York: Atheneum.

Watson, James D. 1980. *The Double Helix: A Personal Account of the Discovery of the Structure of DNA*. [ed by Gunther S. Stent. Revised ed of Watson 1968]. New York: Norton.

Wenger, Etienne 1998. *Communities of Practice*. Cambridge & New York: Cambridge University Press.

Notes on contributors

Andrew J. Barke
Tohoku University
Andrew Barke is a PhD candidate in sociolinguistics at the Graduate School of International Cultural Studies, Tohoku University, Japan. He is currently writing his dissertation *Gender and the Japanese Language: A Prototype Approach to Gender Variation in Japanese*, which investigates the role of politeness in the differentiation of speech act participant gender. He has also written articles on the effect of age on the discourse of Japanese women, and on second-person pronouns in T/V languages and Japanese.

Jennifer Coates
University of Surrey
Jennifer Coates is Professor of English Language and Linguistics at Roehampton Institute, University of Surrey. She went to school in Manchester and studied for a BA in English Language and Literature at Oxford, followed by postgraduate work at University College, London, and then at Lancaster University. Her research and writing have centred on two different areas of linguistics: English mood and modality and language and gender. She has published six books including *Women, Men and Language*, *Women Talk* and a book of readings: *Language and Gender*. While she has made a major contribution to research on women's discourse, her most recent research explores features of male talk.

Nicola Daly
Auckland
Nicola Daly has a PhD in Linguistics from La Trobe University in Melbourne where she researched gender differences in the ways in which people use facial expression when they are speaking to be lipread. She is currently working as a freelance writer and lecturer in linguistics. She has a special interest in sociolinguistics and, in particular, language and gender.

Janet Holmes
Victoria University of Wellington
Janet Holmes holds a Personal Chair in Linguistics at Victoria University of Wellington, where she teaches a variety of sociolinguistics courses. She has published on a range of topics including New Zealand English, language and gender, sexist language, pragmatic particles, compliments and apologies, and most recently on language in the workplace. Her publications include a textbook: *An Introduction to Sociolinguistics*, and a book on language and gender: *Women, Men and Politeness*.

Deborah Jones
Victoria University of Wellington
Deborah Jones is a senior lecturer in Organisational Behaviour at Victoria University of Wellington. She brings her background in linguistics and literature to her work in management studies. Consequently she focuses on organisational culture and communication, and uses interpretive and discourse analytic methods in her organisational research. She has dropped in and out of academic life several times, and has been involved in many kinds of teaching, writing and feminist activism.

Uta Lenk
Universität Augsburg
Uta Lenk studied at the University of Freiburg, Germany, and University of California at Santa Barbara and received her PhD from the University of Augsburg, Germany. She has taught German as a Foreign Language at the College of the Holy Cross, MA (USA) and currently teaches English Linguistics at Augsburg. She is the author of *Marking Discourse Coherence: Functions of Discourse Markers in Spoken English,* and co-editor (with Wolfram Bublitz and Eija Ventola) of *Coherence in Spoken and Written Discourse.*

Sally McConnell-Ginet
Cornell University
Sally McConnell-Ginet is Professor of Linguistics at Cornell University, where she has worked since 1973. She chaired the Department of Linguistics from 1985-1990 and 1997-1999. Currently she is Secretary-Treasurer of the Linguistic Society of America. She is active in Women's

Studies, acting as Director from 1991-1996, and has made a major contribution to research in language and gender issues, including extensive work with Penelope Eckert. She continues to undertake research on formal semantics and pragmatics, exploring connections between this and her language and gender research.

Margaret A. Maclagan
University of Canterbury
Margaret Maclagan is a senior lecturer in Speech and Language Therapy at the University of Canterbury, where she teaches language acquisition and language analysis, including phonetic analysis. She is a phonetician with research interests in the analysis of New Zealand English. With Elizabeth Gordon, she studies sound changes in New Zealand English, including a real-time analysis of the on-going merger of EAR and AIR. Their major current project is research on the Origins of New Zealand English.

Meredith Marra
Victoria University of Wellington
Meredith Marra is a PhD candidate in the School of Linguistics and Applied Language Studies at Victoria University of Wellington. Her thesis investigates the decisions made by corporate project teams in their weekly meetings. As Research Officer for Victoria's Language in the Workplace project, Meredith's research interests include the language of meetings and the use and function of humour in workplace interactions.

Miriam Meyerhoff
University of Hawai'i at Manoa
Miriam Meyerhoff gained her PhD from the University of Pennsylvania in 1997 and since then has worked as an Assistant Professor in Linguistics at the University of Hawai'i at Manoa. Her linguistic interests include the study of synchronic variation, and the implications of variation for the development of linguistic theory, and the development of our understanding of the construction of the social order.

Su Olsson
Massey University
Su Olsson is a senior lecturer in the Department of Communication and Journalism within the College of Business at Massey University. She holds a PhD in English and teaches in the areas of business writing, speech communication and gender issues. She is editor of *The Gender Factor: Women in New Zealand Organisations* and co-editor of *Women and Leadership: Power and Practice Conference Proceedings*. Her current research interests are: organisational myths and storytelling; and women in management.

Damian O'Neill
Massey University
Damian O'Neill is a teacher in the Communication and Journalism Programme at Massey University. His doctoral research, in the field of social psychology, involved the critical evaluation and organisation of a 'stopping violence' programme. He is active as a researcher in the fields of violence, gender and the media, and has a particular interest in Foucauldian Post-Structuralist theory. He has published in international journals including a recent article in *Violence Against Women* on the theoretical literature surrounding wife abuse.

Anne Pauwels
University of Wollongong
Anne Pauwels is Dean of the Faculty of Arts and Professor of Languages and Linguistics at the University of Wollongong, Australia. Previously she held the Foundation Chair in Linguistics at the University of New England, Australia. Her research interests include language and gender, sociolinguistics and bilingualism. Her publications in the area of language and gender research include *Women Changing Language, Non-Discriminatory Language,* and *Women and Language in Australian and New Zealand Society.* She is the co-editor of *Language, Gender and Sexism*, the journal of the AILA Scientific Commission on Language and Gender.

Jennifer J. Peck
University of New England, Armidale
Jennifer Peck is a lecturer in Linguistics at the University of New England, Armidale, Australia. Her main teaching areas include gender and language, language and power, and cross-cultural communication. She is currently engaged in activities with Australian business and industry that aim to advance diversity in business practice. Her work involves research and practical action in the field of communication with minority groups, including women and people with disabilities.

Maria Stubbe
Victoria University of Wellington
Maria Stubbe is a research fellow in the Language in the Workplace Project and is currently working towards a PhD in workplace miscommunication. Her research interests focus on sociolinguistics and the analysis of spoken discourse, with a particular focus on gender and cultural differences. She also has a long-term interest in classroom discourse.

Bernadette Vine
Victoria University of Wellington
Bernadette Vine is manager of both the Wellington Corpus of Spoken New Zealand English and the New Zealand component of the ICE corpus. She is also working towards a PhD thesis in workplace communication focussing on directives and requests. Her recent publications include an article in *English WorldWide* on Americanisms in New Zealand English and in the *ICAME Proceedings* on directives in the New Zealand workplace. She has also co-authored a number of short papers outlining preliminary results from the Language in the Workplace Project.

Paul Warren
Victoria University of Wellington
Paul Warren has a PhD from the University of Cambridge, and is currently a senior lecturer in Linguistics at Victoria University of Wellington. He has teaching and research interests in phonetics and psycholinguistics. His recent research on New Zealand English

intonation has been supported by a grant from the Marsden Fund. Other current research projects include investigations of intonation in speech production and comprehension, and the relationship of sound change and spoken word recognition.

Ann Weatherall
Victoria University of Wellington
Ann Weatherall is a senior lecturer in the School of Psychology at Victoria University of Wellington. Her research interests are in feminist psychology, discourse analysis, and language and social psychology. Her work has appeared in various journals including *Feminism & Psychology, British Journal of Social Psychology, Journal of Language and Social Psychology*, and *Psychology of Women Quarterly*. She is currently writing a book for Routledge called *Women, Language and Society*.